HIKING THE BERKSHIRES

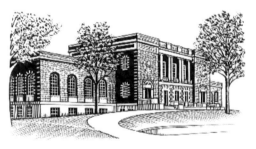

Help Us Keep This Guide Up to Date

Every effort has been made by the author and editors to make this guide as accurate and useful as possible. However, many things can change after a guide is published—trails are rerouted, regulations change, facilities come under new management, and so forth.

We would love to hear from you concerning your experiences with this guide and how you feel it could be improved and kept up to date. While we may not be able to respond to all comments and suggestions, we'll take them to heart, and we'll also make certain to share them with the author. Please send your comments and suggestions to the following email address:

editorial@falcon.com

Thanks for your input, and happy trails!

HIKING THE BERKSHIRES

A GUIDE TO THE AREA'S GREATEST HIKES

Johnny Molloy

FALCONGUIDES

ESSEX, CONNECTICUT

FALCONGUIDES®

An imprint of Globe Pequot, the trade division of The Rowman & Littlefield Publishing Group, Inc.

4501 Forbes Blvd., Ste. 200

Lanham, MD 20706

www.rowman.com

Falcon and FalconGuides are registered trademarks and Make Adventure Your Story is a trademark of The Rowman & Littlefield Publishing Group, Inc.

Distributed by NATIONAL BOOK NETWORK

British Library Cataloguing in Publication Information available

Library of Congress Cataloging-in-Publication Data

Names: Molloy, Johnny, 1961- author.
Title: Hiking the Berkshires : a guide to the area's greatest hikes / Johnny Molloy.
Description: Guilford, Connecticut : FalconGuides, [2022] | Includes index. | Summary: "From families looking for mild walks and day hikes to more adventurous hikers looking for a strenuous summit experience up Mount Greylock or Saddle Ball Mountain, author Johnny Molloy has a hike for everyone"-- Provided by publisher.
Identifiers: LCCN 2021048601 (print) | LCCN 2021048602 (ebook) | ISBN 9781493049769 (Trade Paperback : acid-free paper) | ISBN 9781493049776 (ePub)
Subjects: LCSH: Hiking--Massachusetts--Berkshire Hills--Guidebooks. | Hiking--New England--Guidebooks. | Trails--Massachusetts--Berkshire Hills--Guidebooks. | Trails--New England--Guidebooks. | Berkshire Hills (Mass.)--Guidebooks. | Massachusetts--Guidebooks. | New England--Guidebooks.
Classification: LCC GV199.42.M42 M65 2022 (print) | LCC GV199.42.M42 (ebook) | DDC 796.5109744/1--dc23/eng/20220125
LC record available at https://lccn.loc.gov/2021048601
LC ebook record available at https://lccn.loc.gov/2021048602

CONTENTS

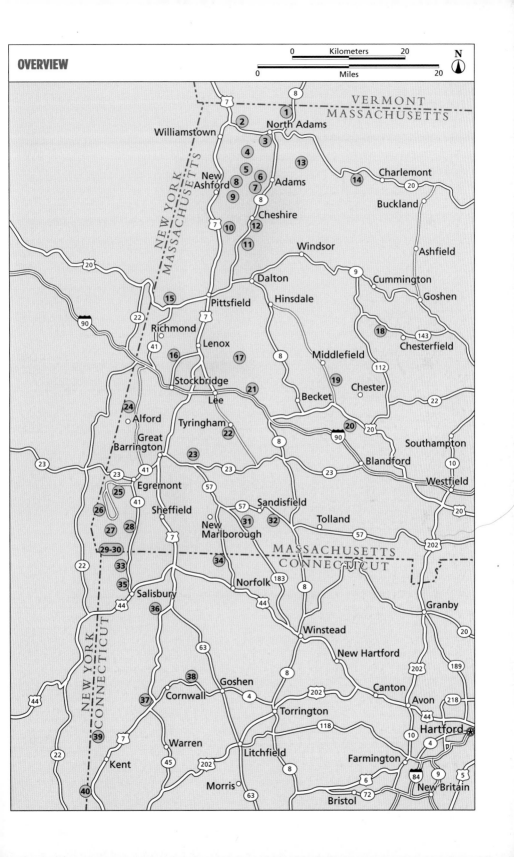

MEET YOUR GUIDE

Johnny Molloy is one of America's most experienced and prolific outdoor writers. His outdoor passion was ignited on a backpacking trip in Great Smoky Mountains National Park. That first foray unleashed a love of the outdoors that led Johnny to spend over 4,500 nights backpacking, canoe camping, and tent camping throughout the United States and beyond over the past three decades.

Friends enjoyed his outdoor adventure stories; one even suggested he write a book. He pursued his friend's idea and soon parlayed his love of the outdoors into an occupation. The results of his efforts are over eighty books and guides. His writings include hiking guidebooks, camping guidebooks, paddling guidebooks, comprehensive guidebooks about a specific area, and true outdoor adventure books covering all or parts of twenty-seven states, including *Hiking Through History: New England* and *Hiking New Jersey*.

Though primarily involved with book publications, Molloy writes for magazines and websites. He continues writing and traveling extensively throughout the United States, endeavoring in a variety of outdoor pursuits.

A Christian, Johnny is an active member of Gideons International. His non-outdoor interests include reading, Christian studies, and University of Tennessee sports. For the latest on Johnny, please visit www.johnnymolloy.com.

INTRODUCTION

Just about everybody in America has heard of the Berkshires. But where exactly are they? The Berkshires are an agglomeration of mountains—a southerly extension of Vermont's Green Mountains—that stretch into western Massachusetts and northwestern Connecticut. They are home to a wealth of peaks rising from the Hoosic, Housatonic, and western Connecticut River valleys, rich with trail-laced public lands where we can hike to overlooks, waterfalls, and historical sites. It all started with area residents acknowledging and preserving the Berkshires' scenic splendor. The citizenry could see that the special places would remain special if they were held in trust for the public to use and enjoy, to create forests and parks, from Mount Greylock State Reservation down to Mount Washington State Forest and Macedonia Brook State Park. Other preserves are privately held but open to the public, such as Clam River Preserve and Chesterfield Gorge.

In a backdrop of southern New England's finest mountain scenery, greater Berkshire hikers can immerse themselves in the region's forests, mountains, and river valleys along which travel hiking trails. Starting in the Northern Berkshires, you can circle picturesque Mauserts Pond at Clarksburg State Park, garnering astounding views of adjacent highlands. Or climb to the overlooks at the Pine Cobble, a scenic destination beheld by locals for two centuries. The hike to The Cascade starts in the town of North Adams then transitions you to the backwoods and a photogenic waterfall.

Moreover, how about the one and only Mount Greylock State Reservation? Hikes here include challenges of all levels through eye-pleasing scenery and varied ecosystems often argued as the Berkshires' finest preserve. Make a loop that not only visits the war memorial atop Mount Greylock, but also takes in other vistas and Massachusetts's only pure boreal forest. Head to lesser-visited Ribbon Falls and Ragged Mountain for overlooks and cataracts. Other hikes take you to still more cascades on a scenic waterfall-hunting loop. The hike to Money Brook Falls is only part of a challenging trek that climbs past peaks and also presents one of the best panoramas in the entire Berkshire region. A longer trek leads you along the Greylock massif to Rounds Rock and more views. Alternatively, work your way up Jones Nose through meadows to more panoramas and an easy, level route back.

Or you can take the famed Ashuwillticook Rail Trail past Cheshire Reservoir, through towns, along wide swamps, and beside raucous river rapids. Hike to the "Grandstand of the Greylock Range" at Spruce Hill. Walk where aboriginals trekked at Mohawk Trail State Forest, visiting the gorgeous Deerfield River as well as Todd Mountain and the Indian Lookout. Make the historic walk near the Hancock Shaker Village up to sacred religious sites within Pittsfield State Forest. The tramp to Cheshire Cobbles and Gore Pond traces the fabled Appalachian Trail from the town of Cheshire up to a rock outcrop that opens a breathtaking landscape north into the Green Mountains of Vermont, west to the Taconics, and south as far as the horizon allows.

Enjoy hiker action like this on Hike 29 Tri State Views Loop, page 168.

The Southern Berkshires present even more opportunities to see the best of this region on hikes of every difficulty. Yokun Ridge South is one of the much appreciated properties managed by the Berkshire Natural Resources Council, with worthy, well-managed trails open to the public that lead to views aplenty as well as an old home site and mountain pond. The hike around Washington Mountain Marsh takes you through a wet wonderland with wildlife-viewing opportunities and boardwalk after boardwalk across a highland swamp ringed in mountains. The hike at Chesterfield Gorge takes you along the federally designated wild and scenic Westfield River then loops back through deep forests. The family hike over the Keystone Arch Bridges Trail returns you to the first Berkshires railroad, now reverted back to wilderness. Hike the Appalachian Trail past an old fire tower site to Finerty Pond, a highland tarn where you might spot a moose. The short loop at Tyringham Cobbles reaps big rewards.

Visit Beartown State Forest to combine a walk around a bucolic pond and to a pair of eye-popping vistas that won't fail to please. Add in some camping, paddling, or fishing while you're at it. Bash Bish Falls is a Berkshires classic, a must-do walk to receive your official Berkshire hiker credentials. Have high expectations for the hike to Alander Mountain—and they will be met. The panoramas are difficult to exceed. Speaking of difficult, the Tri-State Views Loop has some challenging segments, but in the end you can gain stimulating views from Massachusetts, New York, and Connecticut, and even stand in all three states at once!

The Connecticut Berkshires, also known as the Berkshire Hills or sometimes grouped with the Litchfield Hills, may be a little lower in elevation but are no less proud than the Massachusetts Berkshires and also offer a variety of worthwhile hikes that will leave you with a new respect for hiking in the Constitution State. The Bear Mountain Loop leads you to the highest mountain peak entirely within Connecticut and offers far-reaching vistas and a variety of ecosystems. The Appalachian Trail is your conduit to views from the outcrop that is the Lions Head, and is perfect for a family day hike. The unusual vista at Rand View, where a sloping meadow reveals jagged summits to the north as far as the eye can see, is a little more challenging but also uses the one and only Appalachian Trail.

The Pine Knob Loop at Housatonic Meadows is a Connecticut classic that takes you along the Housatonic River and up to rock outcrops that deliver elevated perspectives of the river valley below, and a waterfall, too. Take the Mohawk Trail—the former route of the Appalachian Trail—to a clearing used as an Indian lookout for centuries. The hike at Macedonia Brook State Park will surprise, with its steep rock-slab slopes and a few places where you will be using your hands and feet to reach multiple views. The hike from Bulls Bridge takes you along a crashing river to a lesser waterway, then up a mountain with vistas. Add in a little colonial history to complete the trek. It all adds up to an impressive array of hiking destinations!

It is in the Berkshires where the hikes in this book are found. After having the privilege of researching potential hikes for the book, hiking the hikes, taking photographs, shooting video, finding the ones that made the grade (and the ones that didn't), exploring the parks beyond the trails, mapping the hikes, then actually writing and completing this compendium, I am excited to share these Berkshire adventures with you. The treks are an ideal mix of views and waterfalls, places where the human history of southern New England mixes with the natural history, where a wealth of flora and fauna makes hiking the Berkshires a singular experience.

I think of the treasure trove of trails in this unique region, and how the hikes in this guide—the best hikes in the Berkshires—create a mosaic of trail experiences reflecting the wide array of adventures to be had in this part of the Appalachian Mountains. I hope the trails offered in this book will help you explore, understand, and appreciate the natural and human history of the Berkshires. Enjoy!

WEATHER

The Berkshires from North Adams to Bulls Bridge experience all four seasons in their entirety, and sometimes all at once when you take into account the elevation variations of the region, ranging from a little above 300 feet along the Housatonic River near Bulls Bridge, Connecticut, to 3,491 feet atop Massachusetts's Mount Greylock.

Summer is usually mild, with a few hot spells, though cool breezes can almost always be found along mountain streams and in the high country. Morning hikers can avoid the common afternoon thunderstorms that arise in the mountains. Electronic devices equipped with internet access allow summer hikers to monitor storms as they come up, though coverage can be spotty in places.

Hikers increase in numbers when the first northerly fronts of fall sweep cool, clear air across the Berkshires. Crisp mornings, great for vigorous treks, give way to warm afternoons, more conducive to family strolls.

Winters can be long and will bring frigid subfreezing days and chilling rains, and copious amounts of snow in the lowlands and even more at the higher elevations. Roads leading to highland trailheads may be closed or impassable. Winter brings far fewer hours of daylight; however, wise hike choices, a brisk hiking pace, and reasoned time management will keep you warm and walking. Each cold month has a few days of mild weather. Make the most of them, and seek out lower-elevation hikes.

Spring will be more variable and leads to the mud season, when melting snow and rains can turn paths into quagmires. Avoid trails then to circumvent trail damage and a sloppy hike. In the spring a mild day can be followed by a cold one. Extensive rains bring re-growth, but also keep hikers indoors.

A good way to plan your hiking is to check monthly averages of high and low temperatures and average rainfall for each month in Pittsfield, Massachusetts. Pittsfield averages

70.7 inches of snow and 46.4 inches of rain per year. The following climate data will give you a good idea of what to expect each month. However, remember temperatures can be cooler and precipitation higher in the adjacent highlands.

MONTH	AVERAGE HIGH (°F)	AVERAGE LOW (°F)	PRECIPITATION (INCHES)
January	31	11	2.8
February	35	14	3.1
March	43	21	2.8
April	56	32	3.2
May	67	42	3.6
June	76	52	5.4
July	80	56	4.3
August	80	55	4.3
September	71	47	3.7
October	59	36	4.5
November	47	28	2.9
December	35	18	3.6

FLORA AND FAUNA

The landscape of the Berkshires varies greatly, from the deep valleys of the Hoosic, Housatonic, and Connecticut River tributaries to the rocky, rising peaks extending along the Appalachians. A surprisingly large amount of forested public and private lands create significant swaths and travel corridors for wildlife to roam. At the top of the food chain stands the black bear. You can run into one anywhere in the region and on any trail included in this guide. Although attacks by black bears are very rare, they have happened in the East. Seeing a bear is an exciting yet potentially scary experience. If you meet a bear while hiking, stay calm and don't run. Make loud noises to scare off the bear and back away slowly. Remain aware and alert.

In addition to bruins, another even larger—albeit less dangerous—mammal you may see is the moose. They have made quite a comeback in Massachusetts—and are even spotted in Connecticut. Deer will be the land animal you most likely will see hiking area trails. They can be found throughout the Berkshires. Porcupines are common, too, but are more a threat to your dog than you. A quiet hiker may also witness turkeys, raccoons, or even a coyote. Expect to see beaver around ponds, especially where their dams are visible. Mountain streams and larger lakes may harbor otters. Remember, if you feel uncomfortable when encountering any critter, keep your distance and they will generally keep theirs.

Overhead, many raptors will be plying the skies for food, including bald eagles, hawks, falcons, and owls. Depending upon where you are, other birds you may spot range from kingfishers to woodpeckers. Songbirds are abundant during the warm season no matter the habitat.

The flora offers as much variety as you would expect with such elevational range. Elevation and exposure to the sun fashion differing conditions where varied habitats

Campbell Falls is one of the most picturesque cataracts in the Berkshires.

Hikes in this guide take place in western Massachusetts, northwestern Connecticut, and a little bit of New York.

spring up. The absolute highest elevations harbor the spruce-fir ecosystem, while red spruce and balsam fir commonly mix with northern hardwoods of yellow birch, paper birch, beech, cherry, and maple. Along mountain streams and waterways, rhododendron rises lush, while incredible displays of wildflowers reflect a cornucopia of color—bleeding heart, Dutchman's breeches, trilliums, trout lilies, pink lady's slippers, and jack-in-the-pulpit.

On drier, south-facing slopes, especially in the lower-elevation Connecticut Berkshires, hills harbor chestnut oak, red oak, hickory, and mountain laurel. Moist, low-elevation areas will also see red maple and black birch. It all adds up to vegetational variety of the first order that can be seen and experienced as spring climbs the mountains and fall descends back to the valleys.

WILDERNESS RESTRICTIONS/ REGULATIONS

The best hikes in the Berkshires primarily take place in state forests and parks of Massachusetts and Connecticut, along the National Park Service–held Appalachian Trail corridor, and to a lesser extent privately held preserves open to public use. On one hike you may traverse multiple public parcels of land, going from a state park to a state forest, or from a state forest to a state reservation, and so on. Most of the time you will not know the difference—the flora and fauna of the Berkshires certainly don't. A couple of hikes barely edge into New York. The public lands are managed differently where fees are concerned and are noted in each hike's summary matter. Each unit will have its own backcountry camping regulations. The Appalachian Trail corridor in both Berkshire states allow camping only at specific designated sites.

Detailed trail and road maps are available of almost all public and private lands traveled in this guide. Download them—they will come in handy in helping you get around.

Then there are the private nature preserves. The Berkshire Natural Resources Council (www.brnc.org) and The Trustees (www.thetrustees.org) both preserve lands through which trails travel in this guide. Visit their websites for the latest regulations as well as to download helpful maps.

GETTING AROUND

AREA CODES
The greater Massachusetts Berkshires area code is 413, while the area codes in the Connecticut Berkshires are 860 and 959.

ROADS
For the purposes of this guide, the best hikes in the Berkshires are confined to western Massachusetts and northwestern Connecticut. Specifically in Massachusetts this includes all of Berkshire County as well as a little terrain to the east, and in Connecticut the most northwesterly portion of the state, from Norfolk to Goshen to Bulls Bridge, roughly following the state's Appalachian Trail corridor.

All hikes in this guide are well west of I-91, but I-90 in Massachusetts does cut through the Berkshires en route to the Empire State. Major state arteries include MA 2, MA 9, MA 8, and CT 41. Major federal arteries include US 7 and US 44. Directions to trailheads are given from these arteries or easily identifiable towns.

BY AIR
Pittsfield (PSF) has the only airport of size in the Berkshires. Other options are Springfield, Massachusetts (SFY), or Hartford, Connecticut (BDL). To book reservations online, check out your favorite airline's website or search a travel site for the best price.

BY BUS
Most trailheads are not accessible via bus, but Greyhound serves some towns in the Berkshires; visit www.greyhound.com for more information.

VISITOR INFORMATION
For general information on visiting the Berkshires, visit www.berkshires.org or call (413) 499-1600. For a broader Massachusetts sampling, visit www.visitma.com. The overall official Connecticut tourism website is www.ctvisit.com.

HOW TO USE THIS GUIDE

Take a close enough look, and you'll find that this guide contains just about everything you'll ever need to choose, plan for, enjoy, and survive a hike in the Berkshires. Stuffed with useful western Berkshires–specific information, *Hiking the Berkshires* features forty mapped and cued hikes. The hikes are grouped into three units. "Northern Berkshires" covers hikes in northwestern Massachusetts, including Mount Greylock Reservation. "Southern Berkshires" harbors hikes in southwest Massachusetts, including Mount Washington State Forest. "Connecticut Berkshires" details hikes in the most northwesterly portion of the Constitution State, roughly following the Appalachian Trail corridor.

Each hike starts with a short **summary** of the hike's highlights. These quick overviews give you a taste of the hiking adventures to follow. You'll learn about the trail terrain and what surprises each route has to offer. Following the summary, you'll find the **hike specs:** quick, nitty-gritty details of the hike, each explained more in depth below. Most are self-explanatory, but here are some details on others:

Start: Tells you exactly where you will begin your hike. For example, the hike might start at a picnic area within a state park, allowing you to look for a specific trailhead rather than just the state park. The name of the trailhead often corresponds with those found on mapping apps.

Distance: The total distance of the recommended route—one-way for loop hikes, the round-trip on an out-and-back or lollipop hike, point-to-point for a shuttle. Options are additional.

Difficulty: Each hike has been assigned a level of difficulty. The rating system was developed from several sources and personal experience. These levels are meant to be a guideline only and may prove easier or harder for different people depending on ability and physical fitness.

> Easy—5 miles or less total trip distance in one day, with minimal elevation gain and paved or smooth-surfaced dirt trail.
>
> Moderate—up to 10 miles total trip distance in one day, with moderate elevation gain and potentially rough terrain.
>
> Difficult—more than 10 miles total trip distance in one day, with strenuous elevation gain and rough and/or rocky terrain.

Elevation change: This is the aggregate elevation gained and lost during a hike, whether it is a loop hike or an out-and-back hike. These numbers were found using GPS data obtained during the given hike and loaded onto a mapping program.

Maximum grade: This details the steepest portion of the hike for a sustained distance, whether you will be going up or down that grade on the specific hike. The maximum grade is calculated by dividing the elevation gained or lost by the distance covered.

Hiking time: The average approximate time it will take to cover the route. The number is based on the total distance, elevation gain, and condition and difficulty of the trail. Your fitness level will also affect your time.

Seasons/schedule: This provides information on the best time of year to hike the given hike and/or the specific hours a place is open/closed.

Fees and permits: Tells you whether you need to carry any money with you for park entrance fees and/or permits.

Dog friendly: This details whether dogs are allowed or not and/or specific regulations, but also if it makes sense to take your pet on the given hike.

Trail surface: General information about what to expect underfoot. Is the trail very rocky, smooth, wide, natural surface, etc.? Are parts of the path paved or concrete? This way you know what footwear to use and what conditions to expect.

Land status: States whether the hike is in a state park, state forest, private preserve, or other entity.

Nearest town: Helps orient you to the hike's location, and also to find out what amenities are in the nearest town, such as outfitters, restaurants, or emergency clinic.

Other trail users: Such as horseback riders, mountain bikers, inline skaters, etc.

Map to consult: This lists other maps to supplement the maps in this book. USGS maps are a good source for accurate topographical information, but the local park map may show more recent trails. Use both.

Amenities available: Lets you know if restrooms, picnic areas, campgrounds, or other enhancements are at or near the trailhead. This way you can stop en route to the hike to use the restroom if none are available at the trailhead, know whether to bring a picnic to the trailhead, etc.

Cell service: This helps give you an idea of whether or not your phone will get reception on the hike. In elevationally varied areas such as the Berkshires, you can have reception on a ridge but not down in the valley. Also, what carrier you use can have a lot to do with whether or not you have reception.

Trail contact: This gives you the phone number and website URL for the local land manager(s) in charge of all the trails within the selected hike. Get trail access information before you head out, or contact the land manager after your visit if you see problems with trail erosion, damage, or misuse.

The **Finding the trailhead** section gives you dependable driving directions to where you'll want to park. **The Hike** is the meat of the chapter. Detailed and honest, it's a carefully researched impression of the trail. It also often includes lots of area history, both natural and human. Under **Miles and Directions**, mileage cues identify all turns and trail name changes, as well as points of interest.

HOW TO USE THE MAPS

Overview map: This map shows the location of each hike in the area by hike number.

Route map: This is your primary visual guide to each hike. It shows all of the accessible roads and trails, points of interest, water, landmarks, and geographical features. The map also distinguishes trails from roads, and paved roads from unpaved roads. The selected route is highlighted, and directional arrows point the way.

TRAIL FINDER

To get our readers started on the hikes that best suit their interests and abilities, we include this simple trail finder that categorizes each of the hikes in the book into a helpful list. Your hikes can fall under more than one category. Please choose the categories that are most appropriate for your area.

HIKE #/NAME	BEST HIKES FOR WATERFALLS	BEST HIKES FOR GREAT VIEWS	BEST HIKES FOR CHILDREN
1 Mauserts Pond Loop		•	•
2 Pine Cobble Loop		•	
3 The Cascade	•		•
4 Money Brook Falls Loop	•	•	
5 Mount Greylock Loop		•	•
6 Ribbon Falls Ragged Mountain	•	•	
7 Pecks Brook Falls Loop	•		
8 Greylock Highlands Waterfall Hike	•		
9 Jones Nose Circuit		•	
10 Rounds Rock		•	
11 Ashuwillticook Rail Trail		•	•
12 Cheshire Cobbles Gore Pond		•	
13 Spruce Hill Circuit		•	
14 Todd Mountain Loop		•	
15 Shaker Hike	•		•
16 Yokun Ridge South		•	
17 Washington Mountain Marsh Loop		•	

BEST HIKES FOR DOGS	BEST HIKES FOR POND/STREAM LOVERS	BEST HIKES FOR BACKPACKERS	BEST HIKES FOR NATURE LOVERS	BEST HIKES FOR HISTORY LOVERS
	•			
			•	
	•			
	•			
•			•	•
•	•		•	
•	•	•		
	•	•		
•			•	•
				•
•	•			•
	•	•		
•			•	
	•		•	•
•				•
•				•
	•		•	

HIKE #/NAME	BEST HIKES FOR WATERFALLS	BEST HIKES FOR GREAT VIEWS	BEST HIKES FOR CHILDREN
18 Chesterfield Gorge Loop			•
19 Keystone Arch Bridges Trail		•	•
20 Sanderson Brook Falls Circuit	•	•	
21 Finerty Pond via the Appalachian Trail			
22 Tyringham Cobble		•	•
23 Views at Beartown		•	
24 Alford Springs Preserve		•	
25 Jug End Loop		•	•
26 Bash Bish Falls	•		•
27 Alander Mountain		•	
28 Race Brook Falls and Mountain	•	•	
29 Tri-State Views Loop	•		
30 Sages Ravine and Bear Rock Falls	•	•	
31 York Lake Loop		•	•
32 Clam River Preserve			
33 Bear Mountain Loop		•	
34 Campbell Falls	•		•
35 Lions Head View		•	•
36 Rands View		•	
37 Pine Knob Loop	•	•	
38 Mohawk Mountain via the Mohawk Trail		•	
39 Macedonia Brook Circuit		•	
40 Bulls Bridge Hike	•	•	

BEST HIKES FOR DOGS	BEST HIKES FOR POND/STREAM LOVERS	BEST HIKES FOR BACKPACKERS	BEST HIKES FOR NATURE LOVERS	BEST HIKES FOR HISTORY LOVERS
•	•		•	
•	•			•
•	•			•
•	•			
•				
	•		•	
			•	
•			•	
	•			•
•	•	•	•	
	•	•	•	
			•	
•	•	•		
•	•			
•	•		•	
		•	•	•
	•			
•				
		•	•	
•	•		•	
		•		•
			•	•
•	•	•		•

MAP LEGEND

Municipal

≡⟨90⟩≡	Interstate Highway
≡⟨20⟩≡	US Highway
≡⟨116⟩≡	State Road
―――――	Local Road
= = = =	Gravel Road
= = = =	Unpaved Road
⊢―+―⊣	Railroad
-------	State Boundary

Trails

------	Featured Trail
- - - - - -	Trail

Water Features

⬭	Lake/Reservoir
≛≛	Marsh
∿	River/Creek
∿	Intermittent Stream
⋛	Waterfall
⟁	Spring

Symbols

∩	Arch
⌣	Bridge
▲	Campground
•―•	Gate
▬	Lodging
▲	Peak
⛿	Picnic Area
▪	Point of Interest/Structure
⛺	Ranger Station
⛷	Ski Area
○	Town
①	Trailhead
⚑	Viewpoint/Overlook
❓	Visitor/Information Center

Land Management

�	State Park/Forest
⬚	Reservation/Preserve

NORTHERN BERKSHIRES

Todd Mountain Loop, page 89

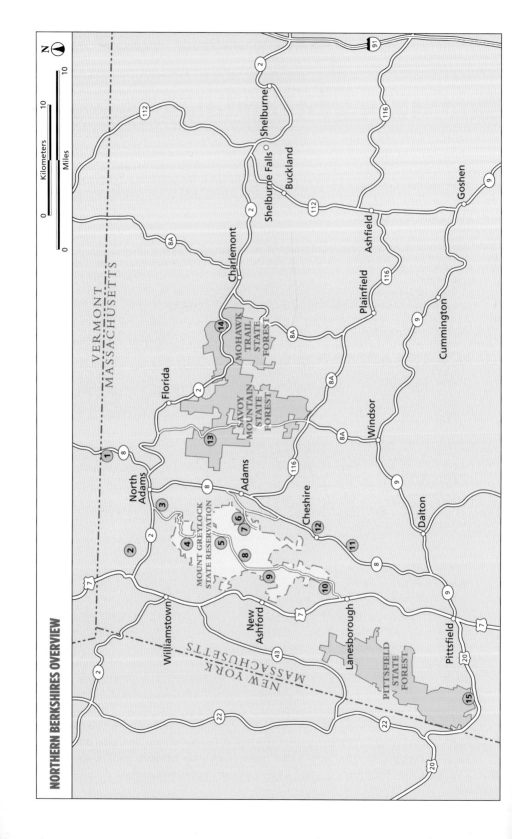

1 MAUSERTS POND LOOP

Set at pretty Clarksburg State Park, nestled in the Hoosic River valley between the Hoosac Range to the east and the Taconics to the west, with the Greylock Range even closer, this loop hike presents first-rate vistas of these nearby mountain ramparts as well as Mauserts Pond, around which this hike travels. Start at the alluring park picnic area, then begin circling the shoreline after crossing Beaver Creek, alternately traveling along the shore, over bog bridges, and back in the hilly woods, before looping past the fine park campground. You may even see a moose!

Start: Picnic area/swim beach parking area
Distance: 3.0-mile loop
Difficulty: Easy
Elevation change: +/-243 feet over entire hike
Maximum grade: 2% grade for 0.4 mile
Hiking time: About 1.5 hours
Seasons/schedule: May through Dec
Fees and permits: Parking permit required
Dog friendly: Yes

Trail surface: Natural surface
Land status: State park
Nearest town: North Adams
Other trail users: None
Map to consult: Clarksburg State Park
Amenities available: Restrooms, picnic area, swim beach at trailhead
Cell service: Good
Trail contact: Clarksburg State Park, (413) 664-8345, www.mass.gov/locations/clarksburg-state-park

FINDING THE TRAILHEAD

From the intersection of MA 2 and MA 8 just east of downtown North Adams, take MA 8 north for 3 miles to Middle Road. Turn left and follow Middle Road for 0.2 mile, then turn right into Clarksburg State Park. Once there, continue right on the main park road to reach the picnic/swim beach parking area on your right. Address: 1199 Middle Rd., Clarksburg, MA. **Trailhead GPS:** 42.736859, -73.075705

THE HIKE

Despite coming in at a mere 368 acres, Clarksburg State Park offers a lot. It certainly seems bigger. Maybe it is the inspiring mountain views to be had from nearly any open space here. Mauserts Pond is the centerpiece of the park and has an intersecting legend to go along with it. Seems the 45-acre man-made pond (now with two dams on outlets of Beaver Creek) was formerly a meadow that was actually farmed. One day, two young men, tired of tilling the soil, decided to have a good ol' fashioned horse race on the meadow, promoting it among the locals. The next thing you know, farmers and towns-folk from miles around gathered at the meadow to watch the contest. And watch they did, betting a pretty penny on which young whippersnapper would win the race.

Other residents were repelled by the gambling and the pride that went along with this horse-racing business. Therefore, to nip this nascent pastime in the bud, local do-gooders dammed Beaver Creek, flooding the meadow and creating Mauserts Pond in the process, eliminating the budding horse track. The pond and surrounding terrain later became a

The Hoosac Range rises from Mauserts Pond.

Massachusetts state park, and a fine one it is, perfect for a family adventure or a relaxing outdoor vacation in the Berkshires. I have camped, picnicked, and enjoyed the waters here, and give it a ringing endorsement. Clarksburg State Park also makes an ideal base camp for hiking nearby trails detailed in this guide.

The hike begins at the picnic/swim beach area. Here, a newer restroom serves an outdoor dining locale with picnic tables in both sun and shade. A long swim beach fronts Mauserts Pond and offers a picturesque spot to cool off on a sunny summer day that will rival any beach in Massachusetts, salt or otherwise. Upon entering the woods, you soon emerge at the shore of Mauserts Pond near a small clearing with picnic tables, beside a small dam at one of the two outlets of Beaver Creek. Mauserts Pond is unusual in that it took two dams to raise the water to an acceptable level, for recreation and for the prevention of horse racing!

Beyond here the trail crosses the outflow of Beaver Creek. There has been a bridge here in the past and will likely be one here in the future (the outflow is subject to floods in the spring), but at the very least there will be stepping stones. After making your way across the creek, enter hummocky ferny woods. Some of the wetter areas will have boardwalks, especially where you span otherwise impassable marshes. At this point you are but a quarter mile from the Vermont border. In fact, the northern park boundary is the Massachusetts-Vermont state line.

And then you return to Mauserts Pond, contrasting with the insect-rich bogs and the lumpy shadowy woods, to gaze upon forest and brush encircling the open waters, from which rise verdant summits of the Hoosacs. Scan for moose. Even if you don't see one, look for their imprints in the shoreline mud and sand.

MAUSERTS POND LOOP

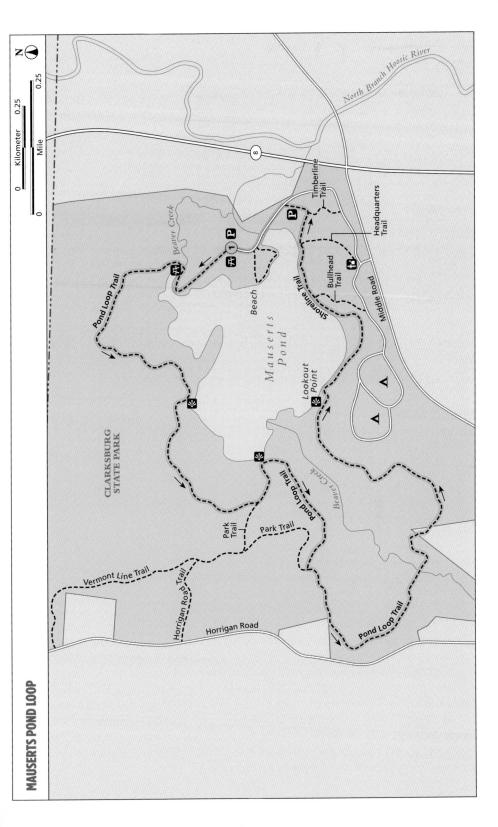

You leave the pond once again, working around another marshy tributary of Mauserts Pond, then come to a trailside boulder, standing proud, a relic of the last ice age when it was dropped by a retreating glacier a couple thousand feet tall! Now the rock is left still and mute, watching the forests grow, fall, and change along with the land, perhaps even hearing the thud of horse hooves from a long-ago horse race, when Mauserts Pond was but a farm field.

The hike leads to another pond view then works around upper Beaver Creek. You next come near the park's highly recommended campground, shaded in evergreens, perfect for a summer or fall family getaway. The camp offers hot showers and flush toilets. Each campsite features a picnic table, fire ring, and bear-proof food storage locker. Reservations are required.

The Pond Loop Trail has been rerouted around the campground but still emerges at the hike's highlight—Lookout Point. Here, a small grassy area opens onto the shore and a thin natural gravel beach. The flat water lays open views of almost the entire lakeshore. Mountains form a backdrop to the scene that is one of my favorites in all of the Bay State. The hike then runs the wooded shoreline of the tarn, popping out for occasional views as well as crossing small bridges and boardwalks. You can see the swim beach getting closer and closer.

After meeting a couple of spur trails, the hike pops out in the large park parking lot, filling on summer weekends and during leaf-peeping season. A short road walk returns you to the trailhead. Consider undertaking more than just a day hike here at wonderful Clarksburg State Park.

MILES AND DIRECTIONS

0.0 Join the Pond Loop Trail at the north end of the picnic parking area, near the large restroom building. Hike a doubletrack path through hardwoods. Just ahead, a short spur goes left toward the shore.

0.1 Reach a foot-only-accessible picnic area along the shore of the pond, in a small cove. Head right from here past a small dam, tracing the outflow of Beaver Creek, then cross Beaver Creek.

0.4 Span a wooden bridge over a marshy stream, more marsh than stream. Enjoy wetland views. Other lesser marshes will have boardwalks as well.

0.7 Return to the shore of Mauserts Pond, opening south to Lookout Point, with the Hoosac Range extending to the horizon. Turn away from the shore and begin working around another feeder branch of Mauserts Pond.

0.9 Bridge the boggy stream feeding Mauserts Pond. From here, make a little climb into thick woods.

1.0 Pass a large glacial erratic, a granite boulder left here during the last ice age.

1.1 Meet the Park Trail on a hillside. It leaves right to meet the Vermont Line Trail. Stay left with the Pond Loop Trail, descending the hill.

1.2 Return to the pond. You are now in the western corner of the tarn. Views open to the north and east. The white swim beach is easy to discern, and the Hoosac Range rises in the distance. Turn away from the water, heading west up the valley of Beaver Creek, draining Sheep Hill above you. Pass an old stone fence of this former farming area.

Hiker circles the brush along Mauserts Pond.

Enjoying the summer breeze blowing in from Mauserts Pond

1.5 Meet the Park Trail a second time. Stay left, circling around upper Beaver Creek along sloped terrain. Come very near the park's western boundary, crossing seeping wetlands.

1.9 Bridge upper Beaver Creek. Rise into drier terrain in shady woods of pine.

2.1 The trail abruptly turns left, working around the campground and dropping toward Mauserts Pond.

2.4 Reach the hike's signature view—Lookout Point. The panorama dispenses first-rate viewscapes of Mauserts Pond and its shoreline in the foreground, with the Hoosac Range rising in the east and northeast and the Green Mountains rising to the northwest in Vermont. From there, head east along the shoreline in woods, bridging occasional wet areas, now on the Shoreline Trail.

2.7 The Bullhead Trail, primarily used as a ski path, leaves right and uphill. Keep east along the shoreline.

2.8 The Headquarters Trail leaves right for park headquarters. Stay straight with the Shoreline Trail, quickly leaving the shore.

2.9 Come to the large park parking lot after passing the intersection with the short Timberline Trail. Head left on the paved main park road, passing the Blueberry Trail.

3.0 Arrive back at the picnic/swim beach parking area, completing the gratifying family hike.

2 **PINE COBBLE LOOP**

This classic Berkshires hike leads you from the town of Williamstown up to the shoulder of East Mountain where the Pine Cobble, an evergreen-bordered outcrop with multiple vista points, delivers fine panoramas. From there the hike leads to the crest of East Mountain and joins the stony Appalachian Trail to reach another overlook. The loop hike then takes the Class of '98 Trail past the rocky shoulder of the mountain to complete the circuit.

Start: Pine Cobble Road parking area
Distance: 5.3-mile lollipop
Difficulty: Moderate to difficult due to stony trail
Elevation change: +/-1,602 feet over entire hike
Maximum grade: 16% downhill grade for 0.9 mile
Hiking time: About 3 hours
Seasons/schedule: May through Dec
Fees and permits: None
Dog friendly: On leash only

Trail surface: Natural surface, some sections extremely rocky
Land status: Private preserve open to public, state forest, Appalachian Trail corridor
Nearest town: Williamstown
Other trail users: None
Map to consult: Pine Cobble Preserve
Amenities available: None
Cell service: Good
Trail contact: Williamstown Rural Lands, (413) 458-2494, https://rurallands.org

FINDING THE TRAILHEAD

From the traffic circle at the intersection of MA 2 and US 7 in Williamstown, take MA 2 east for 0.6 mile, then turn left on Cole Avenue and follow it for 0.8 mile. Cross the Hoosic River, then turn right onto North Hoosic Road and follow it for 0.4 mile to Pine Cobble Road. Turn left and follow Pine Cobble Road for 0.1 mile to reach the trailhead parking on the left. The actual Pine Cobble Trail starts just a little farther up Pine Cobble Road and is on the opposite side of the road from the parking area. **Trailhead GPS:** 42.716115, -73.185288

THE HIKE

When East Mountain was just an unnamed peak above quiet Williamstown, Massachusetts, local residents would climb the west slope of the mount to an open outcrop bordered in evergreens, a place where they could pick out their own house or their neighbor's farm from the stony perch. For students at Williamstown College, the climb to the Pine Cobble has been—and still is—a rite of passage. And when the Appalachian Trail (AT) came rolling through the Hoosac Range, the trails to the Pine Cobble and the AT were linked together, thus enabling us to fashion a satisfying hike with multiple overlooks and a trip through several forest and rock amalgamations.

The word cobble is commonly found around the Berkshires. The term refers to a rock outcrop, or pile of rocks, on a mountainside that often creates an open space that avails views. Numerous hikes in this guide go to or near a place named cobble.

The other word named in our destination is pine. Pitch pines grow around the cobbles found on East Mountain, with no other stands nearby. Pitch pines thrive in fire-prone

Peering down to Williamstown from the Pine Cobble

areas, often the south or west side of mountain slopes, and other areas of poor, shallow, and gravelly soils, leaving a spotty distribution. The evergreens and their limbs grow in poor form, reducing the pitch pine's value as a commercial tree, but increasing its camera-friendly appeal. Pitch pines extend southwest from Ontario and Quebec in Canada down to southeast New England, and along the Appalachian Mountains all the way to Georgia.

Thus, we have the Pine Cobble. The hike uses privately owned preserve property, Clarksburg State Forest, and National Park Service–owned Appalachian Trail corridor lands to cobble together the route. The Williamstown Rural Lands Foundation preserves and conserves lands throughout northwestern Massachusetts, including forests like those here on East Mountain, as well as farms and wildlife habitats. They own and/or manage over 1,200 acres with 100 miles of hiking trails that are actively administered for recreation, with another set of lands held as agricultural assets. Their mission is about conserving land, promoting outdoor recreation, and developing nature-based education. The Pine Cobble property is their largest and most popular natural asset. Visit their website, www.rurallands.org, to learn more or contribute to the organization.

The hike begins off Pine Cobble Road, tracing an old forest doubletrack past where a dwelling once stood, then heads upward on a singletrack well-marked and -maintained path. The rerouted trail works around nearby homes, then climbs to meet the Class of '98 Trail. The path was named for the Williamstown College students from that fine year who built the trail linking to the AT and enabling us to make a loop.

For now, stick with the Pine Cobble Trail as it makes an uptick in very rocky woods, with stony footing. Sassafras, chestnut oak, wild azalea, and bracken fern are more indicators of the xeric woodlands here. Fire is no stranger to these lands. Early residents knew

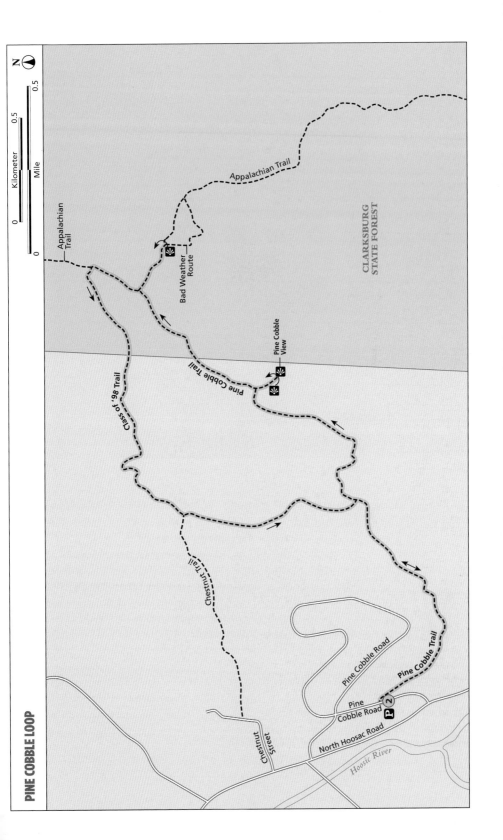

PINE COBBLE LOOP

Crossing a boulder jumble en route to meet the Appalachian Trail

this as a place ideal for blueberries and frequently burned this part of East Mountain to improve berry habitat. One of the more recent fires was in May of 2021, when a conflagration erupted on East Mountain, though it was mostly a ground fire.

You soon reach the Pine Cobble, with its gnarled pitch pines, blueberries aplenty, and open rock outcrops. Explore the numerous overlooks on the perched mountain shoulder. Some of the better views are southeast, up the Hoosic River valley toward North Adams to Mount Greylock and the Hoosac Range beyond. To the southwest another panorama reveals Williamstown below, where you can clearly identify landmarks such as the college, while the Taconics form an emerald bastion beyond the burg. The stunted pitch pines and oaks provide shady spots among the outcrops, where blueberry pickers can munch their fresh treats in late summer.

Beyond the Pine Cobble the hike leads up to the crest of East Mountain and over open rocky pockets where hikers pick their way through sun-bleached boulder jumbles. Partial views can be had from these locales. The Pine Cobble Trail meets the well-trod Appalachian Trail near the hike's high point. You are just above 2,100 feet. Here, a short detour southbound on the AT takes you over more impressive rock gardens then past a highland bog before coming to a point where the AT splits. One way is the main AT, and the other is a bad weather route. The bad weather route leads you to a stone slab and another view. Here you can scan across the Sherman Brook watershed to Bald Mountain. Though inferior to the Pine Cobble panorama, the side trip is worth the effort.

You then trace the AT northbound with some easy ridgetop hiking in foot-friendly woods. And the path is also fine for the first part of the Class of '98 Trail. Then the track becomes more stony as you walk along the base of a boulder-strewn hillside with partial bluffs. The path weaves amidst outcrops and boulders that augment the hardwood forest shading the trail. After completing the loop portion of the hike, you are left with the 0.9-mile backtrack to the trailhead, finishing the long-done Pine Cobble hike.

MILES AND DIRECTIONS

0.0 Pick up the Pine Cobble Trail on the opposite side of the road from the trailhead parking area. Join a doubletrack path, bridging the outflow of a small creek on planks in hardwood-dominant woods of red maple, black birch, and oak with a light understory.

0.4 The Pine Cobble Trail veers left and climbs the mountainside.

0.6 The Pine Cobble Trail levels off. Enjoy the easy hiking.

0.9 Reach the end of the flats and begin to climb. The path becomes rockier as you pass the intersection with the Class of '98 Trail.

1.6 Come to a trail intersection in a gap after an invigorating ascent. Head right toward the views from the Pine Cobble. Make sure to explore all around for multiple views, including Mount Greylock, North Adams, and Williamstown. Backtrack and then continue on the Pine Cobble Trail, ascending toward the crest of East Mountain.

2.1 Cut through a cobble field of white quartzite dotted with wind-bent pitch pines, creating a memorable landscape.

2.3 Intersect the Appalachian Trail. You are only 1.3 miles from the Vermont border to the north. But for now, we hike southbound. Clamber through another boulder garden, then skirt past a small bog.

2.5 The trail splits. Here, the AT keeps straight, but we go right with the bad weather route. Soon come to some open outcrops with views of Bald Mountain and lands beyond. Backtrack to the intersection with the Pine Cobble Trail and stay with the AT northbound, in mixed woods heavy with pine, leaving the rocky terrain.

2.8 Leave left from the AT on the signed but much less used Class of '98 Trail. Begin a prolonged downgrade.

3.6 Enter a rock field, then switchback and soon level off in a shallow valley with huge boulders to the left of the trail.

3.8 The Chestnut Trail leaves right for Chestnut Street. Keep straight with the Class of '98 Trail, with a boulder field rising to your left. More stony spots lie ahead.

4.4 Complete the loop portion of the hike and backtrack down the Pine Cobble Trail.

5.3 Arrive back at the Pine Cobble Trail parking area, finishing the adventure executed by generations of local residents to the Pine Cobble.

3 THE CASCADE

This unusual hike starts in the middle of an urban area then leads up a clear creek draining Mount Greylock State Reservation to a 40-foot waterfall in a natural area so pretty it leaves you in disbelief that you started this hike in a town! Begin at a school/YMCA building with public parking, then bridge Notch Brook. After that you actually hike up a couple of streets to reach the woods. From there wander in deep forest, bridging North Brook again. Finally, turn into a defile where The Cascade makes its tiered white dive into a slender, stone-lined cathedral and shallow plunge pool.

Start: Northern Berkshire YMCA/Brayton Elementary/North Adams municipal lot
Distance: 2.0 miles out and back
Difficulty: Easy
Elevation change: +/-242 feet over entire hike
Maximum grade: 5% grade for 0.8 mile
Hiking time: About 1 hour
Seasons/schedule: Apr through Dec
Fees and permits: None
Dog friendly: Yes, but hike does go through urban neighborhood

Trail surface: Concrete sidewalk, natural surface
Land status: State reservation
Nearest town: North Adams
Other trail users: None
Map to consult: None
Amenities available: All manner of urban offerings nearby
Cell service: Excellent
Trail contact: North Adams Chamber of Commerce, (413) 398-4084, https://explorenorthadams.com

FINDING THE TRAILHEAD

From the intersection of MA 8, Beaver Street, and MA 2, Mohawk Trail, in North Adams, take MA 8 west for 2.2 miles then turn left on Brayton Hill Terrace just before bridging the Hoosic River, then quickly turn left on Brickyard Court to enter the Northern Berkshire YMCA parking lot. Address: 22 Brickyard Ct., North Adams, MA. **Trailhead GPS:** 42.697131, -73.136229

THE HIKE

People have been attracted to naturally beautiful places like The Cascade (as named on official USGS maps, yet locally known as The Cascades in addition to The Cascade) for as long as there have been people in the Berkshires. We don't know what aboriginal Indians thought of The Cascade, but we do know that those who became residents of the town of North Adams (where the waterfall is located)—originally the site of Fort Massachusetts, where during the French and Indian Wars English soldiers were captured after a siege—thought The Cascade a worthy destination worth preserving.

Adams and North Adams were named after Bay State patriot Samuel Adams. The two towns separated in 1878. The Hoosic River provided water power for the mills that sprang up here and led to an inexorable shift from agriculture to industry. Thus, houses in North Adams were built close together in order that mill workers could easily access the mills, resulting in the town growing all around The Cascade, with North Brook flowing from the slopes of Mount Fitch and Ragged Mountain like it had since

The Cascade drops into a dark stone amphitheater.

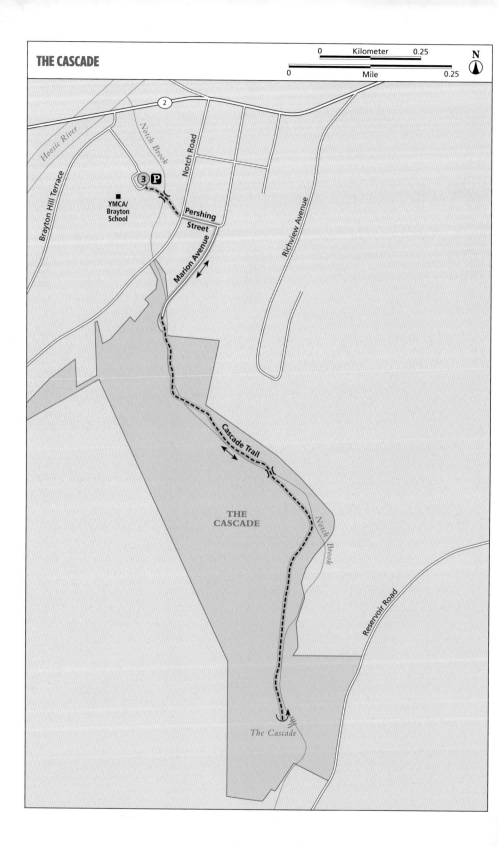

THE CASCADE

0   Kilometer   0.25

0   Mile   0.25

N

Hoosic River

Notch Brook

2

Notch Road

Brayton Hill Terrace

3 P

YMCA/
Brayton
School

Pershing
Street

Marion Avenue

Richview Avenue

Cascade Trail

THE
CASCADE

Notch Brook

Reservoir Road

The Cascade

The Cascade drops 40 feet on its white journey.

recorded time began, tumbling as a picturesque cataract shortly before giving its waters to the Hoosic River then helping to turn a mill wheel. Haggard factory workers, seeking natural refreshment on their day off, went to picnic under the towering hemlocks along North Brook. They would walk a little farther and see the frothing white waterfall, taking mental pictures for daydream fodder as they worked the loom the next week.

The Cascade became a North Adams institution. And you don't mess with an institution. The owner of the local paper mill owned the land around The Cascade, and rumors swirled around town that he was going to take down the forests around it. This never happened, but the threat loomed. Hopes to make this gorgeous vale of North Brook a park weren't realized until the 1970s, when the city bought the property with help from interested groups.

Today we have a natural preserve in the heart of a classic New England Berkshire town. And to access this saved parcel of the lowermost Greylock Range, we actually walk through the town. Take these extra steps and start at the proper trailhead. There is no public parking at the preserve entrance, as it is at the dead end of a neighborhood street.

The hike first leaves the public parking area and bridges North Brook, then enters a neighborhood. In a way, you are following the footsteps of the old mill workers, who walked from their homes to The Cascade. After a few short blocks, you enter the preserve of The Cascade. The transformation is instantaneous. The clear stream flows around big boulders under the shade of regal white pines, nary a house in sight. Weren't you just in a

An erratic boulder lies at the base of The Cascade.

town? Now, the eye-pleasing natural world transforms mind as well as body as you gently climb along the left bank of the creek.

Ahead, the trail bridges North Brook as the wooded hillside steepens, and the path is forced along the creek by this steep bank. The gorge tightens as lesser tributaries flow across the trail. The sounds of tumbling water echo around the corner. It takes a bit of fancy footwork to reach the cataract dry-footed, but then you are looking headlong at The Cascade, making its 40-foot gambit to crash through stone parapets into a shady rock gorge. Following an initial lesser dive, the waterfall gains steam in a small pool before making its final leap into a dark plunge pool, bordered with ferns and complemented by a singular outsized boulder.

Waterfalls like The Cascade are special places. They attract us to visit their realms, where they tumble over ledges in a froth of white, making a visual and audio splash into our lives. However, waterfalls have dangers. Waterfall visitors drown in heavy undertows like that at Bash Bish Falls. Others perish while climbing alongside or even in cataracts, like what occasionally happens at Race Brook Falls. Still others get hurt trying to reach remote off-trail cataracts like lower Bear Rock Falls.

Every warm season, we have accidents around waterfalls, and believe me, I am no alarmist. However, make visiting a waterfall an enjoyable natural experience, not a precursor to an emergency room. Do not climb on slippery rocks or atop a falls. Lovely waterfalls often hide lethal danger.

Developed areas can be just as dangerous as undeveloped areas. As one ranger put it, "It is just the nature of rocks and water and cliffs. You can build observation decks and post signs, but people will be careless and use poor judgment."

The hazards are real. When playing around a waterfall, remember "a single slip could be your last." Here are a few other axioms to follow while visiting waterfalls: Stay on developed trails, and do not stray from observation points or platforms. Watch your footing. Rocks may be slippery, and algae-coated areas are unforgiving. The top of any waterfall is, of course, the most dangerous part. Avoid the temptation to lean over a ledge at the top of the falls. Exercise caution on the trail to the falls, as well as around the falls themselves. Waterfall trails are often treacherous—steep and rocky with sheer embankments. Be especially cautious when taking photographs. You are likely to pay more attention to your camera than to your footing. Watch children carefully. Children should always be under the immediate supervision of an adult. Watch your dog. I saw a golden retriever, who seemed surefooted but did not understand the concept of slick rocks, fall off a 12-foot drop. He was fine, but his master was nearly injured scurrying down to the canine.

With these ideas in mind, you will have a safe waterfall experience. Now go have fun! After enjoying this waterfall, perhaps you can enjoy some of the offerings of North Adams, from art to dining, reflecting on the natural beauty of The Cascade as mill workers did long ago.

MILES AND DIRECTIONS

0.0 Facing the front of Brayton Elementary School, turn around and head east, bridging North Brook in woods. Emerge from the trees and cross Notch Road, keeping east on Pershing Street.

0.1 Turn right on Marion Avenue, southbound through a neighborhood.

0.3 Enter the preserve of The Cascade. Ahead, pass a stone wall along the waterway.

0.6 Cross a bridge over to the right bank of North Brook, continuing upstream in deep woods, with the walls of the valley rising from the water.

1.0 Reach The Cascade after some fancy rock-hopping. The 40-foot spiller crashes in its rock amphitheater. Backtrack to the trailhead.

2.0 Arrive back at the school/YMCA trailhead, completing the hike.

4 MONEY BROOK FALLS LOOP

This hike has it all—incredible views, tall waterfalls, a variety of flora—and challenge. Tighten your laces and get your mojo on for this hike that features over 2,000 feet of climbing and descent on a loop that explores highlights situated on the north end of Mount Greylock State Reservation. First, head up to Mount Williams and a view, then descend into "The Hopper" to view the tiers of 75-foot Money Brook Falls. Next, climb to Mount Prospect and take in more views, then finally top it off with a superlative vantage of Williamstown, framed in fields and mountains.

Start: Wilbur's Clearing parking area
Distance: 5.8-mile loop
Difficulty: Difficult due to elevation changes
Elevation change: +/-2,137 feet over entire hike
Maximum grade: 25% grade for 0.9 mile
Hiking time: About 3.5 hours
Seasons/schedule: May through Dec
Fees and permits: None
Dog friendly: Yes
Trail surface: Forested natural surface, often sloped

Land status: State reservation
Nearest town: North Adams
Other trail users: None
Map to consult: Mount Greylock State Reservation
Amenities available: None
Cell service: Good, except along Money Brook
Trail contact: Mount Greylock State Reservation, (413) 499-4262, www.mass.gov/locations/mount -greylock-state-reservation

FINDING THE TRAILHEAD

From downtown Adams, take MA 8 north for 5.1 miles, then turn left on Furnace Bypass and follow it for 0.1 mile to Furnace Street. Turn left and follow Furnace Street south just a short distance, then veer right onto Reservoir Road and follow it for 2.1 miles. Split left onto Notch Road and stay with it for 2.4 miles to the Wilbur's Clearing parking area on your left. Note: The Wilbur's Clearing parking area is bordered in woods and is no longer a clearing. **Trailhead GPS:** 42.669397, -73.167718

THE HIKE

You will certainly learn all about the ups and downs of Mount Greylock State Reservation on this hike, and will come away with an understanding that the preserve has some steep terrain.

Trail builders face challenges of their own on such declivitous slopes. Ideally, constructors of hiking trails like to keep their grades at 10 percent or less, or 528 feet of climbing/descending per mile (remember, a mile is 5,280 feet). In less than ideal conditions, gradients can be pushed to 15 percent, or 792 feet per mile. However, in the real world, the terrain—i.e., cliffs, valleys, and other areas with sharp declinations—sometimes necessitates steeper grades for brief trail segments. Just about every mountain hike is going to have a brief sharp inclination somewhere, even if just for a few feet.

Money Brook tumbles 65 feet down layered rock.

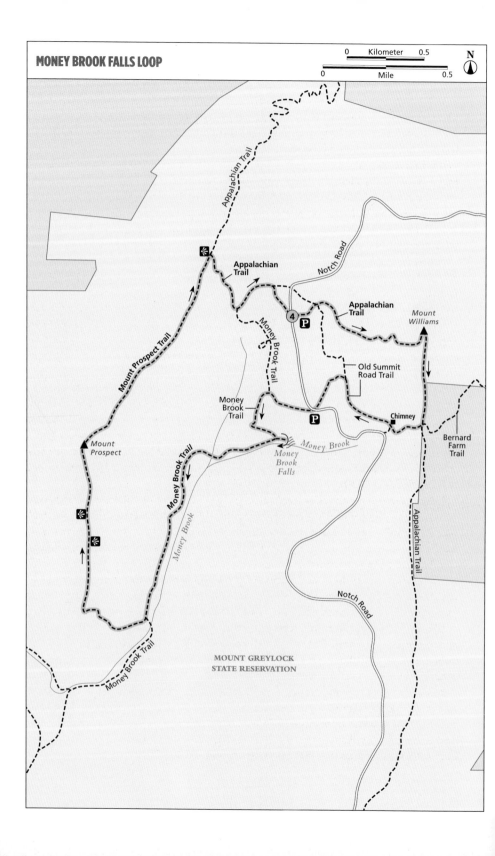

MONEY BROOK FALLS LOOP

0   Kilometer   0.5

0   Mile   0.5

N

Appalachian Trail

Appalachian
Trail

Notch Road

Appalachian
Trail

Mount
Williams

4

P

Mount Prospect Trail

Money Brook Trail

Old Summit
Road Trail

Money
Brook
Trail

P

Chimney

Mount
Prospect

Money Brook Trail

Money Brook

Money Brook

Money
Brook
Falls

Bernard
Farm
Trail

Appalachian Trail

Notch Road

Money Brook Trail

MOUNT GREYLOCK
STATE RESERVATION

Here at Mount Greylock State Reservation, the slopes are such that trail builders have been faced with longer stretches of gradients greater than 10 or 15 percent. You will experience this when leaving the Money Brook valley and The Hopper for the summit of Mount Prospect. Here, the Mount Prospect Trail ascends to the ridgeline of the mountain then tightropes the nose of the ridgeline upward, sans switchbacks, at a 25 percent gradient, or 1,320 feet per mile! Trust me, no matter what shape you are in, this section will get you huffing and puffing.

But isn't seeking challenges part of our quest when hiking the Berkshires? Well, this hike has them in spades! The trek begins at the no-longer-clear Wilbur's Clearing. You will take a short spur to join the fabled Appalachian Trail (AT), tackling challenge number one—Mount Williams. This is a 630-foot climb in 0.8 mile, a 15 percent grade, a solid starter climb right out of the blocks, while trekking under forests of red spruce, yellow birch, and ferns.

Yellow birch trees are found throughout the Berkshires. Look for a yellowish-gold, peeling bark with horizontal stripes. Larger yellow birches will not have bark peeling on their lower trunks, but will still have peeling bark on their upper branches. The twigs and leaves, when crushed, have a slight wintergreen aroma. Primarily a tree of the north, ranging from Minnesota to Maine, it stretches south down the spine of the Appalachians all the way to South Carolina and Georgia mountain regions. It will often sprout on nutrient-rich rotting logs. Later, as the yellow birch grows, the log rots completely away, leaving the tree to look as if it grew up on its root "legs."

A few switchbacks lead you to the summit and an easterly view from an outcrop. The roller-coaster ride heads down as you run the master ridge of the Greylock Range south, leaving the AT for the Old Summit Road Trail. You are beginning a nearly unbroken 2.5-mile descent, dropping 1,483 feet, an average grade of 11 percent. Nowadays, you'd never know this stony eroded path was ever the Old Summit Road, though some parts are still in fine shape. Ahead, you pass a standing chimney, all that is left from an old building from the 1930s.

The hike crosses Notch Road and enters a hardwood cove of maple, oak, and beech. You turn into Money Brook, then make your way to the angled cataract. The waterfall widens as it spills into a deep stony gorge, draining Mount Williams. Money Brook's small watershed makes it a better spring/early summer waterfall destination. Early morning is best for waterfall photographers.

The hike continues down along Money Brook, ensconced in evergreens, into the valley known as The Hopper, purportedly for resembling a grain hopper. Money Brook cascades loudly as you work your way along a rough south-facing slope heavy with oak, maple, and viburnum. You then come to the big climb up to Mount Prospect. This uptick is rough and steep. Luckily, you will pass a couple of fine views to help distract from the climb and allow you to fake like you are stopping only for the view and not because you need to catch your breath.

You've got it made after topping out on Mount Prospect (no views). Roll on a sometimes-rocky ridge north to reach a trail intersection and magnificent view, one of my favorites in the Berkshires. Here, a westerly panorama opens of farms and fields below, along with Williamstown, framed in a menagerie of mountains extending into the Empire State. This is another reward for the effort exerted.

Fields and towns highlight this Appalachian Trail vista.

You are now back on the Appalachian Trail. The trail drops some then runs nearly level. That is known as a 0 percent grade! A final short downgrade returns you to the Wilbur's Clearing parking area.

MILES AND DIRECTIONS

0.0 Join a connector leaving northeast from Wilbur's Clearing parking area, elevation 2,310 feet.

0.1 Meet the Old Summit Road Trail. Stay left with the connector and quickly meet the Appalachian Trail. Head right, southbound on the white-blazed footpath, climbing the west slope of Mount Williams.

0.8 Reach the summit of Mount Williams, 2,953 feet, noted with a sign. Watch for a short trail leading to an outcrop and an easterly view into the Hoosic River valley. Turn south, running the ridge of the Greylock Range on a stony singletrack path.

1.1 Come to a four-way intersection. Here, turn right onto the Old Summit Road Trail. Pick your way through an eroded stony segment.

1.2 Come to a stone chimney. Here, a spur leads left to Notch Road. Stay straight with the Old Summit Road Trail.

1.5 Watch carefully for the signed but obscure connector heading left for Notch Road. The descent continues.

1.7 Cross Notch Road and pass through alternate parking. Keep descending in woods on the connector. The mountainside sharpens.

2.1 Intersect the Money Brook Trail. Head left, continuing the unbroken downgrade. Angle into the very steep gorge of Money Brook.

2.2 Reach the spur to Money Brook Falls. Hike and scramble to boulders at the base of the 65-foot spiller, dropping in stages.

2.6 Cross a tributary of Money Brook in a deep valley.

3.4 Reach the hike's low point and the Mount Prospect Trail. Begin the steepest ascent of the hike, eventually making your way up the nose of the ridge in squat oaks and low blueberry bushes in stony terrain.

3.9 Reach a view to the east of Mount Greylock. Look for the distinct tower.

4.1 Come to another vista, this time to the west, stretching beyond The Hopper. Keep climbing.

4.3 Top out on Mount Prospect. Keep north on a bouldery ridge.

5.2 Meet the AT at a view. Here, a westerly landscape extends as far as the eye can see. Head right, southbound, on the AT.

5.5 Stay with the AT as the Money Brook Trail goes right for the Wilbur's Clearing trail shelter. Roll through level woods.

5.6 Split right on a connector for Wilbur's Clearing parking area, as the AT goes left.

5.8 Arrive back at the trailhead, completing the hike.

5 MOUNT GREYLOCK LOOP

Explore the highest point in Massachusetts, Mount Greylock, at its oldest state preserve. Visit the war memorial tower and view the CCC-built lodge. Soak in the incredible views before striking out on the Appalachian Trail (AT). Head northbound on the AT, then hike to Robinson Point and a worthy vista. Next, the Overlook Trail leads to a view, then you take the AT up the south slope of Mount Greylock, enjoying more highland forest—and a pond—at the historic preserve.

Start: Mount Greylock parking area
Distance: 3.2-mile loop
Difficulty: Moderate
Elevation change: +/-1,046 feet over entire hike
Maximum grade: 27% downhill grade for 0.7 mile
Hiking time: About 2.5 hours
Seasons/schedule: Late May through Oct
Fees and permits: Parking permit required
Dog friendly: Yes, but there are road crossings and explorable buildings on hike

Trail surface: Natural surface, some concrete
Land status: State reservation
Nearest town: Adams
Other trail users: None
Map to consult: Mount Greylock State Reservation
Amenities available: Restrooms and water at trailhead, snacks at lodge
Cell service: Fair to good
Trail contact: Mount Greylock State Reservation, (413) 499-4262, www.mass.gov/locations/mount -greylock-state-reservation

FINDING THE TRAILHEAD

From downtown Adams, take MA 8 north for 5.1 miles, then turn left on Furnace Bypass and follow it for 0.1 mile to Furnace Street. Turn left and follow Furnace Street south just a short distance, then veer right onto Reservoir Road. Follow Reservoir Road for 2.1 miles, then split left onto Notch Road. Stay with Notch Road for 5.9 miles, then turn left onto Summit Road and follow it 0.9 mile to the trailhead parking area. **Trailhead GPS:** 42.637686, -73.166989

THE HIKE

The citizens of Massachusetts and local Berkshires residents hold their high point, Mount Greylock, in literal and figurative high regard. After all, they chose the place for their first designated wilderness reservation. Moreover, it is special—not only is it the highest point in the state at 3,491 feet, but it also has a mountaintop tower built in the 1930s as the state's official memorial to its veterans who have fought for our country. From a natural perspective, the Mount Greylock State Reservation contains the state's only spruce-fir boreal forest, among other God-given attributes.

A reserve for over a century, people have been flocking to Massachusetts's oldest state preserve to see the magnificent views, to smell the evergreens cloaking the mountainsides, and to escape the daily grind. The commissioners first in charge of Mount Greylock Reservation put it succinctly back in 1898: "We are to bear in mind that the utility of the reservation is primarily spiritual, not physical; but the highest purpose is always best attained with some wise reference to lower objects. There will always remain in the

Looking into The Hopper from Robinsons Point

reservation large areas in which the freedom and boldness of nature will constitute the primary impression, and render the chief service."

Today's hikers can find that same spiritual renewal atop Mount Greylock—and find some scintillating history as well. Rising high in western Massachusetts, the mountain first attracted attention in the late 1700s. Farmers had settled the adjacent valleys and were working their way up the slopes, clearing land for pasturage and firewood. In 1830, the faculty and students at nearby Williams College cleared what had become known as the Hopper Trail up the mountain to study its unique climate and vegetation. They also erected a pair of observation towers. Our hike traces a portion of the original Hopper Trail, which some students still use to ascend Mount Greylock on their annual Mountain Day. Later, in 1863, a Williams College professor founded the Alpine Club, ostensibly the first hiking club in the country.

The origin of the name Mount Greylock is now muddled, but the peak has been well established as a New England icon. After all, with views extending up to 90 miles and the ability to see five states on a clear day, why wouldn't it be? Newly laid rail lines brought visitors from Boston and beyond. At the same time, glassmaking, iron smelting, and textile industries were operating in adjacent towns, gobbling up wood from Mount Greylock's hillsides. That, combined with lumber, paper, and charcoal businesses—all requiring wood—alarmed locals. Subsequent fires and floods on Greylock heightened concerns about the future of Massachusetts's master peak.

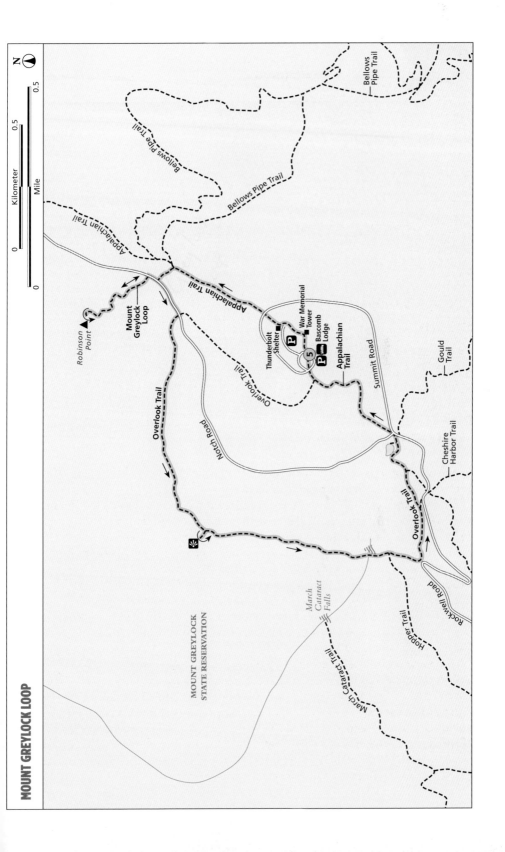

MOUNT GREYLOCK LOOP

N

Kilometer
0   0.5

Mile
0   0.5

Appalachian Trail

Bellows Pipe Trail

Bellows Pipe Trail

Bellows Pipe Trail

Appalachian Trail

Robinson Point

Mount Greylock Loop

Overlook Trail

Notch Road

Overlook Trail

Thunderbolt Shelter

War Memorial Tower

Bascomb Lodge

Appalachian Trail

Summit Road

Gould Trail

Cheshire Harbor Trail

Overlook Trail

Rockwell Road

March Cataract Falls

Hopper Trail

March Cataract Trail

MOUNT GREYLOCK STATE RESERVATION

Hikers descend from Mount Greylock.

Thus, in 1885, a band of citizens formed the Greylock Park Association and purchased 400 acres atop the mountain. This small mountaintop preserve became the heart of what we see today. Seeking to enhance preservation through recreation, the Greylock Park Association constructed a road to the mountain peak and an iron observation tower. A toll was established to pay for the improvements, but the revenue proved insufficient. Eventually, the association became overwhelmed and turned to the state for financial help.

In June of 1898, the Commonwealth of Massachusetts established the state's first public lands atop Mount Greylock. The state eventually increased the 400-acre preserve to the 12,000-plus acres we behold today. That is what makes hiking here so special—among all the lands in the Bay State, we can explore the very first place chosen as a preserve.

Mount Greylock was chosen first again as the site for the official memorial to the state's war veterans. Initially supposed to go in Boston, the memorial now stands as an imposing and inspiring granite tower topped with a light that can be seen from 70 miles away at night. The 93-foot bastion, quarried from Massachusetts stone, was completed in 1932 and forms the centerpiece of the Mount Greylock experience. Gravel paths circle the tower and lead to inspiring views.

More changes were to come in the 1930s. The Civilian Conservation Corps (CCC) came to Mount Greylock, building trails and backcountry lean-tos and completing the Bascom Lodge, a rustic building of native stone and wood. The lodge is located just below the high point and offers overnight accommodations, as well as dining. The CCC also erected the nearby Thunderbolt Shelter, a ski warming hut to go along with the Thunderbolt Ski Trail that they made. The mountaintop structures are on the National Register of Historic Places.

This hike starts atop Mount Greylock. You will want to wander around, heading to the war memorial tower and walking up it if possible. Even if you cannot, extensive panoramas can be had from the ground—five states in all: Massachusetts, New York, Vermont, New Hampshire, and Connecticut. As you walk the nature trails atop the mountain, note the inscribed rocks that have been placed about. They contain inspiring writings about the wonders of creation. Admire the Bascom Lodge, well integrated into the landscape.

After settling down, start your hike at the metal relief map of Mount Greylock. Set out northbound on the Appalachian Trail, routed into the state reservation back in 1930. It takes you by the stone Thunderbolt Shelter. After joining the Robinson Point Trail, find a rock outcrop overlooking a valley known as The Hopper and mountains beyond. Pick up the Overlook Trail, traversing spruce, fir, and northern hardwoods. Grab another view from an overlook. Your circuit around Mount Greylock takes you to the historic Hopper Trail, opened so long ago by college students. Rejoin the AT for your final ascent back to the top of Mount Greylock and pass a picturesque pond on the way, enjoying this special slice of the Massachusetts Berkshires.

MILES AND DIRECTIONS

0.0 Start at the metal relief map of Mount Greylock, located between the parking area and the war memorial tower. Follow the Appalachian Trail northbound directly to the tower. At the tower, angle left, staying with the AT, as other paths spoke away from the tower. Descend into woods. Just ahead, split left and return to the edge of the parking area. Pass the rustic Thunderbolt Shelter. Keep descending on the wide and rocky AT, sharing tread with the Thunderbolt Ski Trail.

0.4 Reach an intersection. Take the signed Robinson Point Trail as it splits left. If you come to where the Thunderbolt Ski Trail and Appalachian Trail diverge, you have gone a little too far.

0.5 Meet Notch Road. Walk right a few steps, cross the road, and resume the Robinson Point Trail. Descend steeply, amid evergreens, moss, rocks, and hardwoods.

0.8 Emerge at Robinson Point. Look down on the rugged wooded valley of The Hopper. Backtrack to Notch Road.

1.1 Reach Notch Road. Turn right here, and walk along the road.

1.2 Join the Overlook Trail, which has come from atop Mount Greylock. Head downhill on a slope.

1.9 Take the short spur on the right to an overlook of the Taconic Mountains above the Green River valley. Resume hiking on the Overlook Trail.

2.4 Meet the historic Hopper Trail, just after passing a closed trail leading right and crossing Hopper Brook. Turn left, uphill on the Hopper Trail.

2.5 Come near Rockwell Road. Turn away, still ascending.

2.6 The Cheshire Harbor Trail leaves right. Stay with the Hopper Trail.

2.7 Reach a trail intersection. Join the Appalachian Trail, left, northbound.

2.8 Come alongside a highland pond, with frogs and tadpoles aplenty during the warm season.

2.9 Emerge at a three-way road intersection. Cross Summit Road and stay with the AT, ascending. The Gould Trail leaves right here from a gravel parking area. Make the final push up Mount Greylock.

3.2 Return to the Mount Greylock crest area, passing a maintenance facility and rest-rooms. Cut through woods and arrive back at the metal relief map, completing the hike.

6 RIBBON FALLS RAGGED MOUNTAIN HIKE

Get a double reward when tackling this hike. Work your way up through Greylock Glen, a once-proposed ski resort/golf course turned park, then climb to Ribbon Falls—a series of eye-popping cataracts along North Branch Pecks Brook. Cross the historic Thunderbolt Ski Trail before climbing to a view from atop Ragged Mountain. Your return trip travels through meadows that present additional vistas.

Start: Bellows South trailhead
Distance: 4.2-mile out and back with a loop in the middle
Difficulty: Moderate to difficult due to 1,348-foot initial climb
Elevation change: +/-1,348 feet over entire hike
Maximum grade: 16% grade for 1.3 miles
Hiking time: About 2.5 hours
Seasons/schedule: May through Dec
Fees and permits: None
Dog friendly: Yes
Trail surface: Packed gravel at first, natural surface with grassy meadows in spots

Land status: State reservation, Town of Adams property
Nearest town: Adams
Other trail users: Mountain bikers
Map to consult: Greylock Glen Trails
Amenities available: None
Cell service: Good
Trail contacts: Mount Greylock State Reservation, (413) 499-4262, www.mass.gov/locations/mount-greylock-state-reservation; Town of Adams, (413) 743-8300, ext. 131, http://greylockglenresort.com

FINDING THE TRAILHEAD

From the intersection of MA 8 and Hoosic Street in the heart of downtown Adams, head south on MA 8 for 0.1 mile to Maple Street. Turn right (west) and follow Maple Street for 0.4 mile to W Road, then turn left and follow W Road for 0.4 mile to Gould Road. Turn right and follow Gould Road for 1 mile to reach the Bellows South trailhead on your right, just before reaching a gate at road's end. **Trailhead GPS:** 42.627293, -73.145237

THE HIKE

Set on the lower slopes of Mount Greylock, the 1,063-acre parcel just west of the town of Adams, Greylock Glen is an outdoor haven with trails linking to Mount Greylock State Reservation. Set on the site of a ski resort that never went into operation and a golf course turned nature preserve, Greylock Glen enhances the greater Mount Greylock trail system. Located a mere mile from downtown Adams, future plans for Greylock Glen include tent and RV campgrounds, a performance amphitheater, and gardens, capped off with a lodge and conference center.

The trail system at Greylock Glen includes a big walking track around a meadow (the former golf course area), as well as mountain biking trails and hiking trails and even winter ski and snowshoe trails. A mind-numbing number of intersections is the only downside of this path network. Make sure to have a trail map, perhaps also a GPS, lucky rabbit's foot, Magic 8 Ball, divining rod, and a deck of tarot cards before you start your hike.

This waterfall is a ribbon of white.

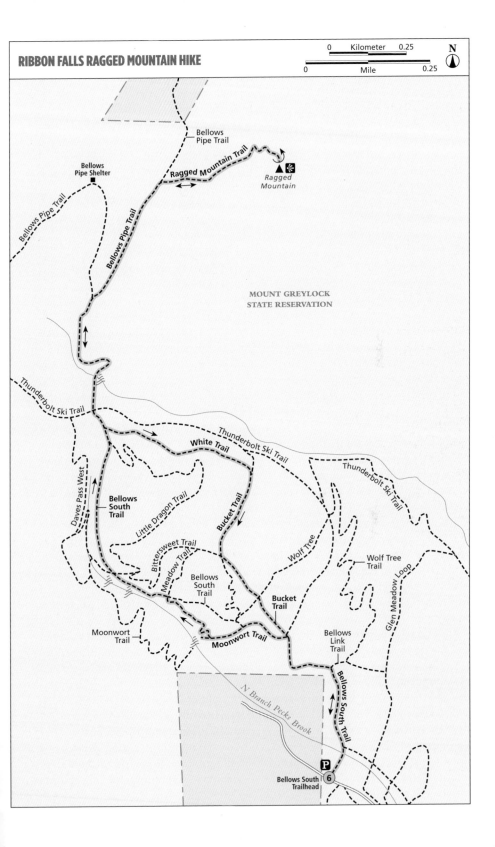

RIBBON FALLS RAGGED MOUNTAIN HIKE

0   Kilometer   0.25

0   Mile   0.25

N

Bellows Pipe Trail

Bellows Pipe Shelter

Ragged Mountain Trail

Ragged Mountain

Bellows Pipe Trail

Bellows Pipe Trail

MOUNT GREYLOCK STATE RESERVATION

Thunderbolt Ski Trail

Thunderbolt Ski Trail

White Trail

Thunderbolt Ski Trail

Daves Pass West

Bellows South Trail

Little Dragon Trail

Bucket Trail

Wolf Tree Trail

Bittersweet Trail

Meadow Trail

Bellows South Trail

Wolf Tree

Glen Meadow Loop

Bucket Trail

Moonwort Trail

Moonwort Trail

Bellows Link Trail

Bellows South Trail

N Branch Pecks Brook

P 6

Bellows South Trailhead

Seriously, though, it's not that bad. Trail intersections are signed. Just make sure to keep up with where you are and ignore unsigned user-created trails. Start your adventure on the Bellows South Trail, crossing North Branch Pecks Brook then entering reforesting land where sumac, witch hazel, quaking aspen, and paper birch grow.

Smooth sumac is known as a pioneering tree, often appearing in old fields and along roadsides. The tree is common throughout southeastern New England, all the way down to Mississippi and Texas and up to Minnesota. The upright berry-like fruit clusters and opposite pinnate leaves make it easy to identify. Aboriginals chewed the sour fruit and made a quasi-lemonade. However, birds and lesser mammals find the fruit quite palatable. Deer browse on the fruit and sumac twigs.

The trail continues as packed gravel for almost a half mile, then the rest of the hike is natural surface. Work your way through a seeming maze of intersections to reach lowermost Ribbon Falls, with the Moonwort Trail crossing between two cataracts. Upstream you have the brook pouring a dozen feet over a wide ledge behind which rises yet another waterfall. Below the trail, the watercourse makes a pair of ledge drops, then follows gravity down an angled slide before flowing out of sight over more ledges.

You will see still more falls while ascending the Ribbon Falls Trail. Some of the cataracts are more difficult to reach. As with all cascades in the Greylock Range, Ribbon Falls has a smallish watershed and is best enjoyed from May through early summer and after rainy events. Winter can be rewarding, too, if you love to photograph frozen waterfalls.

Ahead are more spillers. The tapered whitewater of these faucet-like falls makes it easy to see where the name Ribbon Falls came from. Do continue paying attention at trail intersections, which are as frequent as mosquitoes in a Massachusetts marsh on a summer's eve.

The intersections ease up once you get past the Thunderbolt Ski Trail. A trail with a cool name like that also has to have a cool history to it. Originally carved out by the Civilian Conservation Corps in 1934, the trail was the centerpiece of the 1936 Alpine Ski Championships. The current path starts atop Mount Greylock and beelines down the east slope of the mountain. It is for expert skiers only, dropping over 2,200 feet in 2 miles!

So, on your next steep Berkshire climb, think you could be going up the Thunderbolt Ski Trail . . . Instead, we are keeping straight, northbound, still on the Bellows South Trail, reveling in a much milder gradient to meet the Bellows Pipe Trail. Split right with it, as the other leg of the Bellows Pipe Trail climbs to a lean-to and the Appalachian Trail. With a dozen trail intersections and a bunch of climbing behind us, we can just take it easy on a level doubletrack through the woods—the way we dream of hiking when we're stuck in the office, or an elevator, or in line at the grocery store.

Just like many pleasantries in life, the level hike doesn't last long and we find ourselves descending to a little gap on the Ragged Mountain Trail, then climbing a steep stony knob. But this outcrop reveals a fine view of Mount Greylock, Greylock Glen, and points south, well worth the trek. At this point you will have undoubtedly noticed unmaintained yet marked trails going north on Ragged Mountain. These unofficial paths lead to a view known as Raven Rocks but must be considered off-trail hiking.

Our trek returns to the Greylock Glen trail maze. And with so many paths, why not try some new ones on the way down? The White Trail is a good choice, as it drops to the Bucket Trail. Here you cut through a gap and actually see the bucket for which this trail is named, hung in a tree. Strange but true. From here, drop into a sloped

Another of the cataracts that comprise Ribbon Falls

meadow—Picard's Pasture—delivering easterly views of the Hoosic Range. From the bottom of the meadow, it is a simple backtrack to the trailhead, though with this many trail intersections, you aren't there until you are there.

MILES AND DIRECTIONS

0.0 From the Bellows South trailhead, join the gravel doubletrack Bellows South Trail, northbound, entering a planted evergreen grove to meet and cross North Branch Pecks Brook. Just beyond the stream a connector trail splits right, southeast for the Glen Meadow Loop, a fine, gravel circuit track making a 1.6-mile loop.

0.2 Stay left with the Bellows South Trail, as the Bellows Link Trail splits right.

0.4 Come to an intersection as the gravel footbed ends. Stay left with the Bellows South Trail.

0.5 Come to yet another intersection. Split left onto the Moonwort Trail, though you will reunite with the Bellows South Trail later.

0.6 Meet the Ribbon Falls Trail. You will return to this in just a minute, but for now keep straight with the Moonwort Trail and quickly meet North Branch Pecks Brook. Here, the trail crosses the stream flanked by a waterfall above and below. Backtrack to the Ribbons Falls Trail and begin following it uphill along North Branch Pecks Brook.

0.8 The Ribbon Falls Trail ends. Stay left, rejoining the Bellows South Trail, as the Meadow Trail goes straight. Cruise up an easy doubletrack.

0.9 Reach another trail junction. Here, the Daves Pass West Trail splits left, and a connector leaves right for the Little Dragon Trail. Stay straight with the Bellows South Trail. The trail steepens.

1.2 The Little Dragon Trail leaves right, while we stay straight and quickly pass the White Trail. Take note of the White Trail, as you will be using it on the return trip.

1.3 Come to a four-way intersection on a level part of the mountainside, known as Four Corners. Here, cross the legendary Thunderbolt Ski Trail. Ahead, bridge an unnamed brook just above a 15-foot low-flow sheet cascade.

1.6 Come to yet another intersection and the end of the Bellows South Trail. Stay right, joining the Bellows Pipe Trail as the other end of the Bellows Pipe Trail goes left, up toward Mount Greylock and the Appalachian Trail

1.8 Split right with the Ragged Mountain Trail. Dip to a gap, then climb a stony knob.

2.1 Reach the south peak of Ragged Mountain. Views open to the south framed by mountain ash, while unmaintained trails head north toward Raven Rocks. Backtrack to the White Trail.

3.1 Head left on the White Trail, descending an easy doubletrack.

3.4 Split right with the Bucket Trail. Look for the bucket in a tree.

3.6 Pass the Meadow Trail. Keep descending on the Bucket Trail, entering full-blown meadow. Ahead, cross the Wolf Tree Trail. Scan for apple trees.

3.8 Meet the Bellows South Trail. From here, backtrack to the trailhead.

4.2 Arrive back at the trailhead and congratulate yourself for navigating all the trail intersections on this trek.

7 PECKS BROOK FALLS LOOP

This hike takes you to a cataract in one of the most eye-pleasing gorges of the Greylock Range. Start in the lowlands, crossing Pecks Brook to work up the gorge rim, only to descend back to Pecks Brook and a trail shelter, near which drops the prettiest of the cascades along this mountain stream. Your return trip cuts across the gorge of Pecks Brook, winding down slopes before taking you directly back along the brook for more aquatic enjoyment before closing the loop.

Start: Gould trailhead
Distance: 3.9-mile loop with spur
Difficulty: Moderate to difficult due to 1,100-foot initial climb
Elevation change: +/-1,355 feet over entire hike
Maximum grade: 16% grade for 1.3 miles
Hiking time: About 2.5 hours
Seasons/schedule: May through Dec
Fees and permits: None
Dog friendly: Yes, except near falls

Trail surface: Forested natural surface
Land status: State reservation
Nearest town: Adams
Other trail users: Backpackers
Map to consult: Mount Greylock State Reservation
Amenities available: None
Cell service: Good
Trail contact: Mount Greylock State Reservation, (413) 499-4262, www.mass.gov/locations/mount -greylock-state-reservation

FINDING THE TRAILHEAD

From the intersection of MA 8 and Hoosic Street in the heart of downtown Adams, head south on MA 8 for 0.1 mile to Maple Street. Turn right (west) and follow Maple Street for 0.4 mile to W Road. Turn left and follow W Road for 0.5 mile, then turn right onto West Mountain Road and follow it for 0.9 mile to reach the Gould trailhead on your right. **Trailhead GPS:** 42.619015, -73.150387

THE HIKE

I have a certain fondness for Pecks Brook Falls and the nearby trail shelter, as it was the first place I ever backpacked at Mount Greylock State Reservation. The ground around the shelter and falls is quite sloped, a natural location for a waterfall but not necessarily a campsite! It must've been the waterfall (along with other cataracts on this stretch of Pecks Brook) that attracted the powers-that-be to put the shelter here, along with a pair of tent sites carved into the mountainside.

Even if you aren't camping, the falls themselves are worth the visit. Additionally, a couple other cataracts can be seen near and upstream of the lean-to. There are still other falls on Pecks Brook beyond the scope of this loop, sometimes confusing hikers as to which falls on Pecks Brook they are visiting, most notably Pecks Falls. That short trek starts off Gould Road located within the Greylock Glen sphere of trails. (Note: This area is now also home to mountain bike trails that come near but don't connect to this loop.)

Our hike takes the Gould Trail to enter woods of paper birch with an understory of ferns and bridge Pecks Brook, savoring an upstream view of the waterway and the woods around it. Check the flow. If this part of Pecks Brook is flowing well, then the falls should

Pecks Brook Falls makes its tumble down a stone ledge.

be, too. Climb with the Gould Trail, ignoring unblazed user-created paths that plague the lower eastern slopes of Mount Greylock. Begin a steady climb among beech, oak, and birch, with a smattering of spruce. The long-used Gould Trail is gully-like in places. Quartz outcrops brighten the trailside woods.

The ascent continues all the way to the intersection with the spur to the Pecks Brook lean-to and Pecks Brook Falls. After rock-hopping a tributary of Pecks Brook, drop to the Pecks Brook lean-to and campsite. Level terrain is lacking at the camp, but not beauty. Thick woods cloak the mountainside, and Pecks Brook sings its watery song. The three-sided open-front Adirondack-style shelter faces Pecks Brook. Water can be had by heading upstream from the shelter, above the falls. The shelter is first-come, first-served, and no fee is required.

Reaching Pecks Brook Falls is not easy from the shelter, any way you slice it. Safety first. Work your way down the slope from the front of the shelter, careful to minimize erosive damage. (Some waterfallers approach the falls by walking down along the tributary of Pecks Brook then ascending Pecks Brook to the bottom of Pecks Brook Falls.) Admire the tableau after finding yourself at the base of the cataract. Pecks Brook Falls starts narrow and widens as it dashes curtain-style down a rock ledge for 45 feet, slowing in a plunge pool. Rocks and boulders make for decent observation posts but watch out behind you, as Pecks Brook continues its tumble down the mountainside. Other falls are located upstream of the shelter but may necessitate scrambling.

If you camp overnight at the trail shelter, you will have to get some aqua from Pecks Brook, presenting the dilemma: Do I drink water from the backcountry? So, what can

PECKS BROOK FALLS LOOP

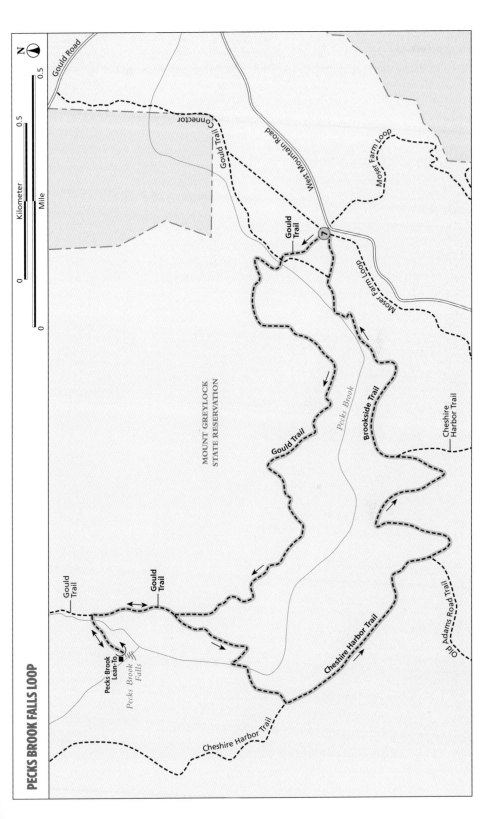

Gould Road

N

Kilometer
0   0.5   0.5
0   Mile

Gould Trail Connector

Gould Trail

West Mountain Road

Moser Farm Loop

Gould Trail

MOUNT GREYLOCK
STATE RESERVATION

Pecks Brook

Brookside Trail

Cheshire Harbor Trail

Gould Trail

Gould Trail

Pecks Brook Lean-To

Pecks Brook Falls

Cheshire Harbor Trail

Cheshire Harbor Trail

Old Adams Road Trail

Moser Farm Loop

drinking bad water do? Microbes such as giardia and cryptosporidium get in your intestines and disrupt your life with excessive gas, diarrhea, and other unpleasantries. Giardiasis—the illness caused by giardia—won't ruin your average hiking trip, as it takes one to two weeks for symptoms to appear. But once symptoms crop up, expect to be ill for two to six weeks. Weight loss and dehydration follow. A doctor's stomach-relieving prescription and plenty of fluids may help with the symptoms, which will eventually run their course, resulting in one painful weight loss program.

Treating your water has become a lot easier these days, but let's harken back for a moment. The old method was to boil your water for at least a minute—there's nothing like hot water to sate a big thirst! It is not convenient either: You have to wait until after your water is boiled, which means you have to have made a fire or broken out a camp stove.

Then came the pump filters—you literally pump your water through a device that filters out the demon microorganisms. Many people use chemical water treatments. Iodine was the choice of days gone by, but it has an awful taste. Nowadays we have products like Aqua Mira, where you mix two drops of chemicals, making chlorine dioxide, and wait thirty minutes, then your water is fine. Again, the wait is a problem, but it is the lightest

This scenic cataract is located just below a trail shelter.

option. Buying a water bottle with a built-in filter is an easier choice. Simply fill your water bottle then suck through a straw, which forces the water through a built-in small filter, which needs to be replaced often.

UV filters are another option—using ultraviolet rays to kill the bad things in the aqua. These products, such as Steripen, use batteries, which can die. Simple filters such as the gravity-fed Sawyer are lightweight, cheap, and last for years. They use special microbe-blocking membranes and operate on gravity—or squeeze pressure if in a hurry. No matter your method, treating your water is smart. Otherwise, you may spend your time being sick instead of hiking.

After returning to the shelter then backtracking on the Gould Trail, you will reach Pecks Brook in easier fashion—by trail—on the connector linking the Gould Trail and the Cheshire Harbor Trail. The short but steep in and out of the ravine will testify to its ruggedness—and scenic splendor, as exemplified by the small but pretty cascade with an alluring plunge pool just upstream from where you reach Pecks Brook.

The hiking is a breeze after meeting the wide Cheshire Harbor Trail, a winter snow-mobile trail, that offers a gentler downgrade than did the Gould Trail's climb. Evergreens become prevalent as you come alongside Pecks Brook a final time before returning to the trailhead.

MILES AND DIRECTIONS

0.0 From the Gould trailhead, take the Gould Trail north, quickly entering deep woods. The Gould Trail Connector leaves right just before the Gould Trail bridges Pecks Brook and another connector enters on the left.

0.2 Split left on the Gould Trail as an unmaintained path keeps straight. Stay with the blue blazes, heading west above the gorge of Pecks Brook.

1.3 Come to an intersection. You will return here later. Stay right with the Gould Trail as a connector heads left to the Cheshire Harbor Trail. Continue the uptick, although you have gained over 1,000 feet.

1.5 Reach another trail intersection. Here, the Gould Trail continues straight, aiming for Mount Greylock. Our hike splits left toward Pecks Brook lean-to and falls. Quickly cross a tributary of Pecks Brook.

1.6 Reach Pecks Brook lean-to. The falls is just below it on a scramble. Use caution. Backtrack to the Gould Trail.

1.7 Return to the Gould Trail, backtracking and descending.

1.9 Split right on the Gould–Cheshire Harbor connector. Drop to Pecks Brook and walk alongside the stream before rock-hopping the waterway and climbing sharply.

2.3 Meet the Cheshire Harbor Trail, a wide, easy, but sometimes eroded track. Head left, south, descending.

2.8 Stay straight at the intersection as the Old Adams Road Trail splits right. The path remains wide and woods thick.

3.3 The Cheshire Harbor Trail splits sharply right. Stay left on the Brookside Trail, a blue-blazed singletrack path still running parallel with Pecks Brook. Beware user-created trails here. Also note the newer mountain bike trails nearby (not shown on map).

3.7 Enjoy good stream views.

3.8 Take the signed spur right toward Mountain Road parking.

3.9 Arrive back at the Gould trailhead, completing the fulfilling hike.

8 GREYLOCK HIGHLANDS WATERFALL HIKE

This hike starts high and stays high while visiting two waterfalls and other cascades flowing off Mount Greylock and Saddle Ball Mountain. Start on gated Sperry Road and walk to Mount Greylock's foot-accessible-only campground, then follow a slender trail on a steep hillside to find comely March Cataract Falls, pouring 30 feet over a stony ledge. After backtracking to the campground, resume the loop, dropping in deep woods to reach tall Deer Hill Falls. Next find a white cascade where the hike bridges Roaring Brook. Earn your rewards while climbing past the Deer Hill trail shelter. Finally, find one last spiller on upper Roaring Brook.

Start: Sperry Road
Distance: 3.5-mile lollipop with spur
Difficulty: Moderate; does have continuous 700-foot descents and ascents
Elevation change: +/-1,235 feet over entire hike
Maximum grade: 23% downhill grade for 0.5 mile
Hiking time: About 2 hours
Seasons/schedule: Mid-May through mid-Nov
Fees and permits: None
Dog friendly: Yes

Trail surface: Forested natural surface, a little bit of gravel road
Land status: State reservation
Nearest town: Pittsfield
Other trail users: None
Map to consult: Mount Greylock State Reservation
Amenities available: Restrooms and picnic tables at campground
Cell service: Fair to good
Trail contact: Mount Greylock State Reservation, (413) 499-4262, www.mass.gov/locations/mount -greylock-state-reservation

FINDING THE TRAILHEAD

From the intersection of US 7 and US 20 in downtown Pittsfield, head north on US 7 for 6.6 miles, then veer right onto N. Main Street and follow it for 0.7 mile. Turn right onto Greylock Road and follow it for 0.4 mile, then veer left onto Rockwell Road, entering the state reservation. After 6.2 miles turn left onto Sperry Road. Parking is immediately on the right after the left turn. Note: Alternate parking is located on Rockwell Road just beyond the turn onto Sperry Road. **Trailhead GPS:** 42.625040, -73.190257

THE HIKE

Here's your chance to see a series of cool waterfalls flowing from the loftiest peaks in Massachusetts—with a caveat. Since these spillers form on the highest mantles of the Bay State, their watersheds are small, meaning when the spring ice melts, the brooks fill and the four cataracts flow strong, white and impressive. However, when the trees leaf out, the temperature warms, and streams dwindle, these waterfalls can disappoint. If you can time your trip after summer thunderstorms or other big rains, the falls will revive. Also, if you can make it up the unplowed roads to the trailhead, winter can be an exciting time to see these streams captured in frozen wonderment.

This cascade on Roaring Brook froths white in ferny woods.

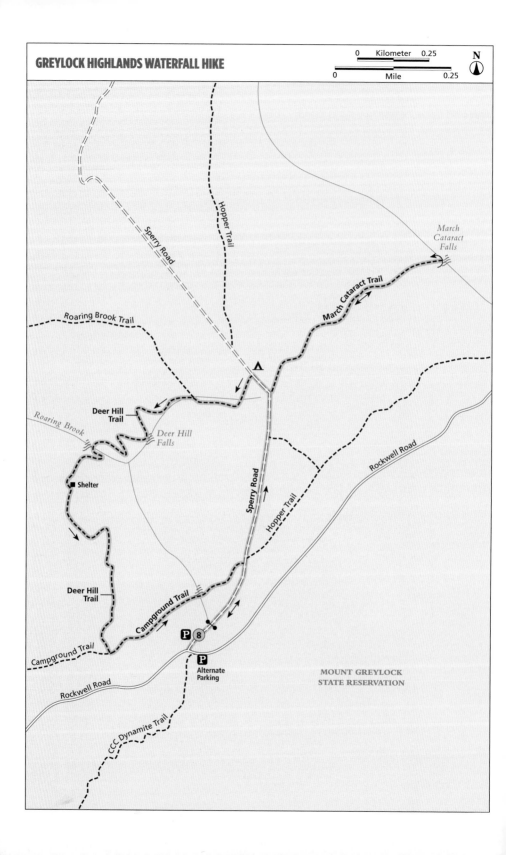

Even without the waterfalls you have a fine highland hike, starting at almost 2,600 feet. The first part of the trail follows Sperry Road, shaded by maple, birch, and spruce, open only to park personnel and used by Mount Greylock enthusiasts for camping. Campsites can be held through Reserve America. Advance reservations are required. The fifteen individual campsites have a picnic table, fire ring, and bear-proof food storage lockers. Drinking water is available during the warm season, solar composting toilets year-round.

Upon reaching the campground (worth a tour), you split right on the March Cataract Trail. The mountain slope steepens the closer you get to the upper reaches of Hopper Brook. The path dead-ends at the waterfall. Here, this stream coursing off the slope of Mount Greylock dives over a creased widening ledge, then slows in a boulder garden and flows on to drop 1,500 feet to feed the Green River, which in turn empties into the Hoosic River at Williamstown.

Our hike backtracks to the campground, which also has group campsites. After returning to Sperry Road, briefly continue down it, then look left for a kiosk and find the Roaring Brook Trail as it passes group campsites. Ahead, bridge a streamlet. Note the old dam here, formerly holding back a quaint pond. After the bridge, the Deer Hill/Roaring Brook Trail splits right as a singletrack path, then you split again, descending by switchbacks on the Deer Hill Trail among evergreens clinging to an insane slope to reach 60-foot Deer Hill Falls. This pourover can be a delight or a dud, depending on recent rain. Either way, the setting displays the rugged nature of these slopes—steep rock gorge, near-vertical falling waters, and deep forests.

Next comes an unnamed cascade at the bridge where the trail crosses Roaring Brook. This 20-foot tongue of whitewater makes an angled tiered drop past ferny woods and is my favorite waterfall of the group. It has the most water and will run longer into the season.

Many hikers are also photographers, and waterfall photographers form an additional hiking subset. As the author of over eighty outdoor guides plus several waterfall-specific books, I photograph just about every waterfall visited, digitally preserving the cataracts. Taking a worthwhile waterfall photo takes time, effort—and a little luck. Capturing the personality of a waterfall may mean several visits during different times of the year.

Here are a few tips that may help you become a better waterfall photographer. A sturdy tripod helps because you cannot hold a camera sufficiently steady when using slow shutter speeds. Set your camera and use a timer, reducing shake caused by pressing the shutter button. Get the correct ISO setting. On most digital cameras the ISO setting is designed to approximate the ISO speed of a chosen film used in a traditional film camera. The lowest ISO number you'll find on a digital camera, usually 100 but sometimes lower, is generally the preferred setting for shooting waterfalls. This number will yield the greatest detail, sharpness, effects, and color accuracy.

Slow shutter speeds give a sense of movement. The movement of flowing water is completely stopped at 1/2000 second. The fastest water will soften starting at 1/60 second. At 1/15 second, water movement will be clearly seen, but not be completely blurred. Most waterfall photographs are shot at 1/8 second or slower to produce a soft quality. Time of day is important. Midday sun creates harsh lighting and shadows. Visit a waterfall at daybreak or an hour before sunset, and use the photogenic light quality. Cloudy days afford more waterfall photo opportunities.

Watch your exposure. The white water of a falls will often cause underexposure of your shot, making the water gray and the foliage slightly dark. With digital cameras you

Find this waterfall just below the bridged crossing of Roaring Brook.

can see what you just shot and adjust aperture, shutter speed, or ISO setting. Use perspective. Waterfall photographs need a reference to indicate their size. To deliver a feeling of depth and space, use foreground elements such as trees, rocks, and people. Try to frame the waterfall.

Mind your position. Shoot from the top, bottom, or side of the falls. Treat the waterfall like a piece of art. Be creative while shooting the waterfall from different perspectives. Consider people. The high reflectance of water tends to underexpose people in waterfall photography. Consider proper lighting for both people and the waterfall.

Seek rainbows. If you are lucky enough to find a rainbow at the end of a waterfall, take as many pictures as you can. Shoot at different settings, then delete pictures back at home. Consider the horizon. Horizon lines should be level, and in general, not placed in the center of the composition. Within the photo, look for wasted space, light and dark spots. Eliminate distracting elements.

The above tips will increase your chances for a remarkable waterfall photograph while hiking the Berkshires.

From the unnamed falls on Roaring Brook, you will climb to the Deer Hill trail shelter. This evergreen-shaded lean-to is set on a declivitous slope, but the land has been leveled at the three-sided wooden refuge. It also has a couple of nearby tent sites cut into the mountain. A spur trail leads to a water source. The climb eases when you reach the Campground Trail, a wide former road. Pass one last set of cascades streaming above and below the trail before returning to Sperry Road and completing this waterfall hike of the Greylock highlands.

MILES AND DIRECTIONS

0.0 From the parking area on Sperry Road just off Rockwell Road, head north on the gravel track, passing around a gate. Keep north on the doubletrack.

0.2 Come to a trail intersection. Here, your return route, the Campground Trail, comes in on your left, while the Hopper Trail leaves right. Stay straight with Sperry Road.

0.5 A leg of the Hopper Trail splits right. Stay straight with Sperry Road. Streams flow under the track.

0.6 Come to the campground entrance. Split right here and briefly walk through the campground before splitting right again on the signed, singletrack March Cataract Trail.

0.9 Descend on a steep slope past large yellow birch trees.

1.1 Come to March Cataract Falls. Pull up a boulder and admire the veil-like 30-foot spiller running over a stone slope. Backtrack to the campground.

1.7 Return to the campground. Head down Sperry Road then turn left, south, near the Cherry Group Camp. Soon bridge a creek, then split right on the Deer Hill/Roaring Brook Trail.

1.9 Split left on the Deer Hill Trail, dropping via switchbacks on an incredibly steep slope.

2.2 Take the short spur left to Deer Hill Falls. This is another low-flow cascade that when running makes an impressive 60-foot splashing descent in veil-like strands over an irregular rock ledge into a boulder garden. Continue dropping by switchbacks as Roaring Brook roars below.

2.3 Bridge Roaring Brook just above a sublime cascade splashing white over a multi-stage stone slide. Begin a demanding climb away from Roaring Brook.

2.5 Come to the Deer Hill trail shelter, set in evergreens on a small flat bordered by steep slopes on all sides. Keep ascending.

2.9 Meet the Campground Trail. Head left, gently climbing an old roadbed.

3.2 Bridge a creek with lively cascades both above and below the trail.

3.3 Return to Sperry Road. Turn right, south, on the doubletrack.

3.5 Arrive back at the parking area on Sperry Road after passing the gate, completing the hike.

9 **JONES NOSE CIRCUIT**

This Greylock highlands hike first tracks through high-country meadows with views then surmounts Jones Nose, a pointy upthrust, topping out on Saddle Ball Mountain to meet the famed Appalachian Trail (AT). You will head south on the AT, losing your hard-won elevation, but are rewarded with distant views. After passing near a trail shelter, the hike uses a trail named Old Adams Road to complete the circuit—passing more mountain meadows—that never goes under 2,000 feet in elevation.

Start: Jones Nose parking area
Distance: 4.0-mile loop
Difficulty: Moderate; does have initial nearly 900-foot climb
Elevation change: +/-1,149 feet over entire hike
Maximum grade: 15% grade for 1.1 miles
Hiking time: About 2.5 hours
Seasons/schedule: Mid-May through mid-Nov
Fees and permits: None
Dog friendly: Yes

Trail surface: Forested natural surface, very rocky in places
Land status: State reservation
Nearest town: Pittsfield
Other trail users: None
Map to consult: Mount Greylock State Reservation
Amenities available: Picnic area 0.1 mile into hike
Cell service: Fair to good
Trail contact: Mount Greylock State Reservation, (413) 499-4262, www.mass.gov/locations/mount-greylock-state-reservation

FINDING THE TRAILHEAD

From the intersection of US 7 and US 20 in downtown Pittsfield, head north on US 7 for 6.6 miles, then veer right onto N. Main Street and follow it for 0.7 mile. Turn right onto Greylock Road and follow it for 0.4 mile, then veer left onto Rockwell Road, entering the state reservation. After 4.3 miles turn right into the Jones Nose trailhead parking lot. **Trailhead GPS:** 42.601587, -73.200407

THE HIKE

Jones Nose harbors meadows at over 2,300 feet. A place where harsh winter winds gash the open terrain, the meadows in spring and summer can be wildflower and birding haven, and in autumn a spot where you can admire fall's colorful cornucopia. The fields of Jones Nose aren't natural. In the late 1700s, a settler named Seth Jones chose this ridgeline for a home and farm. He obviously favored cool summers and brisk winters. Watering his stock from nearby Kitchen Brook, Jones, along with several other farmers, tilled the valley and adjacent hills around the brook.

In addition to farms like Jones's being cleared, other lands were timbered to make charcoal for the thriving iron-ore industry dotting much of the Berkshires landscape. In a story repeated in other parts of the Greylock Range, forests once again rose from the slopes of the highlands after farmers left for western lands, the ore industry cooled, and what is now Mount Greylock State Reservation became a preserve.

But there was something special about the meadows of Jones Nose. The open meadows added biodiversity for disappearing habitat as the Greylock Range reforested.

Hiking through the preserved meadows below Jones Nose

Therefore, the Massachusetts Department of Conservation and Recreation decided to keep the slopes of greater Jones Nose open by mowing and cutting, leaving another distinct jewel in this Berkshire beauty that is Mount Greylock State Reservation. And the meadows shine brightly to this day.

Our hike travels directly through these highland fields, where you can enjoy the flowers, the birds, and the views. It isn't long after starting the hike that you are traipsing through these fields on a narrow singletrack path, with brush crowding your legs by late summer, grasses and flowers blowing in the breeze, and the snout of Jones Nose staring you in the face. To add to the pleasure, a foot-only-accessible picnic area with tables has been set up in the meadow, views included.

The meadow ends all too soon and you make a steady climb up the point of Jones Nose. It wastes no time either, rising sharply through squat hardwoods. The trail levels off while passing the CCC Dynamite Trail before climbing again to a knob of Saddle Ball Mountain, cloaked in balsam fir and red spruce, and at 3,238 feet, one of the loftiest peaks in the Bay State, just 253 feet lower than Mount Greylock. This critically imperiled spruce-fir complex occurs in Massachusetts only on the greater Mount Greylock massif above 3,000 feet.

Paper birch, yellow birch, and mountain ash are deciduous components of this highland forest, along with hobblebush and copious mosses. These forests grow slowly due to the harsh climate, acidic nutrient-poor soils, and excessive exposed bedrock. All the trees up here are generally short, victims of punishing winter winds.

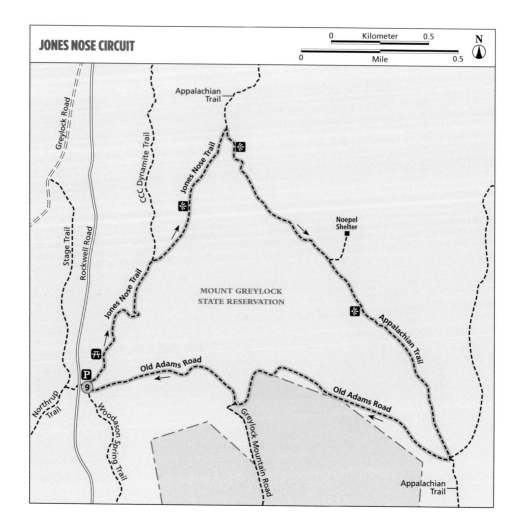

Greylock Road

CCC Dynamite Trail

Appalachian Trail

Jones Nose Trail

Noepel Shelter

Stage Trail

Rockwell Road

Jones Nose Trail

MOUNT GREYLOCK STATE RESERVATION

Appalachian Trail

Old Adams Road

9

P

Northrup Trail

Woodason Spring Trail

Old Adams Road

Greylock Mountain Road

Appalachian Trail

After joining the Appalachian Trail, you descend south from this knob, passing a lesser-used spur left to an outcrop and partial view. The trail remains narrow and rocky, coursing among tightly grown brush and trees. This loop avails a backpacking opportunity as you pass the spur to the Mark Noepel lean-to. This three-sided wooden trail shelter is set on a wooded hillside with a path leading to a nearby tributary of Bassett Brook. The down-grade continues beyond the shelter, guiding you to a better view from a stone perch, with a sharp drop-off below. Here you can look down the Kitchen Brook valley and yonder.

Meet Old Adams Road after winding through a boulder garden. This easy track heads west, closing the loop as it cuts into the Kitchen Brook watershed. Old Adams Road meets Greylock Mountain Road, also closed to public use within the reservation. Remarkably, Greylock Mountain Road was once the route of the Appalachian Trail. The AT reroute is now on the east side of Kitchen Brook. The final part of the hike keeps west, gently rising past another series of picturesque meadows being kept open, adding more opportunities to enjoy the flora and fauna around Jones Nose.

MILES AND DIRECTIONS

0.0 From the Jones Nose parking area, head north through brush on the Jones Nose Trail. Other trails leave in all cardinal directions.

0.1 Come to the small picnic area set up on the fields of Jones Nose. The outdoor dining locale presents superb views to the south of the knob that is Rounds Rock as well as Jones Nose.

0.2 Leave the meadow of Jones Nose and enter woods, climbing steadily.

0.5 Reach a trail intersection in relatively level woods. Here, the CCC Dynamite Trail heads left, working along the west slope of Saddle Ball Mountain. We stay right with the Jones Nose Trail, resuming the uptick.

0.8 A spur trail leads left to a west-facing overlook from a small outcrop.

1.1 Meet the Appalachian Trail after climbing through an increasing number of red spruce and balsam fir trees, a true boreal forest. Head right, southbound, dropping off a knob of Saddle Ball Mountain. Ahead, a spur trail left leads to a decent easterly view.

1.6 A spur trail goes left to the Mark Noepel trail shelter. Keep descending on a narrowing ridgeline.

1.9 Come to a view to the west of the AT, just as the path makes a stony switchback. Panoramas open to the southeast.

2.1 The AT leads you by an overhanging rock, a good escape from a thunderstorm. Wind through a boulder garden on an easy slope.

2.5 Head right, westerly, on the Old Adams Road, a doubletrack trail, now but a gentle downhill, in pleasant hardwoods of birch, beech, and evergreens, bordered with ferns.

2.8 Step over a tributary of Kitchen Brook.

3.3 Bridge a tributary of Kitchen Brook before reaching an intersection with unmaintained Greylock Mountain Road. Head right here, still westbound, making a steady but moderate uptick on a grassy track. Open onto meadows.

4.0 Arrive back at the trailhead after passing around a pole gate, completing the circuit.

Hiker travels toward Jones Nose.

10 ROUNDS ROCK

This long but skinny loop takes you through gorgeous woodlands in the southern end of the Mount Greylock State Reservation to a pair of rewarding overlooks from an outcrop known as Rounds Rock. The circuit, despite being over 7 miles long, is easier than you may think, as the grades are gentle and the trails are in good condition. Additionally, the beginning of the loop traverses a portion of the Bradley Farm Trail, an interpretive path explaining how the area changed from forest to farm and back again.

Start: Mount Greylock Visitor Center
Distance: 7.3-mile loop
Difficulty: Moderate to difficult due to length
Elevation change: +/-1,384 feet over entire hike
Maximum grade: 16% downhill grade for 0.2 mile
Hiking time: About 4 hours
Seasons/schedule: May through Nov
Fees and permits: None
Dog friendly: Yes
Trail surface: Forested natural surface

Land status: State reservation
Nearest town: Pittsfield
Other trail users: None
Map to consult: Mount Greylock State Reservation
Amenities available: Restrooms, picnic tables, visitor center at trailhead
Cell service: Good
Trail contact: Mount Greylock State Reservation, (413) 499-4262, www.mass.gov/locations/mount-greylock-state-reservation

FINDING THE TRAILHEAD

From the intersection of US 7 and US 20 in downtown Pittsfield, head north on US 7 for 6.6 miles, then veer right onto N. Main Street and follow it for 0.7 mile. Turn right onto Greylock Road and follow it for 0.4 mile, then veer left onto Rockwell Road, entering the state reservation. After 0.6 mile turn right into the visitor center lot. The Bradley Farm Trail trailhead is at the far upper east end of the large parking lot. **Trailhead GPS:** 42.553535, -73.211973

THE HIKE

This is a good choice if you are ready to try a longer mountain hike. Though it has a few short, steep sections, overall the trail grades are modest. The trails themselves are in fine shape and well maintained, and are clearly signed as well. The panoramas from Rounds Rock will spur you toward the goal, and the return trip is almost all downhill. Take a spin in the Mount Greylock Visitor Center before or after your hike. Check out the bronze model of the Greylock Range as well as learn more about the human and natural history of the locale.

Our hike leaves east of the visitor center on the Bradley Farm Trail. An interpretive brochure is available at the visitor center and also online for download. The handout details thirteen interpretive stops to help you learn about this part of the Greylock Range, once timbered, then cleared for farmland, and much of it reverted back to forest again. In fact, one of the first things you spot from the trail are apple trees from what once was an open orchard, now woodland. Nature never stands still or allows a void.

Looking southwest into the Empire State from Rounds Rock

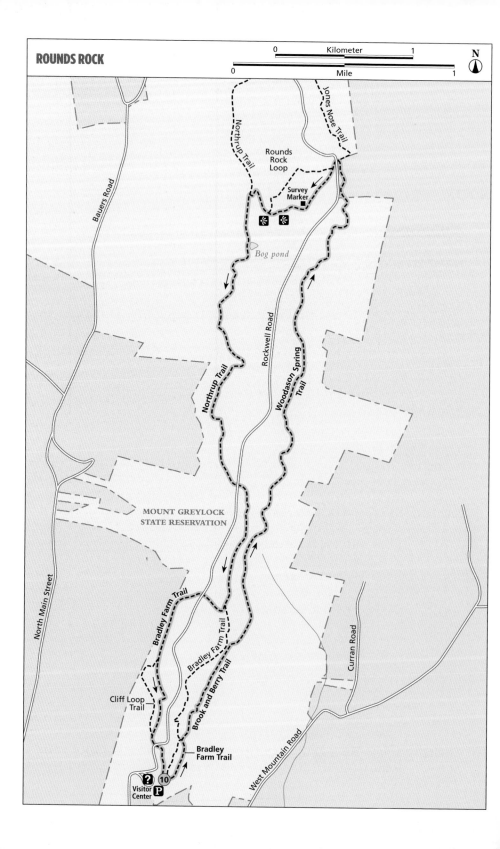

ROUNDS ROCK

0 Kilometer 1
0 Mile 1

N

Jones Nose Trail

Northrup Trail

Rounds
Rock
Loop

Survey
Marker

Bog pond

Bauers Road

Rockwell Road

Northrup Trail

Woodason Spring
Trail

MOUNT GREYLOCK
STATE RESERVATION

North Main Street

Bradley Farm Trail

Bradley Farm Trail

Brook and Berry Trail

Curran Road

Cliff Loop
Trail

Bradley
Farm Trail

Visitor
Center

10

P

West Mountain Road

Author takes a break while enjoying the view from Rounds Rock.

You climb sharply after leaving the farm area. The ascent is short and not sweet, but after surmounting that quick challenge you got it made. After joining the Woodason Spring Trail, the hike traverses the eastern slope of the primary Greylock ridgeline, atop which runs Rockwell Road, part of the scenic auto route that winds through the reservation from one end to the other (USGS quadrangle maps label a knob on this ridge as "South Greylock"). Yellow birch, maple, and cherry grow in ranks with an understory of ferns and grasses. Partial easterly views open through the trees, down to the Hoosic River valley.

You will gently climb, winding in and out of small watersheds, some flowing, some not. The trail often bridges these streambeds, further evidence of the care this path receives. Red spruce begin to appear higher up, joining the northern hardwoods. And then you are on Rounds Rock, walking the rim of this high-country knob and reaching the high point of the hike at 2,581 feet. Wind-stunted trees and blueberry thickets populate the peak. Just ahead is the first of two spur trails that lead south to outcrops and views. The first one is best. It presents a wide-open southward panorama, with a close look at a beaver pond below and distant views of peaks and valleys down the Berkshires and on to New York. The second view isn't as rewarding.

Leave Rounds Rock. This is the steepest descent of the hike, albeit very short. Your return trip on the Northrup Trail first passes a small beaver pond that allows you to look back up at Rounds Rock. Can you spot the stone outcrops where you stood earlier? I personally find it astonishing that beavers found a refuge and created a home high in these mountains.

Beyond the beaver pond, the Northrup Trail cruises south, bridging Town Brook, then crosses Rockwell Road before bisecting an old clearing, now growing up in trees. Note the widespread branches of the trees, revealing they grew up amid fields. You are back in former farm country. Look for more evidence until the hike's conclusion back at the visitor center.

MILES AND DIRECTIONS

0.0 From the east end of the visitor center, at a kiosk, join the Bradley Farm Trail. The Brook and Berry Trail leaves nearby. Work your way up a wooded valley.

0.2 Come to a four-way intersection. Here the Brook and Berry Trail comes in from your left, while the Bradley Farm Trail keeps straight. Turn right here, joining the Brook and Berry Trail, dipping to step over a small mountain stream, then make the only sharp climb of the hike.

0.7 Come to an intersection. Here, the Brook and Berry Trail ends, while the Bradley Farm Trail enters on your left and continues left. Our hike splits right with the Woodason Spring Trail.

1.3 Bridge small Pettibone Brook.

1.6 Level off atop a highland flat, just above 2,200 feet.

2.3 Red spruce find their place in the forest.

3.1 Make a sharp but quick jump up the slope of Rounds Rock.

3.3 Head left at an intersection toward Rounds Rock. Cross Rockwell Road, climb just a bit, and reach the loop portion of the Rounds Rock Loop. Stay left at this split. (If you go right, that trail passes the site of a 1948 small plane crash.)

3.5 Find a survey marker embedded in stone, marking the high point of Rounds Rock.

3.7 Come to the better overlook after taking the spur to it. Here, a stone perch opens a southward view as far as the eye can see, mountains distant and near, and also a little beaver pond below by which you will hike. Cheshire Reservoir and downtown Pittsfield are easily identifiable.

3.8 Pass a second, lesser view, accessed via a spur trail. It offers a more westerly perspective. After visiting that overlook, continue the Rounds Rock Loop and come to an intersection. Here, stay left, westerly, descending off Rounds Rock.

4.0 Meet the Northrup Trail. Head left, south, on a gentle, nearly level track in pleasant woods. Spruce are scattered among the hardwoods.

4.3 Pass by a bog pond, bridging it near a beaver dam. Look up toward Rounds Rock.

4.9 Bridge the upper headwaters of Town Brook.

5.6 Cross Rockwell Road, still in mixed spruce and hardwoods, with scads of ferns in summertime.

6.2 Head right on the Bradley Farm Trail, then quickly cross Rockwell Road again. Keep descending in woods.

6.7 Pass the first of two intersections with the Cliff Loop Trail, which drops right on a steep slope.

7.1 Cross Rockwell Road a final time after passing the second intersection with the Cliff Loop Trail.

7.3 Arrive back at the east end of the visitor center parking lot, finishing the hike.

11 ASHUWILLTICOOK RAIL TRAIL

This fine rail trail, despite being in and out of populated areas, delivers fun, good scenery, and better views. Start at pretty Cheshire Reservoir, behind which rises majestic highlands, then make your way up the greater Hoosic River valley through the town of Cheshire then into the undomesticated wetland flats of Stafford Hill Wildlife Management Area, finally making your way to historic Adams, ringed in mountains. Thus, the rail trail offers easy flat lake, river, mountain, and urban views. Furthermore, you can alter the distance of your hike from 1 to 14.2 miles in length, according to your desire of distance covered.

Start: Farnam's Crossing parking area
Distance: 1 to 14.2 miles out and back or 7.1 miles one way
Difficulty: Easy to difficult depending on distance
Elevation change: +/-354 feet over entire hike
Maximum grade: 1% grade for 0.9 mile
Hiking time: 1 to 6 hours
Seasons/schedule: Year-round
Fees and permits: None
Dog friendly: Yes, if your dog doesn't mind paved trails
Trail surface: Asphalt
Land status: State park
Nearest town: Cheshire
Other trail users: Bicyclers, rollerbladers, anglers
Map to consult: Ashuwillticook Rail Trail
Amenities available: Restrooms and picnic tables at trailhead and parking areas
Cell service: Good
Trail contact: Ashuwillticook Rail Trail, (413) 499-7003, www.mass.gov/locations/ashuwillticook-rail-trail

FINDING THE TRAILHEAD

From the intersection of MA 8 and MA 9 in Pittsfield, take MA 8 north for 5.9 miles and turn left on Farnam's Road. Drive just a short distance west and reach the parking area on your right. **Trailhead GPS:** 42.538643, -73.182842

THE HIKE

You will be happily surprised at the sights and scenes that the Ashuwillticook Rail Trail delivers on this journey. For starters, it runs along the shores of 418-acre Cheshire Reservoir, from which rise the loftiest peaks in Massachusetts. While passing through Cheshire, the former rail line crosses paths with the one and only Appalachian Trail. And then your eyes will savor the wetland flats of Stafford Hill Wildlife Management Area, where the Hoosic River lazily winds its way through this unexpected natural interlude. In still other places, the rapids of the Hoosic provide visual and audio enhancements while Mount Greylock towers in the distance. Upon entering Adams, you can appreciate the sightly brick structures located along the old rail line. And downtown Adams makes a worthy end/turnaround point.

Being a rail trail, the path presents multiple access points, though I recommend the full hike. Alternatively, you can do the whole enchilada by executing a 7.1-mile one-way endeavor. Simply plant a shuttle vehicle in Adams or get a ride back to the trailhead.

This rail trail takes you along the shore of Cheshire Reservoir.

During its century-and-a-half life, starting in the 1840s, what was originally the Pittsfield and North Adams Railroad first served booming textile mills in the Hoosic River valley, then later moved limestone and other minerals out of the region. Passengers were also served as the line struggled to survive, changing hands a few times before ceasing operations in 1990. By that time, the rail trail concept had gained a toehold in the nation and local leaders saw the train right-of-way as a path linking the communities for recreation, exercise, and transportation. Thus, they preserved the right-of-way in the critical early stages, and today it is a linear Massachusetts state park.

The 10-foot-wide, 12.7-mile-long (one-way) rail trail came to be in 2001. Since then, hikers, bicyclers, roller-bladers, and anglers have enjoyed the universally accessible track that is a mandatory bucket list destination for Berkshires enthusiasts in the know.

You start the trek at Farnham's Crossing, a small park on the shore of Cheshire Reservoir. Here you will find parking, picnic tables, restrooms, and fishing opportunities—along with your first rewarding views of the lake and highlands that rise from its west side. The trail is open overhead more often than not—bring a hat and sunscreen during the warm season. You are also mere feet from the shore of Cheshire Reservoir most of the time. Cherish the aquatic intimacy.

Occasional waterside repose benches beckon. Before long you can see the church steeples and other structures of Cheshire. Marshes occasionally stretch out the east side

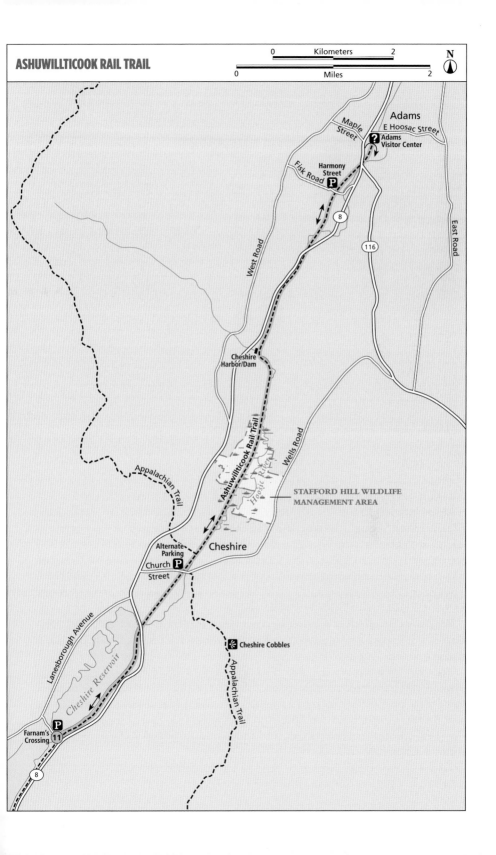

0   Kilometers   2

0   Miles   2

N

Adams

Maple Street

E Hoosac Street

Adams Visitor Center

Harmony Street

Fisk Road

West Road

8

116

East Road

Cheshire Harbor/Dam

Ashuwillticook Rail Trail

Wells Road

Hoosic River

Appalachian Trail

STAFFORD HILL WILDLIFE MANAGEMENT AREA

Alternate Parking

Church Street

Cheshire

Lanesborough Avenue

Cheshire Reservoir

Cheshire Cobbles

Appalachian Trail

Farnam's Crossing

11

8

Even the geese like the Ashuwillticook Rail Trail.

of the rail trail. Enter Cheshire after leaving the lake. Next you get to enjoy the winding Hoosic River as it works around brushy little islands.

Enter Stafford Hill Wildlife Management Area after leaving Cheshire behind. Here, a huge wooded swamp flanks the serpentine watercourse, pushing back the boundaries of civilization in appearance if not in fact. In summer, red-winged blackbirds will cheer you on, while other avian life echoes over the flats. The rail trail runs on a berm through this marshy locale, neither water nor land, but naturally picturesque all the same. This is a place not to be missed.

You enter Cheshire Harbor, site of an old railroad station, after bridging the Hoosic River. Bassett Brook enters the river here, just before the Hoosic loudly spills over a dam then runs in sonorant rapids through a shady wooded corridor. The trail in this part is shadier, too.

The river keeps up its lively flow, a contrast to the slow flow through the swamps. You enter Adams, passing neighborhoods then the brick-structure-rich downtown area, viewing old mills the railroad once served. Enjoy looks at downtown as well as the adjacent mountains, then reach the Adams Visitor Center. If you haven't set up a shuttle or have a ride, turn around and walk an encore performance through the many faces of the Ashuwillticook Rail Trail.

MILES AND DIRECTIONS

0.0 From the parking area at Farnam's Crossing, walk east toward MA 8 then join the signed, paved Ashuwillticook Rail Trail, northbound. The trail is bordered with gravel, and a few trees and bushes rise above it. Cheshire Reservoir extends to your left, with houses nearby. Watery views are nearly continual.

0.4 Cross Mallard Cove Road. Keep north as the trail is mostly directly along the shoreline. Note the lake islands.

1.5 Cross MA 8 at a traffic light just after passing the Cheshire Reservoir Dam outflow. Ahead, the aquatic scenery morphs from lake to watercourse as the unleashed Hoosic River winds north, bordered by willow trees, reeds, and brush.

1.7 Bridge Kitchen Brook. Walk through the town of Cheshire.

2.2 Come to the large Church Street trail parking area. The Appalachian Trail crosses the river and briefly follows the rail trail corridor before heading for the Greylock Range. The Ashuwillticook Rail Trail continues through Cheshire, keeping north-northeast. The river winds in and out of view.

3.2 Enter Stafford Hill Wildlife Management Area. A vast marsh extends on both sides of the trail beyond a screen of sumac, willow, and alder. Beaver ponds are scattered throughout the swamp.

4.4 Leave the wetland and enter a tunnel of greenery.

4.6 The rail trail bridges the Hoosic River to enter historic Cheshire Harbor. Cross Harbor Road, then pass a trailside dam. Look for stone walls hemming in the Hoosic River.

5.0 A trail sign welcomes you to Adams. Enjoy looks at the fast-moving Hoosic.

5.8 The rail trail goes under MA 8.

6.0 Bridge the Hoosic again. You are now on the west bank of the river and will remain so for the duration of the hike.

6.4 Pass under Harmony Street and reach the Harmony Street trail parking on your left. Enter the more urbanized older part of the town. Pass a mill on your right.

6.8 Cross MA 8 again, also known as Park Street. Mount Greylock looms over the town.

7.1 Come to the Adams Visitor Center, with parking, restrooms, water, and information. Backtrack to Farnam's Crossing.

14.2 Arrive back at the Farnam's Crossing trailhead, completing the rail trail hike.

12 CHESHIRE COBBLES GORE POND

This Appalachian Trail adventure starts in the community of Cheshire, then climbs the world's most famous footpath up North Mountain. Reach the outcrop known as the Cheshire Cobbles. Here you can delight in expansive vistas of the Hoosic River valley, Cheshire Reservoir, and the Greylock Range, as well as the towns below. From there, ramble south along North Mountain, reaching a high point to then drop to highland Gore Pond, where you can relax by this mountain-top body of water before returning to the trailhead.

Start: Railroad Street parking area
Distance: 7.2 miles out and back
Difficulty: Moderate to difficult due to rocky trail in places
Elevation change: +/-1,445 feet over entire hike
Maximum grade: 11% grade for 1.5 miles
Hiking time: About 4 hours
Seasons/schedule: May through Nov
Fees and permits: None
Dog friendly: Yes
Trail surface: Natural surface, some rocky sections

Land status: National Park Service Appalachian Trail corridor
Nearest town: Cheshire
Other trail users: None
Maps to consult: Chalet Wildlife Management Area, National Park Service–Appalachian Trail
Amenities available: Restroom, benches, picnic tables at trailhead
Cell service: Good
Trail contact: Appalachian National Scenic Trail, (304) 535-6278, www.nps.gov/appa

FINDING THE TRAILHEAD

From the intersection of MA 8 and MA 9 in Pittsfield, take MA 8 north for 7.3 miles to Church Street. Turn right and follow Church Street for 0.4 mile, then turn left on Railroad Street, just before crossing the Ashuwillticook Rail Trail. Go a very short distance on Railroad Street, then turn right into the trail parking area.
Trailhead GPS: 42.562564, -73.156555

THE HIKE

Massachusetts is the proud home to 90.4 miles of the 2,193-mile Appalachian Trail (AT) as it travels from Georgia to Maine. Elevations of the AT in Massachusetts range from 650 feet to 3,491 feet, the high point being the highest point in the state at Mount Greylock. From the south the AT enters Massachusetts at Sages Ravine in Mount Washington State Forest and works its way north to many highlights detailed in this guide, including Bear Rock Falls, Mount Race, Tyringham Cobble, Finerty Pond, Mount Greylock, and of course the Cheshire Cobbles, which you can enjoy during this hike.

The Appalachian Trail was completed in 1937. It is a privately managed unit of the National Park System. On its journey from Georgia to Maine, the AT touches fourteen states. The lowest elevation of the entire AT is 124 feet near Bear Mountain, New York, and the highest elevation is 6,625 feet on Clingmans Dome in Tennessee.

The Cheshire Cobbles provides expansive views of valleys and mountains.

Hikers that trek the Appalachian Trail end to end in one fell swoop are known as thru-hikers. Others who complete the AT piece by piece are known as section hikers, literally tackling it segment by segment. More than 21,000 people have reported hiking the entire Appalachian Trail.

A thru-hike of the AT takes the average hiker anywhere from four to six months to complete. This entails hiking miles and miles per day, day after day, and camping out most nights. It means trekking through temperatures ranging from 20 to 95 degrees and through an equally wide range of weather, from snow to sleet to rain, blasting wind to blaring sun, high humidity to thunder and lightning.

Most aspiring thru-hikers fail in their quest. Success rate estimates range from 15 to 25 percent, with hikers dropping out for various reasons, whether from the daily physical rigors or mental challenge of hiking day after day. Or perhaps it is being away from family, friends, and home, or simply running out of money while hiking.

You may see some thru-hikers on your trek to the Cheshire Cobbles and Gore Pond. Most of them take on a trail name rather than using their own name while on their AT quest. The new name is part of the Appalachian Trail experience. Trail names symbolize the transition from the old life to the new life, a tangible break from what was to what is.

Trail names add anonymity among a new set of comrades thrown together by chance, each independently concluding this was the time to hike the AT. Then their daily pace and trail experiences further spin the roulette wheel of with whom they hike, and from whom they might receive a trail name. The trail name becomes their identity among

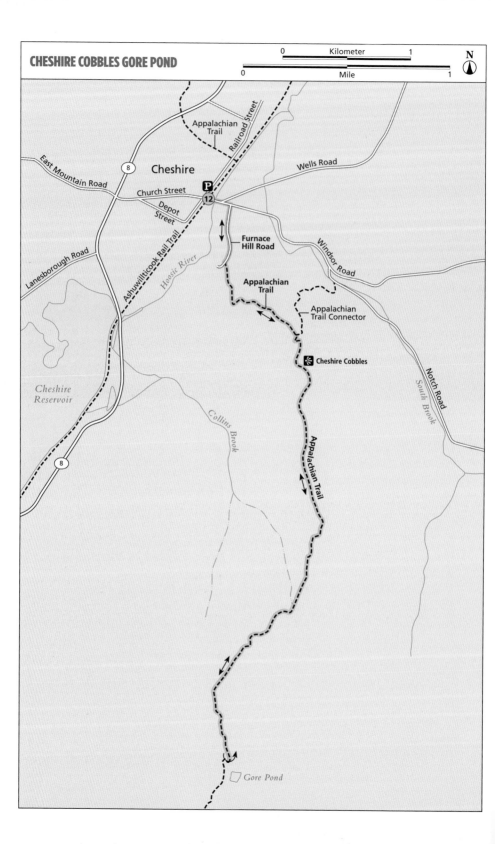

CHESHIRE COBBLES GORE POND

0   Kilometer   1

0   Mile   1

N

East Mountain Road

8

Cheshire

Railroad Street

Appalachian Trail

Wells Road

Church Street

P

12

Depot Street

Furnace Hill Road

Windsor Road

Lanesborough Road

Ashuwillticook Rail Trail

Hoosic River

Appalachian Trail

Appalachian Trail Connector

Cheshire Cobbles

Notch Road

South Brook

Cheshire Reservoir

Collins Brook

Appalachian Trail

8

Appalachian Trail

Gore Pond

Gore Pond reflects the summer sky.

other hikers after they finish the AT, and represents the freedom of life on the trail long after their return to the regular world.

To make the AT a contiguous path the trail must route through communities, known in the hiking world as "trail towns." In these trail towns, such as Cheshire, thru-hikers often rest, resupply, shower, and enjoy the comforts of home we take for granted.

Since this is a day hike, we are seeking a respite in nature rather than return to civilization. After leaving the Railroad Street parking area, you walk a few streets east and south, actually traveling through a neighborhood before the AT joins the National Park Service corridor (this corridor protects the AT lands from being developed and forcing a trail reroute), where you trek through woods. The natural aspect of the trail corridor is effectively widened by much of the adjacent property being part of the Chalet Wildlife Management Area.

Upon reaching the Cheshire Cobbles, you may believe that this is one of the finest panoramas in the Berkshires. For starters, it presents views near and far. In the northern distance, the Green Mountains hold sway, while nearer you can easily identify the communities of the Hoosic River valley—Adams, Cheshire, and North Adams. To the south you can look through the valley to the Taconics and beyond to distant peaks. And Mount Greylock holds sway to the west. Wow!

Keep along the ridge of North Mountain, passing a rocky knob dubbed on official USGS maps as The Cobbles, with some views, then work up along a small highland stream. Note the red spruce up here. After topping out on a knob, the AT dips toward

Gore Pond, first passing a vegetated highland bog. Then suddenly you are at Gore Pond. The small body of water is ringed in forest but near the AT has some alluring rocks that make great seats to sit and observe the watery oasis. On your return trip, be wary of old forest roads you may cross. They don't all lead back to the trailhead.

MILES AND DIRECTIONS

0.0 From the parking area on Railroad Street, walk south to Church Street, then head east on Church Street, cross the Ashuwillticook Rail Trail and Hoosic River, then join Main Street. Keep east, then split right on East Main Street.

0.1 Turn right on Furnace Hill Road. Walk south, gently uphill through a house-lined neighborhood. You can see the rock outcrops of the Cheshire Cobbles while hiking up the road.

0.4 Enter woods left at the dead end of Furnace Hill Road (no parking). A mantle of maple, hemlock, and birch rises overhead. The climb is easy. Beware joining old woods roads.

1.0 Reach a trail intersection. Here, a connector trail leads left 0.5 mile to an alternate parking area on Notch Road. We stay southbound with the AT, working up the slope of North Mountain.

1.3 Head left on the spur trail to the Cheshire Cobbles after working through a boulder field. Quickly open up to a wide outcrop with spectacular views north to the Green Mountains and immediately to the town of Cheshire, Cheshire Reservoir, and the rampart that is the Greylock Range on the west side of the Hoosic River valley. Return to the AT and continue southbound.

1.6 Come to USGS-named The Cobbles. Note the survey marker. Keep south, climbing into the headwaters of Collins Brook, which you will cross numerous times ahead.

3.2 Top out on the hike's high point at 2,220 feet. Descend, passing a highland bog.

3.6 Reach Gore Pond near where its outflow crosses the AT. Rock outcrops here provide looks at the small but scenic body of water. Backtrack to Railroad Street.

7.2 Arrive back at the Railroad Street trailhead, completing the hike.

13 SPRUCE HILL CIRCUIT

This loop hike at Savoy Mountain State Forest delivers a top-notch Berkshires vista across the Hoosic River valley to the towering Greylock Range—and beyond. What could be called the "Grandstand of Mount Greylock," the Spruce Hill panorama is worth the effort alone. Yet, onward you trek beyond Spruce Hill, through the Hoosic Range, wandering past home sites, along hills, and near untamed swamps of the Staples Brook watershed. Come near North Pond before returning to the trailhead.

Start: Busby Trail parking area
Distance: 5.3-mile loop with spur to Spruce Hill
Difficulty: Moderate
Elevation change: +/-1,060 feet over entire hike
Maximum grade: 17% grade for 0.3 mile
Hiking time: About 3 hours
Seasons/schedule: May through Dec
Fees and permits: Parking permit required
Dog friendly: Yes

Trail surface: Natural surface woodland trail
Land status: State forest
Nearest town: North Adams
Other trail users: None
Map to consult: Savoy Mountain State Forest
Amenities available: None
Cell service: Good atop Spruce Hill, less so elsewhere
Trail contact: Savoy Mountain State Forest, (413) 663-8469, www.mass .gov/locations/savoy-mountain -state-forest

FINDING THE TRAILHEAD

From downtown North Adams, take MA 2 east for 5.8 miles, then turn right onto Shaft Road and follow it for 0.5 mile. Stay right on Central Shaft Road and follow it for 1.6 miles, then turn right at a three-way intersection, still on Central Shaft Road. Continue 1 mile to reach the Busby Trail trailhead, on your right as the road curves left and Old Florida Road enters on your right, just a little ways beyond the ranger station. **Trailhead GPS:** 42.658137, -73.055499

THE HIKE

The first part of this fine loop uses the Busby Trail to reach Spruce Hill. Savoy Mountain State Forest offers a downloadable interpretive brochure about the Busby Trail that can enhance your hike, the first part of which traces an old farm road, more difficult to imagine as the trail is now in complete woods. You are already at 1,800 feet when the hike begins, on the east slope of the Hoosac Range, once one of the tougher obstacles on the east–west running Mohawk Trail.

When railroads came to western Massachusetts, the Hoosac Range was unclimbable for trains of the day, and thus construction was begun on the famed Hoosac Tunnel, an underground passage cutting through the Hoosac Range. The nearly 5-mile-long hole took almost twenty-five years to build and over 175 lives were lost in the process. The railroad tunnel made possible a rail corridor between points east and west in Massachusetts. The railroad builders of the 1800s learned well the meaning of the word Hoosac— "place of stones"—using a variety of techniques to blast, drill, and otherwise force their

Gazing down on North Adams and East Mountain from Spruce Hill

way under the mountain. The ambitious undertaking was a mere idea in the early 1800s. Financing, machinery, and evolving technology combined with American determination led to the tunnel's opening in 1875. The shaft is still in use today.

You will be way above the engineering marvel while heading north on the Busby Trail in attractive woods, going under a pair of power lines, a decidedly less arduous infrastructure undertaking than the tunnel. Beyond the power lines the Busby Trail starts a gentle upgrade up the greater Staples Brook valley. The woods and path both become rockier. You then come to the Busby home site, marked with a cellar hole, home foundation, and stone fences.

Ol' Busby located his home well. A spring is nearby, and the home site faces southeast, with Spruce Hill providing some protection from the northwesterly winds of winter. The locale was occupied here at 2,177 feet from the early 1800s until the farm was bought in 1933, just one of many tracts purchased to create what became Savoy Mountain State Forest. The Busby clan may have had rough winters and solitude, but at least they didn't suffer from electronics overload like so many of us do today. And that is one of the great pluses of hiking—a woodland venture allows you to return to nature, seeing, feeling, hearing, and smelling the real world, nothing virtual about it, including the post-hike aftereffects such as sore legs, sweaty clothes, and a pleasant memory.

Savoy Mountain State Forest is one of Massachusetts's bigger preserves, coming in at 10,200 acres. With over 50 miles of trails overlain on this mountainous park, hikers, mountain bikers, and other nonmotorized trail enthusiasts can have a ball.

In addition to this hike to Spruce Hill, another popular state forest destination is Tannery Falls/Parker Brook Falls, located southeast of Spruce Mountain. These two cataracts are accessed by the same path, and if you stand in just the right spot, you can view both waterfalls at the same time. Other Savoy Mountain State Forest pursuits include camping

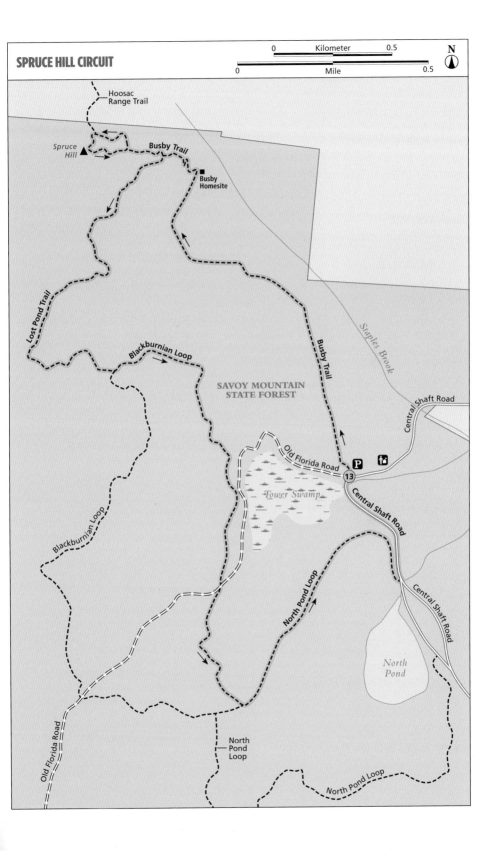

SPRUCE HILL CIRCUIT

0   Kilometer   0.5
0   Mile   0.5

N

Hoosac
Range Trail

Spruce
Hill

Busby Trail

Busby
Homesite

Lost Pond Trail

Blackburnian Loop

SAVOY MOUNTAIN
STATE FOREST

Busby Trail

Staples Brook

Central Shaft Road

Blackburnian Loop

Old Florida Road

Tower Swamp

P

13

Central Shaft Road

North Pond Loop

Central Shaft Road

North
Pond

Old Florida Road

North
Pond
Loop

North Pond Loop

at South Pond, located just a few miles south of this hike, with forty-five reservable sites available. The campground offers on-site showers. Anglers and nonmotorized boaters can ply both North Pond and South Pond, also home to four rental cabins.

The hike changes character beyond the Busby home site, making the only significant climb of the loop, passing the Lost Pond Trail while making your way up to Spruce Hill. Soon you are making the final ascent to the rock knob that is your viewing perch atop Spruce Hill. Warm-up views open to the north, but you'll know when you've reached the main overlook atop a wide-open rock slab. The valley of the Hoosic River forms a grand gulf between Spruce Hill and easily visible Mount Greylock with its distinctive tower, as well as the entire Greylock Range. Additional far-flung landscapes open both north and south along the valley below, including the outcrop of the Pine Cobble, also detailed in this guide. This is easily one of my favorite overlooks in the entire Berkshires, truly the "Grandstand of the Greylock Range."

Continue the loop hike after descending from Spruce Hill. Enjoy the upland woods walk on the Lost Pond Trail, first paralleling one of farmer Busby's rock walls, then coursing in and out of lesser vales flowing toward Staples Brook. Stinging nettle can crowd the trail by midsummer. Consider long pants if hiking that time of year. Next you meet the Blackburnian Loop, likely named for the Blackburnian warbler, a habitué of northern forests in summer. Its orange throat is the bird's identifying characteristic. This bird is no dummy, spending its winters in the tropics.

After crossing Old Florida Road, a once-significant travel route now relegated to backwoods forest road, the trail levels off, crossing another tributary of Tower Swamp, above which you have been circling. You then pick up the more heavily used North Pond Loop. The hiking is easy as you traipse through ferny woods, circling around a hill to reach Old Shaft Road. You are near the forest picnic area, a great place for a post-hike meal, near North Pond. Our hike treads the forest road past the outflow of Tower Swamp before returning to the trailhead, finishing the circuit.

MILES AND DIRECTIONS

0.0 Leave the Busby Trail parking area, immediately entering spruce, birch, and maple woods. The Busby Trail joins a gravel track and passes under a pair of power lines, then becomes more primitive. Climb on gently sloping terrain, former farmland.

1.0 Reach the Busby home site. Begin climbing in earnest by switchbacks in brushy woods on a trail reroute (the old path was straighter and steeper).

1.2 Meet the Lost Pond Trail. You will return here later. For now, stay straight with the Busby Trail, climbing.

1.3 Stay right at the easily missed upper mini-loop around Spruce Hill. Stay right, still climbing the Busby Trail to pass the Hoosac Range Trail, entering on your right and heading north to MA 2. Hike over wind-stunted trees and rock slabs.

1.5 Top out on the wide-open slab of Spruce Hill. A spectacular panorama opens before you of the Hoosic River valley separating you from the Greylock Range to the west. The towns of Adams and North Adams are visible below, with the Green Mountains of Vermont visible in the distant north. Look for the outcrop of the Pine Cobble on East Mountain near Williamstown. Resume toward the Lost Pond Trail after soaking up your fill of this all-star vista.

1.8 Head southwest on the Lost Pond Trail, going downhill more than not.

The Greylock Range as seen from Spruce Hill

2.6 The trail turns abruptly left, east, still descending.

2.7 Curve around a beaver pond, crossing a couple of smallish brooks feeding the pond.

2.9 Intersect the Blackburnian Loop. Head left, crisscrossing a widening branch.

3.4 Cross the two power lines and after the second one briefly join Old Florida Road, then look carefully for the blazes splitting right back into woods. Many hikers miss this split and continue down Old Florida Road, a rugged four-wheel-drive track.

3.8 Cross Old Florida Road. Bridge a stream, then make a moderate ascent in evergreens.

4.1 Intersect the well-used North Pond Loop then turn left, heading north on the North Pond Loop, making an easy, level, splendid woods walk.

4.9 Reach the entrance road to North Pond and gravel Central Shaft Road. Head left on the gravel road, circling Tower Swamp.

5.3 Arrive back at the Busby Trail trailhead, finishing the circuit.

14 TODD MOUNTAIN LOOP

This fun hike takes you on a highlight tour of Mohawk Trail State Forest. Join the historic Mahican-Mohawk Trail along the Deerfield River, absorbing aquatic vistas aplenty while also coming alongside bottomland fields. Next climb Todd Mountain to find views of Deerfield and Cold River valleys from the Indian Lookout. From there drop down the rugged Indian Trail to the Cold River, passing by the campground and other facilities of this state forest before completing the circuit.

Start: Mohawk Trail State Forest entrance
Distance: 5.1-mile loop with spur
Difficulty: Moderate to difficult due to 1,000-foot climb
Elevation change: +/-1,401 feet over entire hike
Maximum grade: 21% grade for 0.25 mile
Hiking time: About 3 hours
Seasons/schedule: May through Dec
Fees and permits: None if parking on MA 2
Dog friendly: Yes

Trail surface: Natural surface woodland trail
Land status: State forest
Nearest town: Charlemont
Other trail users: None
Map to consult: Mohawk Trail State Forest
Amenities available: None at parking lot; picnic, restrooms, camping nearby
Cell service: Not good
Trail contact: Mohawk Trail State Forest, (413) 339-5504, www.mass.gov/locations/mohawk-trail-state-forest

FINDING THE TRAILHEAD

From the intersection of MA 2 and MA 8A in Charlemont, take MA 2 west for 4.2 miles to the parking area on MA 2 just before the bridged entrance to Mohawk Trail State Forest. **Trailhead GPS:** 42.636025, -72.935041

THE HIKE

The Mohawk Trail was a pre-Columbian Indian path connecting tribes of what is now eastern New York in the Hudson River valley with the people and lands of the Connecticut River valley to the east. A portion of that east–west trail cut through the Berkshires. Later, when English colonists arrived, they also trod the Mohawk Trail. And when a fledgling United States broke from England, the Mohawk Trail was used to move American troops and supplies during the war, including Benedict Arnold's famous march from Boston to Fort Ticonderoga, after which he captured British cannons and returned them to Boston, giving the Patriots a great shot of confidence early in the War for Independence. Much of today's MA 2 highway follows the old Mohawk Trail.

There is also an auto-based Mohawk Trail that was the first scenic highway in New England, established in 1914. It travels from the New York–Massachusetts state line to Millers Falls and the Connecticut River, a distance of 63 miles. Along the way you can enjoy many natural, cultural, and historical sites.

Back in 1992, a group of students at nearby Williamstown College checked into the possibility of reviving the Mohawk Trail as a footpath, and out of that effort the

Mahican-Mohawk Trail was born. This route tries to faithfully follow the Mohawk Trail where possible, even using water routes. They identified a still-original segment of trail along Todd Mountain, and we travel part of that on this hike. It is not often that we can hike an original segment of trail that could be up to thousands of years old and trammeled with innumerable footfalls by people from long ago.

Many other paths lace Mohawk Trail State Forest in addition to the Mahican-Mohawk Trail, and we will explore some of them, too. This state forest offers many activities for the outdoor enthusiast. You will walk near the riverside campground on this trek. The park offers forty-seven campsites during the warm season and also has six rustic cabins for rent in case you want to rough it a little smoother. Anglers can vie for trout in both the Cold River and Deerfield River, or just cool off on a hot day with a dip.

Enjoying a view from the Indian Lookout

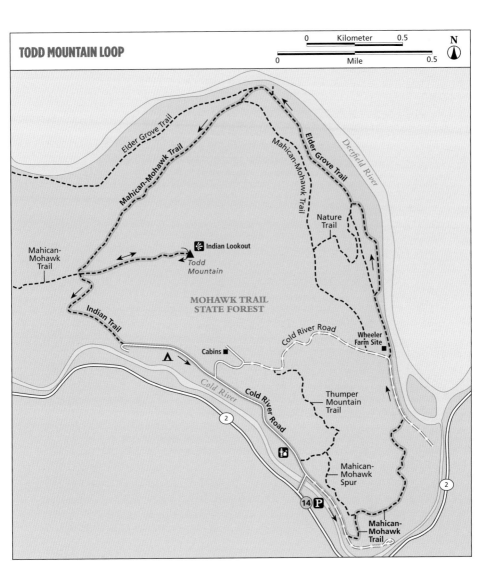

0   Kilometer   0.5

0   Mile   0.5

N

Elder Grove Trail

Mahican-Mohawk Trail

Mahican-Mohawk Trail

Elder Grove Trail

Deerfield River

Nature
Trail

Mahican-
Mohawk
Trail

Indian Lookout

*Todd
Mountain*

**MOHAWK TRAIL
STATE FOREST**

Indian Trail

Cold River Road

Wheeler
Farm Site

Cabins ■

Cold River

Cold River Road

2

Thumper
Mountain
Trail

Mahican-
Mohawk
Spur

14 P

2

Mahican-
Mohawk
Trail

The circuit hike starts by trekking along the Cold River, one of two major waterways encircling this hike, located on a peninsula just before the two waterways merge. This is part of the Mahican-Mohawk Trail, marked with a yellow blaze with a maple leaf inside it. Pines, mountain laurel, and hardwoods shade the path as you wind along Thumper Mountain before dropping to the banks of the attractive Deerfield River, its clear-tea-colored waters rushing over a stony bottom, surrounded by rising mountainous forests.

You stay along the river in bottomland, some of which is being kept open in meadows. Todd Mountain rises from the flats. The walking has been quite easy thus far, with little elevation change. Watch for unmarked mown paths. Just stay right, closest to the river, and you won't get lost. Remain in easy-walking wooded flats after joining the Elder Grove Trail, ensconced between the Deerfield River on one side and the sharply rising Todd Mountain on the other.

The Deerfield River flows majestically through the Berkshires.

Speaking of deer, they are the most widely distributed large mammal in Massachusetts and the Berkshires, as well as the most-sought game species by hunters. It's always exciting to spot a deer in the woods, or in meadows like those along the Deerfield River. Let's face it—fawns are among the cutest of all wild animals. We are in no danger from deer while hiking but rather from deer/vehicle collisions en route to the trailhead.

Eventually the flats end and you work along the lower slope of Todd Mountain, where you rejoin the Mahican-Mohawk Trail. Now the scramble begins, up the shady wooded north slope of Todd Mountain. The narrow, singletrack path works around rocks and beneath evergreens. You will be second-guessing the trail constructors as the last part of this section rises 280 feet in a quarter-mile, a 21 percent grade!

But the ascent reaps benefits as you reach a gap and an original segment of the Mohawk Trail. But for now, after that climb, head east for the views on Todd Mountain and the Indian Lookout. The uptick is gentle through oak–mountain laurel woods, along stone slabs, and up minor rock-and-tree-covered knobs. Most people stop at the first, less rewarding view south. But if you keep following the official trail, it leads to a small loop atop the very crown of Todd Mountain, where you find a stone slab providing an opening through the trees into the wooded, wild-appearing Cold River chasm and across to the forests of Hawks Mountain. This is the Indian Lookout.

From there a short backtrack leads to the Indian Trail and down an authentic portion of the original Mohawk Trail. This path is pretty rough—rocky and steep as it works over stone slabs and through ragged south-facing forests, and suffering from erosion in still other places while dropping 600 feet in 0.4 mile. Just think of all the travelers these trailside stones have seen.

Emerge near the forest campground, now tracing the paved road past facilities. Pick out your favorite campsite as you stroll east, with the Cold River humming in the distance. Take in the developed part of the state forest, passing near the cabin access road then park headquarters before returning to the bridge over the Cold River. After spanning the water, you are back at the parking area on MA 2, a historic hike completed.

MILES AND DIRECTIONS

0.0 Leave the parking area on MA 2, then cross the Cold River on an auto bridge. Turn right, joining gated Cold River Road/Mahican-Mohawk Trail, open only to park personnel and also used by anglers. Walk parallel to the Cold River.

0.3 Split left with the singletrack Mahican-Mohawk Trail, as Cold River Road goes straight. Climb into white pines with contrasting green ferns.

0.4 Pass a spur going to the Thumper Mountain Trail.

0.9 Emerge on a bluff at the Deerfield River, just above its confluence with the Cold River. Head left, tracing an old roadbed, looking upon where the Deerfield River splits around an island.

1.1 Reach an intersection. A left takes you toward the park cabins. Stay right, closer to the river, toward the Elder Grove Trail, passing the signed Wheeler Farm Site, then walking near meadows. Watch for user-created trails leading down to the Deerfield River.

1.3 Stay right at an unsigned junction near meadows. Enter an area with unsigned mown paths. Stay right at these intersections, closest to the river.

1.6 Come to a signed intersection. Stay right, joining the Elder Grove Trail. Continue in flats alongside the Deerfield River. Pass through a planted red pine grove.

2.1 A short spur trail goes right to the river. Here you can look on Zoar Road and the confluence of Pelham Brook and the Deerfield River. Grab this last river view, then return to the Elder Grove Trail.

2.2 The Elder Grove Trail stays right, running along the Deerfield River, while we split left up a short connector toward the Mahican-Mohawk Trail, climbing an ever-steepening mountain slope.

2.3 Intersect and join the Mahican-Mohawk Trail. Keep climbing.

3.0 Reach a gap in the ridge and trail intersection. Head left toward the views on Todd Mountain. Keep going beyond the first view.

3.4 Reach the mini-loop atop Todd Mountain, the Indian Lookout. Enjoy a southerly view, then backtrack.

3.8 Return to the gap, then head south on the Indian Trail. This is an original portion of the Mohawk Trail. The descent is steep, rugged, and irregular. Watch your footing— more than a few ankles have been twisted here.

4.2 Come out on the main paved road near the campground. Head left, cruising the level road, with the Cold River in sight. Pass along the campground.

4.6 A road leads left toward the forest cabins. Keep straight on the main park road.

4.9 Walk past the ranger station, entrance booth, and nature center, then the Thumper Mountain trailhead to your left.

5.1 Arrive back at the trailhead on MA 2, completing the historic hike.

15 **SHAKER HIKE**

Arguably the most historic hike in the Berkshires, this loop takes you along a stream and up a mountain peppered with interpretive information about the Shakers, a religious sect that dwelt in the area and worshipped in the mountains of what is now Pittsfield State Forest. Along the way you will pass a water-source pond, a waterfall, dwelling foundations, and the Shakers' stone quarry, as well as sites deemed holy by the Shakers. Consider timing your hike with a visit to the preserved Hancock Shaker Village, open April through October, located just south of the trailhead.

Start: US 20 trailhead
Distance: 5.5-mile lollipop
Difficulty: Moderate; does have solid climb
Elevation change: +/-1155 feet over entire hike
Maximum grade: 11% downhill grade for 1.0 mile
Hiking time: About 3 hours
Seasons/schedule: Year-round
Fees and permits: None
Dog friendly: Yes

Trail surface: Forested natural surface
Land status: State forest
Nearest town: Pittsfield
Other trail users: ATVs on parts of the trail
Map to consult: Pittsfield State Forest
Amenities available: None
Cell service: Good
Trail contact: Pittsfield State Forest, (413) 442-8992, www.mass.gov/locations/pittsfield-state-forest

FINDING THE TRAILHEAD

From downtown Pittsfield, take US 20 west for 4.6 miles to the Shaker trailhead on your right. It is a large pullover on the north side of US 20. **Trailhead GPS:** 42.431513, -73.339947

THE HIKE

Set in the 11,000-acre Pittsfield State Forest, very near where the preserved Hancock Shaker Village stands, this loop hike, collectively known as the Shaker Trail, uses several paths in the state forest to fashion a circuit that not only enhances your appreciation of the Berkshires, but also helps you travel back in time to 1790, when the Hancock Shaker Village was established. It was one of many Shaker communities in New England and New York. Originating in England, the religious sect members were dubbed "Shakers" for their ecstatic dance when worshiping God.

Despite the sect's celibacy vow and ban on marriage, Hancock Village grew (via recruits), and its residents became known for their industriousness of labor and quality craftsmanship, as well as being efficient agronomists. Hancock had over 300 members at its high point in the 1840s, working an estimated 3,000 acres. The members lived in six communal groups known as "Families." By the early 1900s, the group was down to fifty individuals. Most of the land was sold, and eventually the community died off. However, one relict Shaker community survives in Maine to this day, still following the Shaker motto, "Put your hands to work and your hearts to God."

These dam remnants now help form a waterfall.

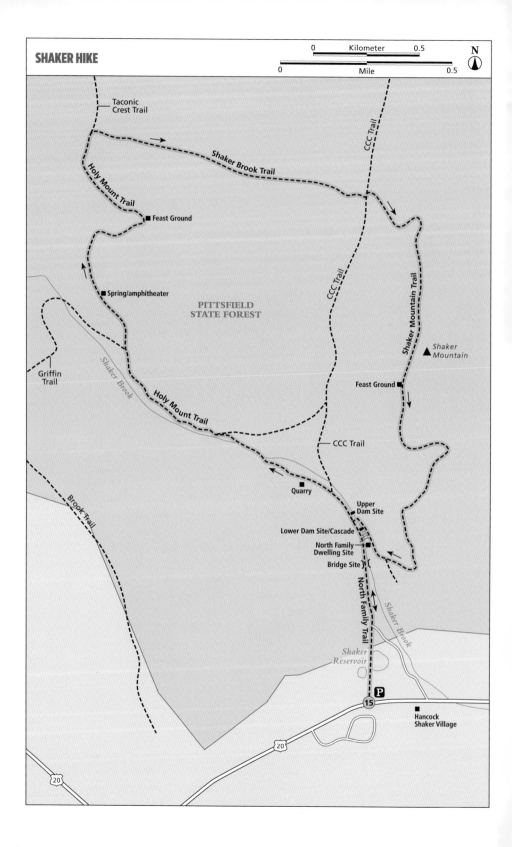

SHAKER HIKE

0   Kilometer   0.5

0   Mile   0.5

N

Taconic
Crest Trail

Shaker Brook Trail

CCC Trail

Holy Mount Trail

■ Feast Ground

■ Spring/amphitheater

PITTSFIELD
STATE FOREST

Shaker Brook

Griffin
Trail

Holy Mount Trail

Shaker Mountain Trail

▲ Shaker
Mountain

Feast Ground ■

CCC Trail

CCC Trail

■ Quarry

Upper
Dam Site

Lower Dam Site/Cascade

North Family
Dwelling Site ■

Bridge Site ■

Brook Trail

North Family Trail

Shaker Brook

Shaker
Reservoir

P
15

■ Hancock
Shaker Village

20

20

Evidence of a Shaker milldam and flume lie in repose.

Though most Shaker activity took place in the level valley below where our hike travels, they did expand up what became known as Shaker Brook and Shaker Mountain. The whole interpretive route, blazed with a triangle with a circle in its center, passes several sites right off the bat, including a water reservoir, the North Family dwelling site (occupied from 1821 to 1867), bridge locations, and even a sawmill locale. It continues past dam remnants and a marble quarry, reflecting the practicalities of the industrious Shakers.

Beech trees grow thick near the marble quarry site. It is theorized they might produce a chemical that discourages other vegetation. These second-growth forests lack the splendor of virgin old-growth woods but are still attractive in their own right. Beech trees, a very shade-tolerant species, are a common element of northern hardwood forests like those found at Pittsfield State Forest, along with yellow birch, sugar maple, and cherry. Beech trees are the only northern hardwood to produce a nut. Bears, raccoons, squirrels, and game birds love beech nuts. In fall you can often find opened husks beneath this tree.

Beech leaves turn yellow in autumn before falling off. Younger beech trees will hold the dried, curled leaves all winter. Beech wood has a wide variety of uses including charcoal, railroad ties, furniture, and flooring. Some like beech for firewood, being dense and not too smoky, but I find it either too green or too rotten for fuel. Beech trees range throughout New England, west to Michigan, and down the Mississippi River to northwest Florida and up the Eastern Seaboard.

Next the hike aims for Holy Mount, visited biannually by the Shakers to worship the Lord. Non-Shakers would stand outside the walls and watch the singing and worship. This was welcomed by the Shakers, as it might inspire someone in the audience to become a member. After cutting across formerly cultivated lands, now regrown in forest, the hike aims for Shaker Mountain, or Mount Sinai as it was known to the Shakers. This site is still kept cleared, though not much evidence of Shaker activities or works remains. Yet here they also gathered for outdoor worship. Beyond this site the hike makes a prolonged descent and returns to the concentration of sites along Shaker Brook. From there it is a short backtrack to the trailhead.

While here, consider visiting the full Hancock Shaker Village, preserved from the 1800s, where you can get an in-depth look at Shaker life in the Berkshires and see the intriguing architecture up close, including the Round Stone Barn, as well as get a taste of farm life from the mid-1800s. Special events are held in time with the seasons. For more information, visit www.hancockshakervillage.org.

MILES AND DIRECTIONS

0.0 With your back to US 20, walk around a gate and join a doubletrack path, the North Family Trail, heading due north. Quickly come to and pass along the Shaker Reservoir. It supplied water to the community and is still in use to this day.

0.2 A spur trail leading down along Shaker Brook enters from your right. Just ahead, find steam boiler remnants. Enter full-blown woods and Pittsfield State Forest. Come alongside Shaker Brook, then reach the signed location of an old Shaker bridge.

0.5 After passing the lower dam site and cascade, come to a bridge and the loop portion of the hike. Here, stay left with the North Family Trail, ascending along Shaker Brook in thick woods.

0.6 Come to another intersection and the end of the North Family Trail. Here, split left with the Holy Mountain Trail, as the CCC Trail keeps north. Soon pass the signed location of the Shaker marble quarry, keeping up Shaker Brook under a mantle of birch, beech, and oak, along with viburnum and goosefoot maple.

1.0 Cross Shaker Brook then meet the Griffin Trail, open to ATVs. Keep up Shaker Brook.

1.4 The Griffin Trail splits left. Stay right as the hiker-only Holy Mount Trail splits right. Ascend through hardwoods, angling up the mountainside in fits and starts.

1.6 Come to the lower end of the 45-acre Sacred Lot. The Shakers came to this marked spring and amphitheater site for personal reflection and contemplating God. Continue up the mountainside. Note the Shaker-built stone walls.

2.0 Top out on the Holy Mount and reach the Feast Ground, a 1-acre spot for worship. Split right to view an ideal stone wall, then resume the trail, heading northwest in ferny woods. This area was once completely open. You are at 1,900 feet. Descend.

2.4 Reach a gap and intersection. Head right on the Shaker Brook Trail, open to ATVs, passing rock walls and formerly cultivated areas. Step over a tributary of Shaker Brook. Keep easterly, passing more rock walls.

3.2 Come to an intersection. Here, take a few steps left on the CCC Trail, then split right, joining the Shaker Mountain Trail. Gently ascend in woods.

4.0 Come to the Feast Ground on what the Shakers called Mount Sinai, now officially named Shaker Mountain, after passing a user-created trail that goes to the top of Shaker Mountain. This 1/3-acre spot remains cleared. It once had a shelter, altar, and fountain. Songs were sung and other worship went on here, also biannually. Reenter woods and begin a prolonged descent.

4.3 Pass under a power line for the first of two times. Keep descending.

4.7 Wander through thick pines. Ahead, the trail curves sharply right, westerly, aiming for Shaker Brook. Pass a spur aiming for fields below. Head upstream on Shaker Brook, noting more mill remains. View the lower dam and cascade a second time.

5.0 Cross the bridge over Shaker Brook, completing the loop portion of the hike. From here, head south, backtracking.

5.5 Arrive back at the US 20 trailhead, completing the hike.

SOUTHERN BERKSHIRES

Views at Beartown, page 137

16 YOKUN RIDGE SOUTH

This challenging hike encompasses two rewarding loops (that can be done individually) on Berkshire Natural Resources Council lands outside of Stockbridge. Head along the south slope of Stockbridge Mountain, then climb to its crest and a view. Next, savor famed Olivia's Overlook before making a circuit along Lenox Mountain, where you will grab another view, stop by an old home site, and visit a quiet pond before completing the hike.

Start: Brothers Trail parking area
Distance: 6.5-mile figure-eight loop with spur
Difficulty: Moderate to difficult due to elevation change
Elevation change: +/-1,330 feet over entire hike
Maximum grade: 14% grade for 0.7 mile
Hiking time: About 3.5 hours
Seasons/schedule: May through Nov
Fees and permits: None
Dog friendly: Yes

Trail surface: Natural surface singletrack
Land status: Private preserve open to public
Nearest town: Stockbridge
Other trail users: Bicyclers
Map to consult: Yokun Ridge South
Amenities available: None
Cell service: Good
Trail contact: Berkshire Natural Resources Council, (413) 449-0596, www.bnrc.org

FINDING THE TRAILHEAD

From exit 3 on I-90 in West Stockbridge, take MA 41 north for just a short distance to MA 102 west/MA 41 north. Turn left and follow MA 102/41 for 0.3 mile, then turn right onto Swamp Road and immediately turn right onto Lenox Road. Follow Lenox Road for 2 miles, then turn right onto Richmond Mountain Road and stay with it for 0.7 mile to reach the Brothers Trail parking area on your left. Parking is limited, so be considerate. **Trailhead GPS:** 42.354224, -73.329129

THE HIKE

You won't find "Yokun Ridge" on older topographic maps. That's because Yokun Ridge didn't come to be until 2009, when the term officially applied to a 9-mile-long ridge composed of several linked mountains—including Stockbridge Mountain and Lenox Mountain that you will visit on this hike—was accepted by the United States Board on Geographic Names. (Did you even know there was such a board?) See, the Berkshire Natural Resources Council, owners and managers of the property on this hike, began using the term Yokun Ridge to honor an early Mohican Indian named Jehoiakim Yokun, who adopted Christianity as his religion and also fought in the French and Indian Wars. (His son Timothy fought on the American side in the Revolutionary War.) Before that, back in the 1740s, Yokun bought the land that now bears his name.

Later, Yokun sold the tract. Despite being hardscrabble ridgetop terrain, much of it was farmed and logged, the trees being used for charcoal to power nearby iron foundries during the Civil War. The open ridges provided distant views, and the mountaintops became coveted places for wealthy residents to build homes. One such majestic dwelling dubbed "Shadowbrook Cottage" eventually became a Catholic seminary but burned to

Olivia's Overlook delivers lake and mountain views.

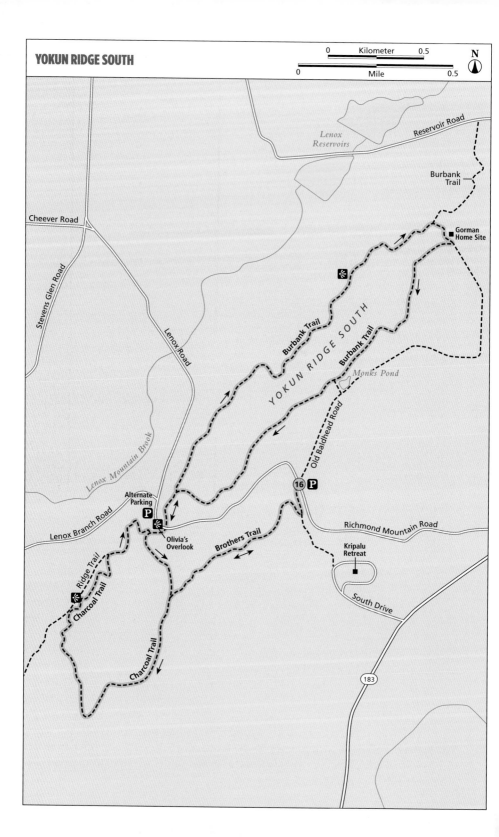

0   Kilometer   0.5

0   Mile   0.5

N

Lenox Reservoirs

Reservoir Road

Burbank Trail

Cheever Road

Gorman Home Site

Stevens Glen Road

Burbank Trail

YOKUN RIDGE SOUTH

Burbank Trail

Lenox Road

Monks Pond

Lenox Mountain Brook

Old Baldhead Road

Alternate Parking

P

16 P

Richmond Mountain Road

Lenox Branch Road

Olivia's Overlook

Brothers Trail

Kripalu Retreat

Ridge Trail

Charcoal Trail

South Drive

Charcoal Trail

183

This pond once provided water to a Catholic monastery.

the ground in 1956. The property is now a yoga retreat center named Kripalu, and our hike actually passes a spur path to the health center.

Over time, the forests returned to Yokun Ridge. Today, this 734-acre tract provides a wonderful place to hike, with a wealth of forests, panoramas, and a little history you can enjoy along the way. The two loops you explore can easily be done as individual shorter hikes of 1.6 and 3.2 miles respectively, if starting at the Olivia's Overlook trailhead. Our adventure begins on the Brothers Trail, westbound, then joins the Charcoal Trail, skirting the south slope of Stockbridge Mountain. A short but steep climb takes you to the top of the mountain and a westerly view.

The trek then drops to an alternate trailhead at highly acclaimed Olivia's Overlook, with the waters of Stockbridge Bowl below. You then join the Burbank Trail, rolling along Lenox Mountain to another vista, then descend to the 1800s highland home site of one John Gorman. From there the Burbank Trail leads past small, rustic, and scenic Monks Pond, built as the water source for the former Catholic seminary. After an encore visit to Olivia's Overlook, you complete the loop part of the Charcoal Trail then back-track on the Brothers Trail, finishing the trek.

MILES AND DIRECTIONS

0.0 Head south from the Brothers Trail parking area, crossing Richmond Mountain Road to join the Brothers Trail, a well-built singletrack path under hardwoods and evergreens.

0.1 Reach an intersection. Here, a spur goes straight for Kripalu Retreat, while we turn right with the Brothers Trail to rock-hop an unnamed stream flowing off Lenox Mountain. Keep westerly.

0.7 Meet the Charcoal Trail after cutting under a cleared power line right-of-way. Stay left here, continuing on the rocky mid-slope of the mountainside in mountain laurel, witch hazel, and birch.

1.0 Begin a prolonged climb. Look for circular flats cut into the mountainside, where wood was burned to make charcoal. Use steps in places beneath tall pines.

1.7 Top out on the ridge near an outcrop. Head to a bench and an easterly view, then join a short spur to a westerly view into the Cone Brook valley. The Ridge Trail leaves the westerly view in both directions. Stay with the Charcoal Trail, descending in rocky woods.

2.2 Reach an intersection. Stay left here toward Olivia's Overlook, then soon emerge at the cleared easterly view into the Stockbridge Bowl, aka Lake Mahkeenac, and distant ridges. This is Olivia's Overlook. Cross Richmond Mountain Road, then join the Burbank Trail, climbing the ridgeline of Lenox Mountain.

2.4 Come to the loop portion of the Burbank Trail after cutting across a gas line clearing. Stay left on the Burbank Trail, ascending Lenox Mountain.

3.0 Reach the crest of the mountain. Continue north among open rock slabs, chestnut oaks, and bracken fern.

3.5 Top out and head left on a short path that leads to an outcrop and westerly vista.

3.8 An unnamed spur keeps north toward Reservoir Road. Stay right with the Burbank Trail, still descending.

3.9 Reach the signed home site of John Gorman, who resided here from 1838 to 1898. Note the foundations, flats, and walls. Come to an intersection a little beyond the home site. Here, Old Baldhead Road leads left 1.2 miles to the Brothers Trail parking area. Our hike cuts right, staying on the Burbank Trail, beginning a prolonged descent toward Monks Pond. Come along a stream in a half mile.

4.6 Find serene Monks Pond, the former water supply for the Catholic seminary. A short trail heads left across the pond dam to Old Baldhead Road. This is another chance to shortcut the hike. Note the spillway creating a minor cataract. Stay right with the well-constructed Burbank Trail as it continues along a steep mountainside.

5.3 Complete the loop portion of the Burbank Trail. Stay left, descending to cross Richmond Mountain Road a second time, then enjoy an encore view from Olivia's Overlook before rejoining the Charcoal Trail, hiking the rest of the loop. Descend in woods.

5.8 End the Charcoal Trail. Head left, backtracking on the Brothers Trail.

6.5 Arrive back at the Brothers Trail parking area, completing the hike.

17 WASHINGTON MOUNTAIN MARSH LOOP

This loop explores a mountaintop wetland with a bevy of views and wildlife-viewing opportunities in season. Located in remote and lofty October Mountain State Forest, the mostly level trek visits former farms before reaching Washington Mountain Marsh. From there, climb a woodsy hill before returning to the marsh. Alternate in woods and open wetlands, traversing one boardwalk after another. The trek also includes a side trip to a rock outcrop with fine vistas.

Start: West Branch Road trailhead
Distance: 3.2-mile loop
Difficulty: Easy to moderate
Elevation change: +/-378 feet over entire hike
Maximum grade: 19% grade for 0.1 mile
Hiking time: About 1.5 hours
Seasons/schedule: May through Oct
Fees and permits: None
Dog friendly: No; lots of narrow boardwalks over wetlands

Trail surface: Forested natural surface, boardwalks
Land status: State forest
Nearest town: Lee
Other trail users: None
Map to consult: October Mountain State Forest
Amenities available: None
Cell service: Iffy at best
Trail contact: October Mountain State Forest, (413) 243-1778, www .mass.gov/locations/october -mountain-state-forest

FINDING THE TRAILHEAD

From exit 10 on I-90 (Mass Turnpike) in Lee, take US 20 east for 4.2 miles. Turn left on Becket Road, then stay with it for 1.9 miles and veer left as Becket Road becomes Yokum Pond Road. Continue for 1.7 miles, then turn left onto County Road and stay with it for 3.7 miles. Veer right onto Lenox–Whitney Place Road and follow it for 1.2 miles to reach a four-way intersection. Here, turn left onto West Branch Road and follow it for 0.4 mile to the Washington Mountain Marsh trailhead on your right. Parking is just beyond the trailhead on your left. Much of the drive is over slow, uneven gravel roads, so give yourself plenty of time to get there and back. Note: Beware online directions that lead onto gated and/or very rough roads. **Trailhead GPS:** 42.352960, -73.187966

THE HIKE

Washington Mountain Marsh came about by accident. This upland plateau, rising from the Housatonic Valley to the west, is dotted with peaks and ponds that drain into the Housatonic River. The highlands were once part of the vast country estate and summer cottage of financier William C. Whitney, prominent in the late 1800s, who also had a home in nearby Lenox. The estate later formed the heart of October Mountain State Forest, and it is here we find Washington Mountain Marsh.

Forest officials wanted a new lake. An area was surveyed, then in 1973 a dam was completed to hold back the waters of Washington Mountain Brook. Problem was the would-be lake never filled and became a marsh, whose waters are also dammed by beavers. Their dams have created open water pockets among the vast wetlands ringed in forested hills.

Beavers are active at Washington Mountain Marsh.

About a decade later, October Mountain Lake was successfully created and is located just a half mile south of Washington Mountain Marsh, accessed on an easy road from the parking area for this hike. Picnic tables, a restroom, and a hand boat launch are located on the shore of October Mountain Lake and would make a fine complement to this adventure.

Though the Washington Mountain Lake never came to be, October Mountain State Forest officials saw a diamond in the rough. They then created a loop trail exploring the marsh, building a remarkable number of boardwalks to cross the bog. Thus, the hike traverses forests of spruce and hardwoods as well as the open boggy areas that present fine views of these mountaintop wetlands, where wild iris and pink lady's slippers rise, where red-winged blackbirds twitter among the reeds and marsh grasses, and where beavers do their part in keeping this marsh marshy.

Beavers were once found all over Massachusetts, but trapping for their pelts and the change to an agrarian society eliminated them from the Bay State entirely. However, in the 1920s, beavers were reintroduced into Berkshire County, beginning a sustained comeback for the massive rodents. They are now all over the state save for far southeastern Massachusetts, Cape Cod, and the coastal islands.

Beavers can live up to twenty years or more. They are known for staying with the same mate for life, and have one to nine kits in the spring. The kits typically stay at their home den for two winters until setting out on their own. Their dam-building skills are unique among mammals in that they can alter the environment to help produce food for

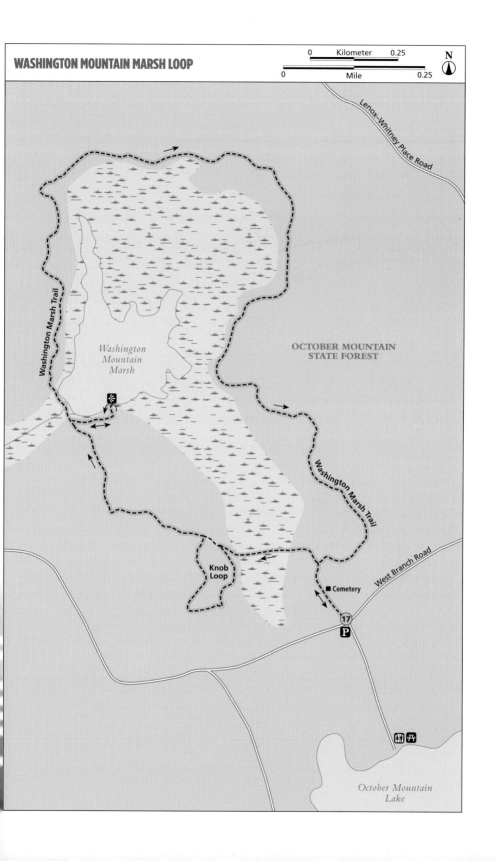

0   Kilometer   0.25

0   Mile   0.25

N

Lenox-Whitney Place Road

Washington Marsh Trail

Washington Mountain Marsh

OCTOBER MOUNTAIN STATE FOREST

Washington Marsh Trail

Knob Loop

■ Cemetery

West Branch Road

17

P

October Mountain Lake

Boardwalks lead you through much of the marsh.

themselves. Washington Mountain Marsh is a great place to see this phenomenon—and the beavers themselves in a wild setting.

The numerous boardwalks you will traverse are constantly being replaced, as time and the elements lead to decay. On your hike expect to pleasantly cruise over newer boardwalks while tight-roping and jumping over weak spots on other boardwalks. Furthermore, the rise and fall of beaver dams within the greater marsh change water levels and affect the boardwalks. Consider the ever-changing state of the boardwalks as part of the challenge, as you go on and off forested land.

You first leave the trailhead in a long-ago settled area, now a remote part of October Mountain State Forest. Life had to be tough on this plateau two centuries back. Look for rock walls and cellar holes before passing the West Branch Cemetery (also known as the October Mountain Cemetery), established in 1811. Almost all the interred were laid to rest in the 1800s. Later, these simple farmers were bought out by the aforementioned William C. Whitney when he established his country estate.

Now we walk past the silent graves and walls to enter spruce woods, then begin the loop portion of the hike. You will soon cross your first open marsh, then make the hike's only climb on the Knob Loop. From there, return to open marsh to then climb a rock and get a fine rock-top vista. Next, cross one of the main arms of the swamp past open waters. The trail settles into a pattern of traversing woods on standard foot trail then crossing bogs on boardwalks, circling the entire greater marsh in this manner. It's a special hike in the Berkshires and makes for a fine destination in summer and autumn. Try it for yourself.

MILES AND DIRECTIONS

0.0 Leave West Branch Road, north-bound on a singletrack foot trail, cutting through a formerly logged area and before that farmland. Ahead pass rock walls and the West Branch Cemetery.

0.1 Begin the loop portion of the Washington Mountain Marsh Trail. Head left and soon dip to a marsh. Make your first boardwalk crossing of the marsh that is neither land nor water, thick with vegetation and tall with cattails, with scads of black spruce. This first boardwalk goes for a full 0.1 mile before regaining terra firma.

0.3 Head left on the lesser-used Knob Loop. It takes you away from the marsh and into a hilly, rocky forest of yellow birch, cherry, and ferns. This is the only climb of the hike and it is only a 105-foot ascent.

0.6 Rejoin the main loop, wandering through a forest dotted with vernal pools and its own boardwalks, though much shorter than the boardwalks of the open marshes.

Pink lady's slipper brightens the woods near the marsh.

1.0 Return to the marsh. First take the spur trail right to an overlook from atop a rock. From there you can see open waters and vegetated wet-lands as well as the forested hills that frame the marsh. Backtrack to the main loop.

1.2 Resume the main circuit, traveling across what would've been open lake. Today the boardwalk leads north across wetlands, just below a beaver dam and open water. A bridge crosses the outflow of the beaver dam. Return to dry land and woods of red spruce, paper birch, and oak. Continue circling around the west side of the swamp.

1.7 Come to marsh and a series of boardwalks, alternating off and on with short stretches of forest. The light of the marsh and the dark of the woods create but one of many contrasts on this trail.

2.0 Return to a more continually forested segment of trail, circling the north side of the bog.

2.2 Cross an old jeep road, now heading south.

2.3 Resume boardwalks. Note how this highland swamp is truly in the back of beyond. Look for more beaver dams.

2.6 Turn away from the marsh. Wind through lightly hilly woods.

3.1 Complete the loop portion of the trail. Backtrack to the trailhead.

3.2 Arrive back at the trailhead, finishing the marshy trek.

18 CHESTERFIELD GORGE LOOP

This super-scenic hike first winds along the edge of an impressive tight stone gorge of the East Branch Westfield River then continues down along the watercourse, where you can savor first-rate stream scenes framed in mountain delight—and perhaps determined anglers vying for wily trout. Keep along the waterway, pulling up a boulder to admire the wide river rapids, maybe even enjoying a summertime dip. The circuit then climbs an upland ridge, walking its woodsy slopes then visiting a highland marsh, eventually returning to the river to complete the adventure.

Start: Chesterfield Gorge Reservation trailhead
Distance: 5.7-mile lollipop
Difficulty: Moderate; does have 450-foot climb
Elevation change: +/-770 feet over entire hike
Maximum grade: 10% grade for 0.8 mile
Hiking time: About 3 hours
Seasons/schedule: May through Nov
Fees and permits: Parking fee required at Trustees lot and adjacent private lot
Dog friendly: Yes

Trail surface: Doubletrack gated dirt road, then singletrack natural surface foot trail
Land status: State forest
Nearest town: Chesterfield
Other trail users: Autos on first part of East Branch Trail, bicycles on entirety of East Branch Trail
Map to consult: Chesterfield Gorge Trail
Amenities available: Restroom, picnic area at trailhead
Cell service: Fair to poor in the gorge
Trail contact: The Trustees, (617) 542-7696, www.thetrustees.org

FINDING THE TRAILHEAD

From the intersection of North Road, South Road, and MA 143 in Chesterfield, take MA 143 west for 2.2 miles, bridging the East Branch Westfield River, then turn left on Ireland Street. Follow Ireland Street south for 0.9 mile, then turn left on River Road and follow it for 0.1 mile to the left turn into the Chesterfield Gorge Reservation parking area. If that lot is full, continue just a short distance down River Road to a private fee lot on your right, the Chesterfield Four Seasons Club. **Trailhead GPS:** 42.393321, -72.880191

THE HIKE

This cool hike presents multiple trail and scenery conditions. Starting at the 166 acres of privately held but open to the public Chesterfield Gorge Reservation, managed by The Trustees since 1929, you will follow a trail along a sheer stone-sided gorge through which flows the federally designated wild and scenic East Branch Westfield River. This designation gives us a hint of the aquatic splendor found where this waterway courses through rugged highlands rising nearly 1,000 feet above the flow, augmenting the river's beauty. Within the Chesterfield Gorge Reservation, you will also find the stone abutments of a Revolutionary War–era stagecoach road linking Boston and Albany, used by the British after retreating from their loss at the Battle of Saratoga in the autumn of 1777.

Peering down the slot canyon of Chesterfield Gorge

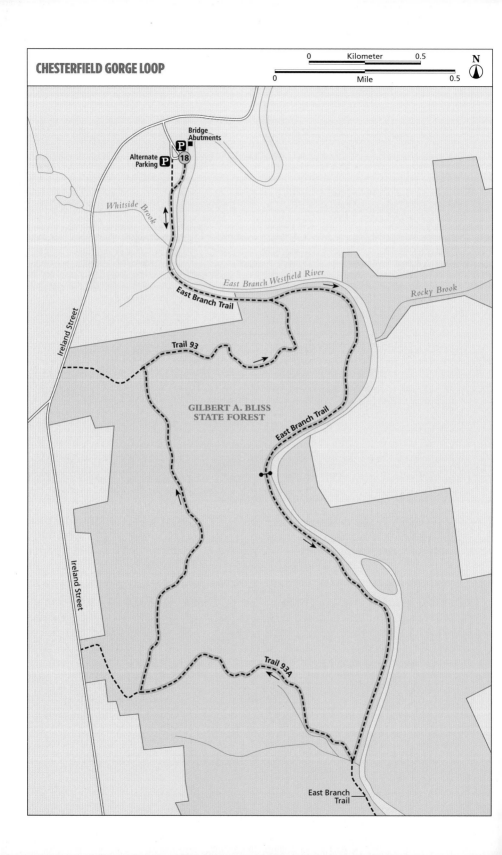

East Branch Westfield River deserves wild and scenic designation.

You then leave The Trustees property and join the East Branch Trail as it mimics the curving East Branch Westfield River to enter Gilbert A. Bliss State Forest, a 2,770-acre tract that encompasses both sides of the Chesterfield Gorge, though it's broken in spots by private property. Even the private property tracts are forested and wild, since most of the gorge land is too steep or flood-prone to be developed. The East Branch Trail continues 9 miles along the waterway down to Knightville Dam. Bicyclers often pedal down to the dam and back, using this trail. By the way, the trails of Chesterfield Gorge are well used by snowmobilers—and cross-country skiers—in the winter, so be apprised of that if coming here during the cold season.

The trip along the wild and scenic river is a feast for the eyes, presenting everywhere-you-look finery. You will be lured to the water sooner or later, so go ahead and succumb to the temptation. There's something about sitting by a rushing mountain rapid or a sublime pool that mesmerizes and relaxes. Maybe it is the combination of moving water, fixed rock, and swaying trees roofed with the changing sky that turns the trick. Or maybe this natural exquisiteness shows what we're missing by looking at phone and computer screens all too long.

Instead, seek out small beaches accumulating along the water's edge. Other banks will display rocky cobble bars and bigger boulders. In still other spots vegetation grows to the water's edge. No matter where you are, the song of whitewater echoes through the gorge. Occasional spur trails lead to the river's banks. Ahead, the trail enters Gilbert A. Bliss State Forest, but scenically there's no difference.

Continue downriver, passing wooded islands in the stream. Then attain another trail junction at a stream bridge. Here, the hike leaves East Branch, climbing wooded slopes of the gorge. The walking is pleasant up here as you near an elevated swamp. Rock-hopping the outflow of this marsh dry-footed can be a challenge if the water is high. The upland hiking in maples and hemlocks remains easy. You then execute a decline on a winter snowmobile trail, finding yourself back at the East Branch Trail. While backtracking to the trailhead, reflect on what a "gorge-ous" hike this is.

MILES AND DIRECTIONS

0.0 From the Chesterfield Gorge Reservation parking lot, walk toward the river and reach the gorge and a fence. First go left, upstream, to soon find the old bridge abutments of the historic post road. Turn downstream and admire the sheer cliffs, wild waters, and verdant forests. Shortly meet the East Branch Trail, tracing a wide doubletrack with the East Branch Westfield River to your left, mountains rising from the water.

0.3 Bridge Whitside Brook, then bridge another smaller stream as the river curves easterly.

0.7 Come to a trail intersection. Trail 93 leads right, away from the river. This will be your return route. For now, stay with the East Branch Trail, continuing downriver, curving with the curve of the gorge. Steep wooded hills rise high on the far side of the East Branch. Soon enter Gilbert A. Bliss State Forest.

1.5 The East Branch Trail is crossed by a gate. Continue around the gate, curving with the river. Look for places where the East Branch divides around picturesque islands bordered in quickening shoals.

2.6 Come to a trail intersection where the East Branch Trail reaches a wooden bridge over a bubbling mountain stream. Here, turn right, climbing on Trail 93A, a winter snowmobile path. Make an initial sharp ascent, then keep uphill along a cascading stream. Cross old stone walls.

3.1 Level off on a bench of the mountainside. The hiking eases.

3.3 Reach a trail intersection. Here, a spur keeps straight to reach Ireland Street after a quarter mile. But we turn right, northbound, paralleling the East Branch flowing 400 feet below. Mosey through piney woods, viewing more stone walls ahead.

4.1 Rock-hop a brook draining a big beaver-dammed marsh to your left. The open marsh seems bright after trekking through leafy summertime woods.

4.3 Come to another intersection. Here, another spur goes left to Ireland Street but we turn right with Trail 93 as it makes a lengthy downgrade in bouldery woods for the East Branch Westfield River.

5.0 Return to the river and the East Branch Trail. Head left, backtracking upstream, feasting on more river scenes.

5.7 Arrive back at the Chesterfield Gorge Reservation parking lot, completing the river circuit.

19 KEYSTONE ARCH BRIDGES TRAIL

Follow one of America's first mountain railways on one of the Berkshires' most scenic streamside hikes, traveling along—and over—the West Branch Westfield River. Relish eye-appealing beauty as you first view Double Arch Bridge, still in use by CSX Railroad, then travel beside the lovely Westfield as singsong tributaries cross your path. Join the old 1841 railroad grade, then cross two intact hand-built stone arch bridges replete with views into the Westfield River gorge before reaching the trail's west end, then returning with a backtrack.

Start: Keystone Arches trailhead
Distance: 5.0 miles out and back
Difficulty: Moderate
Elevation change: +/-536 feet over entire hike
Maximum grade: 3% grade for 0.9 mile
Hiking time: About 2.5 hours
Seasons/schedule: Year-round
Fees and permits: None
Dog friendly: Yes
Trail surface: Packed dirt road, natural surface

Land status: Public right-of-way, wildlife management area
Nearest town: Chester
Other trail users: Bicyclers
Map to consult: K. A. B. Trail
Amenities available: None
Cell service: Decent
Trail contacts: Friends of the Keystone Arches, www.keystone arches.com; Massachusetts Wildlife Field Headquarters, (508) 389-6300, www.mass.gov/orgs/division-of -fisheries-and-wildlife

FINDING THE TRAILHEAD

 From US 20 in Chester, take Middlefield Road north for 2.5 miles to reach the signed parking area on your left. Additional parking is available down the short gravel road leaving from the upper parking area. **Trailhead GPS:** 42.311510, -72.992625

THE HIKE

After the 1825 opening of the Erie Canal—creating an aquatic trade route from New York City to the Great Lakes—merchants in Boston felt the pinch of lost trade and determined to do something about it. They decided to invest in one of those newfangled railroads. Under the engineering of United States Army Major George Washington Whistler—father of famed painter James Abbott McNeill Whistler (remember the painting *Whistler's Mother?*)—a railroad was completed in 1841, traveling from sea level Boston over the lowest point in the Berkshire Mountains (1,458 feet) and thus to Albany. The gambit had paid off. Western trade returned to Boston.

And in doing so, the Western Railroad of Massachusetts achieved some remarkable feats for its time: At 150 miles, it was the world's longest railroad. Where it passed through the gap in the Berkshires, it was also the highest railroad in the world. (At that time, climbing grades of any steepness was very difficult.)

Looking down from one of the famed Keystone Arch bridges

Before the rail line was established, naysayers said it couldn't be done. The act of building the railroad through the wild and mountainous Berkshires was madness. And it may have been except for the genius and persistence of Major Whistler—and his arched bridges.

In laying out his way west through the Berkshires, Major Whistler decided to follow the West Branch of the Westfield River, as it led to the low Berkshire crossing. From there he could drop into the Hudson River valley and reach Albany and the Erie Canal trade. However, following the river meant bridging it on several occasions. To that end stonemasons constructed ten special bridges, using dry-laid cut stone (read: no concrete binding the stone together) to bear the weight of the locomotives and their freight over the waterway. These are the keystone arch bridges, and are still in use today.

Fast-forward to 1912, when a short portion of the Western Massachusetts Railroad through the Berkshires was relocated, leaving a segment of the old rail line unused. Visitors would come to see the keystone arch bridges in this abandoned section to admire their splendor as well as the scenery of the West Branch Westfield River. This area later became part of Walnut Hill Wildlife Management Area. Ideas came about to build a trail to and along the abandoned section of line, and including a section of the even older Pontoosic Turnpike, an old stagecoach road linking western Massachusetts to Albany.

Soon after the new millennium, the Keystone Arch Bridges Trail was opened. And today you can hike along the banks of the West Branch Westfield River as it courses through the Berkshires, then walk some newer foot trail, skirting around still-active CSX Railroad property, and join that Berkshire marvel—the historic rail line. There you can tread the route Whistler laid out, gaining exquisite views from the keystone arch bridges,

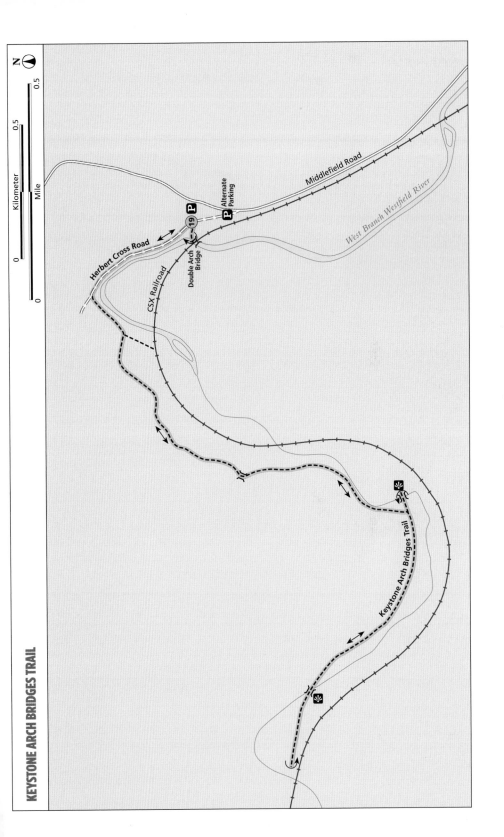

KEYSTONE ARCH BRIDGES TRAIL

N

Kilometer
0   0.5   0.5

0   Mile   0.5

Herbert Cross Road

CSX Railroad

Middlefield Road

Alternate Parking

19

Double Arch Bridge

West Branch Westfield River

Keystone Arch Bridges Trail

Looking down on West Branch Westfield River

as well as cutting through forests that comprise a portion of Massachusetts's largest road-less area.

You are certain to appreciate both the human and natural history that can be found on this trek. Your eyes aren't deceiving you while admiring the West Branch Westfield River—78 miles of the Westfield River's headwaters as well as its three major branches are designated as a National Wild and Scenic River. This particular segment of the watershed is known for whitewater kayaking, as well as clean water and trout and bear habitat. In fact, there's a lot to love on this trail.

In 2021, the keystone arch bridges were designated a National Historic Landmark.

MILES AND DIRECTIONS

0.0 From the lower parking lot, take the spur trail to Double Arch Bridge, part of the still-active CSX line. Join the main trail, bridging an unnamed cascading tributary flowing from Johnnycake Hill, looming 800 feet above. Trace a riverside doubletrack road under hemlock, beech, and ferns.

0.3 Overlook a big deep pool in the river, an alluring summer sight. Curve to the southwest.

0.5 Pass around a pole gate. Ahead, a spur road leaves left for the river, but we stay right with the blazed trail as it turns away from the West Branch Westfield River. Follow the foot trail through flats of the valley, passing an old home site and rock walls.

0.9 Trace the foot trail along the lower slopes of Johnnycake Hill.

1.0 A footbridge leads you across a mountain stream.

1.2 Return to the old doubletrack, part of the Pontoosic Turnpike.

1.4 Reach the old Western Railroad of Massachusetts rail bed. Turn left here, heading out to one of the keystone arch bridges. Look down on the rapids and pools of the river below, admiring the stone construction in the near. You can also see the newer rail line. A user-created trail leads down to the Westfield. Turn around and head west on the old grade, cutting through blasted rock walls that allow the railroad to maintain a manageable grade.

1.9 Pass a concrete structure on either side of the line. The walking is easy, though you do have muddy sections.

2.1 Come to the second keystone arch bridge on the trail. This span allows a scenic upstream view. In summer the open bridges contrast mightily with the deep woods of the Walnut Hill Wildlife Management Area, which along with October Mountain State Forest comprise the largest roadless area in the commonwealth.

2.5 Reach trail's end after pushing through another blasted hill. Backtrack to the trailhead.

5.0 Arrive back at the trailhead, completing the historic hike.

20 SANDERSON BROOK FALLS CIRCUIT

This hike presents an ideal combination of Berkshire history and beauty. Hike up Sanderson Brook on a trail system developed by the Civilian Conservation Corps in the 1930s to visit 60-foot Sanderson Brook Falls. From there, climb toward Observation Hill. Detour by an old mica mine, then loop your way back to the trailhead, stopping for inspiring vistas from a trio of overlooks.

Start: Sanderson Brook trailhead
Distance: 5.4-mile lollipop with spur
Difficulty: Moderate; does have sustained climbs
Elevation change: +/-1,430 feet over entire hike
Maximum grade: 18% grade for 0.5 mile
Hiking time: About 3 hours
Seasons/schedule: Year-round, May and June for bold waterfall
Fees and permits: None
Dog friendly: Yes
Trail surface: Natural surface, some forest roads

Land status: State forest
Nearest town: Huntington
Other trail users: Bicyclers and possibly illegal ATVs in places
Map to consult: Chester Blandford State Forest
Amenities available: None
Cell service: Iffy to decent
Trail contact: Chester Blandford State Forest, summer (413) 354-6347, winter (413) 269-6002, www.mass.gov/locations/chester-blandford-state-forest

FINDING THE TRAILHEAD

From exit 3 on I-90 near Westfield, bear right after tolls and follow MA 10/202 south for 3 miles into downtown Westfield. Turn right onto US 20 west and follow it 16 miles to the Sanderson Brook trailhead on your left. **Trailhead GPS:** 42.255770, -72.946960

THE HIKE

The Great Depression hit in 1929, and eventually made it to Chester, Massachusetts. The United States government sought a remedy, and it took the form of the Civilian Conservation Corps (CCC), a group of young men employed by the Feds, ostensibly to create jobs where there were none. The 113th CCC Company was situated in a flat along the Westfield River, just below a tract of land that was to be Chester Blandford State Forest, where this fun loop hike takes place. The hundred or so young men set about to improve the forest, first combating the gypsy moth which was defoliating oak trees. They left an additional legacy, including the trails and roads you will use on this trek, even the path to Sanderson Brook Falls.

Besides being paid a wage, the men learned the value of teamwork and camaraderie. Said one CCC boy, "All the time we grew closer together. In the winters, we froze together, and in the summers, we baked together. We were bruised with the same rocks and banged with the same picks. Sore backs soon became strong backs. Stringy bodies,

Blooming mountain laurel catches a hikers's eye.

iron bodies . . . and if you see some pal wiping his eyes as he goes out, don't say a thing because you will do the same when you go out. "

Remember these fellows while making your way up to Sanderson Brook Falls. From there you will enjoy more CCC handiwork, stopping by a still-standing chimney, then climbing a ski trail they built. Snow skiing had just become popular in New England, and the CCCers added this path that takes you to Observation Hill Road. Enjoy a mountaintop trek to Mica Mine Road. Here you will drop into the Gold Mine Brook valley, which, true to its name, was an area where small mines yielded mica, emery, and corundum, as well as a little gold. Yes, people prospected for gold in the Berkshires, and hobbyists still do it today.

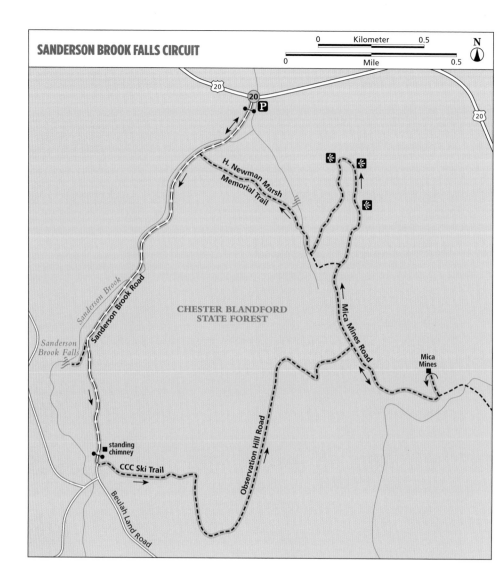

Kilometer

Mile

N

CHESTER BLANDFORD
STATE FOREST

Sanderson Brook

Sanderson Brook Road

Sanderson
Brook Falls

H. Newman Marsh
Memorial Trail

Mica Mines Road

Mica
Mines

standing
chimney

CCC Ski Trail

Observation Hill Road

Beulah Land Road

However, if you seek visual treasures, take the spur trail to a couple of old mica mines. Upon the ground of this spur trail, the shiny pliable stuff that peels off in layers and looks like broken mirrors will be scattered on the ground. The first mica mine opening is on the left. Water oozes from a rectangular opening in a sheer stone wall. Continue up the spur, passing irregular slag piles on your left before the trail dead-ends at another mine.

The hike then heads for the vistas along Observation Hill. Beyond there, a steep path leads back down to Sanderson Brook, passing a seasonal waterfall. This path was originally developed by the CCC as a firebreak. Be prepared to keep your brakes on! And be grateful not to be hiking up this trail. The return to the Sanderson Brook trailhead is a simple backtrack.

Sanderson Brook Falls tumbles in distinct stages.

MILES AND DIRECTIONS

0.0 Leave the Sanderson Brook trailhead up a wide gravel road, built by the CCC, entering woods.

0.1 Pass around a pole gate, then bridge Sanderson Brook. Continue up the densely wooded mountain valley.

0.2 Meet the Marsh Memorial Trail. It heads left, steeply up Observation Hill, and is your return route. Keep straight on Sanderson Brook Road, overlooking the crystalline mountain rill below, ascending mildly among rocks, ferns, and mossy boulders underneath northern hardwoods.

0.6 Bridge crystalline Sanderson Brook again. You are now on the right bank climbing a narrow part of the vale. This is a good wildflower area. Quickly bridge the stream again.

0.9 Split right on a singletrack path toward Sanderson Brook Falls. Skirt a wetland, then reach the cataract as it spills 60 feet in stages over a rock face. Backtrack and return to Sanderson Brook Road. Continue up an incline. Look for a view of Sanderson Brook Falls from the road.

1.3 Bridge a small tributary of Sanderson Brook. Keep working uphill.

1.4 Pass around a pole gate with a standing chimney to your right. Ahead, roads split left and right. You take a third track heading sharply left, the CCC Ski Trail. Soon pass a concrete spring box to the right of the trail. The climb sharpens. A small brook flows to your left.

2.4 A track leaves right to a dead end. Keep straight on Observation Hill Road. Hike parallel to a rock escarpment.

2.9 Come to a triangular trail intersection. Split right on Mica Mine Road. You will return to this junction later. Descend a rocky path.

3.2 The spur to the mica mines leaves left. Take this trail left. Mica Mine Road keeps straight. You know you have missed the turn to the mica mines if you reach a ford of Gold Mine Brook. Following the spur to the mica mines, you will quickly come to the visible mine opening on your left, with water oozing out. Look for the mica layers on the ground. Keep forward to pass overgrown slag piles and another mine to the left before dead-ending. Backtrack, then continue back up Mica Mine Road.

3.7 Return to the three-way trail intersection. Go straight on Mica Mine Road.

3.9 Join the Marsh Memorial Trail, a blazed singletrack path at the end of Mica Mine Road. Begin bending around the narrow north ridge of Observation Hill. The land drops sharply off to your right. Views open through the trees.

4.3 Open to a prominent vista on a piney rock outcrop, enhanced with mountain laurel. Look below for the Westfield River and US 20, the Jacobs Ladder Scenic Byway. Fayes Hill and Gobble Mountain frame the valley. From here, curve south, gently ascending.

4.7 Turn sharply right, and begin stepping downhill along a streamlet.

4.8 Rock-hop the streamlet. You are now on the left bank. Keep descending steeply, often on stone steps, dropping a total of 600 feet in 0.4 mile! Along the way a user-created spur leads right to a 40-foot low-flow cataract.

5.2 Return to Sanderson Brook Road and backtrack toward the trailhead.

5.4 Arrive back at the trailhead, completing the hike.

21 FINERTY POND VIA THE APPALACHIAN TRAIL

This hike in big October Mountain State Forest uses the Appalachian Trail to take you from a pass in the Hoosac Range where US 20 crosses the Berkshires, up to Becket Mountain, site of a former fire tower. Enjoy easy hiking on a ridge crest, rolling over Walling Mountain before dropping to 25-acre Finerty Pond, the headwaters of Washington Mountain Brook. Enjoy a waterside respite before backtracking to the trailhead.

Start: US 20 Appalachian Trail parking area
Distance: 6.0 miles out and back
Difficulty: Moderate
Elevation change: +/-1,050 feet over entire hike
Maximum grade: 10% grade for 1.5 miles
Hiking time: About 3 hours
Seasons/schedule: Apr through mid-Nov
Fees and permits: None
Dog friendly: Yes, but trail can be busy in summer

Trail surface: Forested natural surface
Land status: State forest
Nearest town: Lee
Other trail users: None, but hike crosses ATV trail
Map to consult: October Mountain State Forest
Amenities available: None
Cell service: Good
Trail contact: October Mountain State Forest, (413) 243-1778, www.mass.gov/locations/october-mountain-state-forest

FINDING THE TRAILHEAD

To reach the Appalachian Trail parking area on US 20 from exit 10 on I-90 (Mass Turnpike) in Lee, take US 20 east for 4.3 miles to the large parking area on your right, the south side of US 20. This is also a parking area and informational stop for the Jacobs Ladder Scenic Byway. **Trailhead GPS:** 42.292794, -73.161087

THE HIKE

Harken back to the year 1948. The United States—and the soldiers who fought—are still emerging from the trials of World War II. One man by the name of Earl Shaffer sought a way to put his experiences in the conflict behind him. Shaffer served in the army, and as a radioman advancing island to island in the Pacific Ocean, had seen the hells of war firsthand.

Upon returning to the United States, Shaffer came up with the idea to hike the entire length of the Appalachian Trail (AT) from its southern terminus at Georgia's Mount Oglethorpe to Maine's Baxter Peak in one single adventure. In his own words, he decided to do it "to walk the war out of my system." Perhaps the mountain splendor combined with good ol' fashioned daily exercise would do the trick.

And Shaffer did exactly as he planned, covering the 2,100-or-so-mile distance in 124 days, becoming the first Appalachian Trail thru-hiker. Truth is, the term "thru-hiker" didn't even exist then. Nobody did such a thing as hike the whole trail end to end in one

The Appalachian Trail takes you directly by Finerty Pond.

fell swoop. Officials of the Appalachian Trail Conference initially thought Shaffer was telling tall tales (they later recognized and lauded his achievement).

On Shaffer's hike he covered the same ground we do on this trek to Finerty Pond. We know because he wrote that in his trail diary from his 1948 adventure (it is preserved in the Smithsonian Institution). While crossing US 20 he met a man named Chuck Anderson, who gave him a ride into Lee for supplies and even bought Shaffer breakfast. In Shaffer's own words that he wrote in his trail diary, "Such favors are priceless to the backpacker." Shaffer later executed Appalachian Trail thru-hikes in 1965 as well as 1998, when he was 79. Interestingly, these two hikes also established records: 1965—first person to hike the AT in both directions (he went from Maine to Georgia that time); 1979—oldest person to thru-hike the AT. The last record has been beaten by M. J. Everhart, who did it at age 83.

So, while at the trailhead, imagine life on the trail for Shaffer, and then appreciate all the memories others before have made on the AT. US 20 is a lot busier than in Shaffer's day, which is why you first take a spur trail from the parking area to meet the AT. From there the trek makes a steady but moderate ascent in woods, where you cross quiet Tyne Road. The famed footpath angles up the southwest slope of Becket Mountain, and you top out at the site of a fire tower lookout. The 30-foot metal structure had a short life span here on Becket Mountain. It was erected in 1915, and had a telephone line run up to it to report fires, but forest managers thought better of its location and removed the tower in 1916. They rebuilt it, making it taller, on top of Lair Mountain in Tolland, then replaced the tower in 1934.

From the Becket Mountain tower site, the hike is easy—cruising, dipping, and lightly rising in woods broken by picturesque fern glades to reach the hike's high point on 2,220-foot, wooded Walling Mountain (no views). From here, drop to the banks of

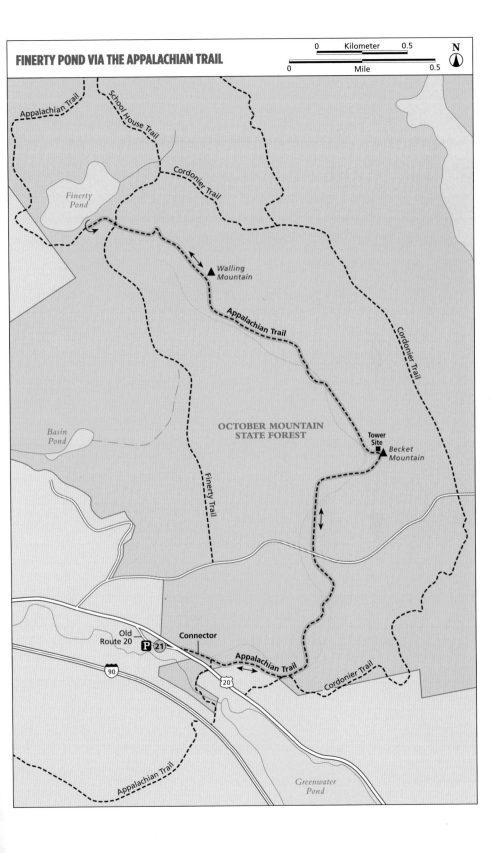

Appalachian Trail

School House Trail

Cordonier Trail

Finerty
Pond

Walling
Mountain

Appalachian Trail

Cordonier Trail

Basin
Pond

OCTOBER MOUNTAIN
STATE FOREST

Tower
Site

Becket
Mountain

Finerty Trail

Old
Route 20

P 21

Connector

Appalachian Trail

Cordonier Trail

90

20

Appalachian Trail

Greenwater
Pond

0   Kilometer   0.5

0   Mile   0.5

N

A fern garden lines the Appalachian Trail near Becket Mountain.

Finerty Pond as the AT swings around its southwest shore, presenting pond views. Find yourself a stopping spot and relax, imagining Earl Shaffer as he trod this same track by the pond.

You may even see a moose around Finerty Pond. While Massachusetts has not turned into "Moose-achusetts," nor has Connecticut become "Cow-necticut," both states do have populations of this large mammal. After being extirpated by unregulated hunting and loss of habitat through widespread farming in the Berkshires back in the 1700s, moose were absent from the landscape until they moved back into the area on their own in the 1980s, roughly corresponding with the reforestation of old farms. Today, moose are well established in western and central Massachusetts, though they are surprisingly elusive for such a large mammal, standing up to 6 feet at the shoulder and weighing from 500 to 1,000 pounds! Unfortunately, the biggest threat to moose is from being hit by vehicles (also very dangerous for the drivers).

Stick with the AT on your return trip. The ATV trails in October Mountain State Forest can be a muddy, rocky mess for those on foot.

MILES AND DIRECTIONS

0.0 Walk to the east end of the long parking area on US 20. Look for the blue blazes. At the far east end of the parking area, cross US 20 north and join the blue-blazed connector trail as it works east in woods on a very steep slope above US 20.

0.2 Meet the Appalachian Trail. Head left, northbound in oaks, pines, and maples. Step over a little bog.

0.4 Cross a boulder garden, then join an old roadbed. Ahead, the AT runs parallel to an ATV track. Stay to the left of the ATV track, then pass under a power line in a boggy section spanned with boardwalk bridges.

0.6 Cross a mossy brook that is more rock than water at normal flows. Gently ascend.

1.0 Cross Tyne Road after stepping over a wide, shallow brook. The slope and trail steepen beyond Tyne Road.

1.3 The AT curves easterly. You are now on the crown of Becket Mountain, aiming for the summit. Travel through a dense thicket of beech and birch.

1.5 Make a final jump just before reaching the top of Becket Mountain. Note the footings from a fire tower that once stood here more than a century back. The wooded stony crown is a popular stopping spot, with a trail register. From here, the AT turns northwest along the ridge crest. The hiking is easy, level, and gentle. Note the spruce growing in these highlands, along with ferns aplenty in summer.

2.6 Top out on Walling Mountain after crossing a small knob between Walling and Becket Mountain. Walling Mountain is wooded, with squat oaks. Descend toward Finerty Pond.

2.9 Cross Finerty Trail, an ATV trail. Finerty Pond is shimmering in the distance. Stay with the AT, running parallel to the shore.

3.0 A spur trail goes right to a pond observation area. Check out the highland tarn, then find a stopping spot. Backtrack to the trailhead.

5.8 Take the connector trail leaving right, westerly, to reach the US 20 parking area.

6.0 Arrive back at the AT parking area, completing the hike.

22 TYRINGHAM COBBLE

With the iconic Appalachian Trail (AT) as its centerpiece, this short and relatively easy family loop hike near Tyringham Village takes you through open meadows with vistas opening on either side of the Hop Brook valley. You then join the AT and climb over Cobble Hill, with outcrops that deliver a worthy top-down panorama. Drop through a mix of field and wood before passing a strange and notorious rock outcrop, completing the loop.

Start: Jerusalem Road trailhead
Distance: 2.1-mile lollipop
Difficulty: Easy
Elevation change: +/-500 feet over entire hike
Maximum grade: 9% grade for 0.9 mile
Hiking time: About 1 hour
Seasons/schedule: Year-round
Fees and permits: None
Dog friendly: Yes

Trail surface: Natural surface singletrack
Land status: Private preserve open to public
Nearest town: Tyringham
Other trail users: Appalachian Trail thru-hikers
Map to consult: Tyringham Cobble
Amenities available: None
Cell service: Good
Trail contact: The Trustees, (617) 542-7696, www.thetrustees.org

FINDING THE TRAILHEAD

From the intersection of Main Road and Jerusalem Road in Tyringham, take Jerusalem Road south for 0.2 mile to the parking area on your right. **Trailhead GPS:** 42.243252, -73.205498

THE HIKE

A short but scenic part of the Appalachian Trail courses through the property that is Tyringham Cobble. Owned and managed by a philanthropic outfit known as The Trustees, the 206 acres from which rises 1,348-foot Cobble Hill rests just outside the Berkshire village of Tyringham. Hemmed in by Baldy Mountain to the northeast and Mount Wilcox in the southwest, Tyringham is set in the lowermost valley of Hop Brook (a fishing haunt of President Grover Cleveland), just before the stream delivers its waters to the Housatonic River.

Such a fertile vale attracted westward settlement from eastern Massachusetts, and by the late 1700s settlement was such that farmers began clearing Cobble Hill for their expanding crop and grazing operations. The Shakers, a pious religious group originating in England, settled in the shadow of Cobble Hill, specializing in sheep raising. The slopes of Cobble Hill proved to be productive for the sheep, but the Shakers weren't so fruitful, especially considering their vows of celibacy and a ban on marriage that cut into their numbers, eventually selling out in 1875.

Cobble Hill remained mostly cleared by subsequent agriculturists. Fast-forward to the 1930s, when recreational interests sought Cobble Hill as the centerpiece of a ski resort. A group of six preservation-minded citizens bought the tracts comprising Cobble Hill

A hike at Tyringham Cobble leads through meadows and woods.

to keep it as it was. They dubbed themselves "The Cobblers." Eventually the saved tract was deeded over to The Trustees, along with an endowment to manage the scenic parcel.

Today, the village of Tyringham is home to less than a third of the residents than back in the Shaker days, numbering under 350 souls. Yet the slope of Cobble Hill remains partly pastoral and partly wooded, enhanced by the routing of the Appalachian Trail over the top of the hill in 2008. Formerly, the AT skirted the southwest slope of Cobble Hill. (The AT is linked to the Cobble Hill parcel on either end with National Park Service Appalachian Trail corridor land.) To enhance Tyringham Cobble even more, a loop trail was added, allowing you to trek the open slopes of Cobble Hill then join the world's most famous footpath southbound. Here, a steady little climb leads you to the rocky top of the knoll, feasting on the views from this Berkshire treasure, savoring a triumvirate of stone outcrops, and delivering panoramas of the adjacent mountains and little ol' Tyringham nestled in the valley of Hop Brook.

When on rocky segments like the part of this hike atop Tyringham Cobble, whether you are day hiking or backpacking, footwear is important. When choosing trail shoes, consider the terrain. Is the trail rough and rocky like at Alander Mountain? Is it steep like up to Race Brook Mountain? Or is the trail a smooth, widely graded path like the Ashuwillticook Rail Trail? Day hikers can get away with low-top hiking shoes if the trail is easy, though if you aren't blessed with strong ankles like mine, go with shoes that give ankle support. If the trail is rough, consider even more support.

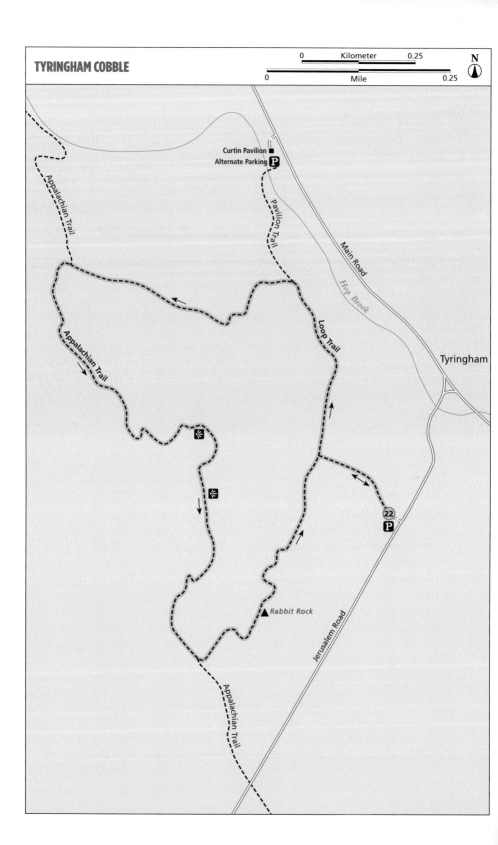

TYRINGHAM COBBLE

0   Kilometer   0.25

0   Mile   0.25

N

Curtin Pavilion
Alternate Parking

Pavilion Trail

Appalachian Trail

Appalachian Trail

Loop Trail

Main Road

Hop Brook

Tyringham

22

Appalachian Trail

Rabbit Rock

Jerusalem Road

Appalachian Trail

Gazing down on the New England Village of Tyringham

Backpackers may have the biggest dilemma when it comes to shoes. They desire boots that will support a fully loaded backpack while hiking, and also comfortable shoes in which they can hang around the campsite. Big, heavy boots aren't so fun at the campsite, unless it's winter. Having two pairs of shoes on your person during a backpacking trip can add weight, though camp shoes get lighter by the year. Crocs are popular camp shoes.

If you are going to do a lot of hiking, or going on a very long trip, I strongly recommend having good trail shoes with ankle support and a sturdy sole. Proper fit is key—have someone that knows what they are doing help fit you. And if you find a brand that works for you, stick with that brand, and size. A good hike starts from the ground up—your shoes.

The final part of the circuit leads past a sandstone outcrop informally known as "Rabbit Rock," as the stone protrusion recalls the body and ears of a bunny. I think this an accurate description.

MILES AND DIRECTIONS

0.0 From the parking area on Jerusalem Road, pass the trailhead kiosk, pass through a stile, then enter a field that may have animals grazing. Head northwest on the Loop Trail connector, toward Cobble Hill. The buildings of Tyringham, including the

Wildflowers grace the meadows of summertime at Tyringham Cobble.

spire of the picturesque Congregational Church, are visible to your right, north. The entirety of the scene is prototypical New England.

0.1 Reach the loop portion of the hike, officially joining the Loop Trail. Head right, northbound. You are still in meadow, with scattered maple and apple trees mixed in. Notice the widespread branches of these mid-meadow trees, free from competition with other trees.

0.4 A spur trail continues straight, toward the Terrence F. Curtin Pavilion, located on Main Road in Tyringham. Our hike heads left, still on the Loop Trail. Climb the north slope of Cobble Hill, then level off after entering full-blown woods of white pine, maple, beech, and cherry. Watch for rock fences from the early days.

0.8 Intersect the Appalachian Trail near the north end of The Trustees property. Head left, southbound, climbing Cobble Hill. Parts of the ascent are broken by switchbacks.

1.2 Top out and level off in mixed field and wood. Reach a bench and view to the north. Tyringham is clearly visible below. Continue climbing.

1.3 A spur trail leads left to the stone summit of Cobble Hill. Here you can look down on Tyringham, including a large cemetery, backed by the rising slopes of Baldy Mountain. Descend a rock slope, wandering through a partly grown area presenting more views amidst scrubby trees, including cedar and sumac.

1.7 Leave the Appalachian Trail, rejoining the Loop Trail in brushy woods.

1.8 Come to a sandstone outcrop. Decide for yourself whether or not it looks like a rabbit. Remain in brushy woods that may be overgrown and briery in summer.

2.0 Reach a trail intersection after coming along a fence line. You have been here before. Head right on the spur leading to the parking lot on Jerusalem Road.

2.1 Arrive back at Jerusalem Road, completing the hike.

23 VIEWS AT BEARTOWN

This fine hike at Beartown State Forest takes you to multiple vista points within the 12,000-acre preserve. First, hike along the shores of 35-acre Benedict Pond, then join the fabled Appalachian Trail to command a view from the Ledges. Next, return to walk along more of Benedict Pond then break off, climbing to a sweeping vista of the Housatonic Valley from the Lookout, followed by a return to the pond. Consider enjoying not only the trails of Beartown State Forest but also its camping, paddling, swimming, picnicking, and fishing.

Start: Benedict Pond boat ramp
Distance: 4.4-mile loop with 2 spurs
Difficulty: Moderate
Elevation change: +/-800 feet over entire hike
Maximum grade: 9% grade for 0.5 mile
Hiking time: About 2 hours
Seasons/schedule: Best when the skies are clear
Fees and permits: Parking fee required between Memorial Day and Labor Day
Dog friendly: Yes

Trail surface: Forested natural surface
Land status: State forest
Nearest town: Great Barrington
Other trail users: Mountain bikers on part of loop
Map to consult: Beartown State Forest
Amenities available: Restrooms, picnic tables at trailhead
Cell service: Okay, better at lookouts
Trail contact: Beartown State Forest, (413) 528-0905, www.mass.gov/locations/beartown-state-forest

FINDING THE TRAILHEAD

To reach the Beartown State Forest trailhead from Great Barrington, take US 7 north from downtown a short distance, then turn right onto MA 183 south. Follow MA 183 for 5.3 miles, then turn left onto Blue Hill Road and follow it for 2.2 miles to Benedict Pond Road. Turn right and follow Benedict Pond Road for 0.4 mile to reach the trailhead parking, boat ramp, and picnic area of Beartown State Forest. **Trailhead GPS:** 42.202857, -73.288692

THE HIKE

Like many of Massachusetts's public lands, Beartown State Forest has a history of standing for eons before being cleared for farming and timbered for charcoal and wood, then growing back and returning to wildlands, except this time with recreational facilities first built by the Civilian Conservation Corps then improved and managed by the state. A large, well-drained plateau, what is now Beartown State Forest, is laced with pathways, including the Appalachian Trail as well as a large mountain biking loop. The campground, with reservable sites, draws in warm-season visitors, as does Benedict Pond, with its swim beach and fishing and paddling opportunities on the electric-motors-only lake.

But we're hikers first, thus first we will hike. The Benedict Pond Loop Trail is undoubtedly the most popular path in the state forest, and deservedly so. You can walk alongside the scenic body of water from which mountains rise, enjoying aquatic vistas aplenty, as well as delight in wildlife-rich wetlands and rocky areas. And you can cruise by the dam

Looking out on Benedict Pond

spillway fishing area, campground, and swim beach. There's a lot to see at Benedict Pond. And if you are looking for an easy family hike, just make the loop around the pond.

Yet our hike literally goes the extra mile to capture more views. From Benedict Pond, fed by the headwaters of Stony Brook, we join the Appalachian Trail northbound, climbing above wetlands to a bluff, where another pond awaits, an upland aquatic tableau fashioned by beavers. Beyond here, you walk the bluff line to the Ledges, where you can gaze south and west on a host of wooded ridges and East Mountain State Forest as well as Butternut Mountain ski area.

From the view we return to Benedict Pond, walking the shoreline where verdant forests rise amidst massive boulders, while other trail segments lead across grassy marshes, home to frogs and other amphibians, as well as functioning as a filter for any pollutants and a place where excessive rain runoff is absorbed, reducing potential flooding. Between these wetlands, the trail takes you to waterside perches, where you can grab more panoramas of the pond, identifying the swim beach and pond dam across the water.

Your next leg leaves the pond north, traversing flatwoods rich with mountain laurel before gently rising to the shoulder of Benedict Pond Peak. Mountain laurel, with smaller evergreen leaves in contrast to the larger evergreen leaves of rhododendron, prefers dry, south-facing ridges and pine-oaks forests. The pinkish-white flowers bloom here in June. Mountain laurel ranges down the Appalachians from southern Maine and over to northwest Florida, and throughout the Berkshires. The leaves of mountain laurel are poisonous to livestock and as a result are seldom browsed. The wood has historically been used for spoons, tobacco pipes, and tool handles.

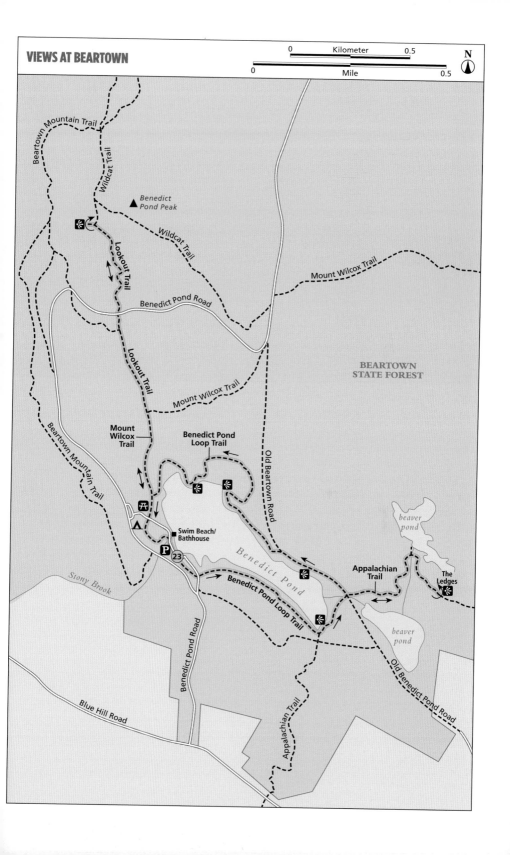

The Lookout truly deserves its name.

After reaching the outcrop on the shoulder of Benedict Pond Peak, matchless views of the Housatonic Valley open wide, including ski slopes, valley fields, and ridgelines to the north and west, all the way to the Taconics and Catskills in the yon.

The final leg of the hike works around the woodsy west end of Benedict Pond, before emerging at the pond dam, where Stony Brook is once again released. A walk by the beach may tempt you for a swim on a hot summer's day, while the shady picnic tables nearby present an ideal post-hike dining repose. Taken as a whole, Beartown State Forest presents a cornucopia of outdoor activities for the Berkshire hiker.

MILES AND DIRECTIONS

0.0 As you face Benedict Pond from the boat launch, leave right on the Benedict Pond Loop Trail, eastbound. Ahead, a spur goes left to a picnic area overlooking the lake. Stay with the well-used, somewhat rocky track in maples, keeping the lake to your left.

0.2 Meet a rock slab and good view of the pond's east end. Continue east.

0.4 Intersect the Appalachian Trail, at the pond's east end. Head left, northbound on the AT, crossing a headwater of Stony Brook. Just ahead a short spur leads left to an outcrop and watery vista stretching the length of Benedict Pond.

0.5 Reach an intersection after crossing the primary headwater stream of Benedict Pond. Here, Old Beartown Road splits right, while the Benedict Pond Loop Trail heads left. We keep straight on the AT, leaving the pond in maple, yellow birch, witch hazel, and goosefoot maple, wandering at the base of a rock-strewn hill.

0.7 Climb in earnest and in 0.1 mile a spur trail leaves left to a blufftop pond. After visiting this "hidden pond," resume the AT, crossing the outflow of the hidden pond, now back on level trail cruising a cliff line in a xeric environment heavy with mountain laurel and chestnut oaks.

1.0 Reach the Ledges, a linear rock promontory along which the Appalachian Trail runs. Here, a southwesterly view opens. Backtrack on the AT.

1.5 Resume the Benedict Pond Loop Trail, westbound. Here, Old Beartown Road and the Benedict Pond Loop Trail run in conjunction. Ahead, a spur leads left to an elevated pond view.

1.7 Old Beartown Road splits right while we split left, now on singletrack path, passing big boulders in rugged terrain. Look for beaver lodges along the lake.

1.9 Come to another pond view, this time to the south of the swim beach and dam, then swing around a marshy wetland with the aid of boardwalks and small bridges.

2.3 Return to the pond for a southeasterly panorama, then immediately turn away from the water again, working around another marsh.

2.5 Meet and join the Mount Wilcox Trail, open to bicycles but only lightly used by them, and head north in flatwoods. You are now headed for the Lookout, leaving Benedict Pond for the second time. Ahead, bridge an intermittent stream flowing off Benedict Pond Peak.

2.7 Come to an intersection. Here, the Mount Wilcox Trail splits right while we stay straight on the Lookout Trail. Bridge another branch.

2.9 Reach a trail junction. Here, a connector leads left toward the Beartown Mountain Trail. We stay straight on the Lookout Trail, climbing a bit to cross Benedict Pond Road. Keep gently climbing.

3.3 A spur trail leads left a short distance to the Lookout. Savor astonishing views to the northwest of the Housatonic Valley in the fore with the Taconics and Catskills in the distance. Picnic tables enhance the vista. Backtrack toward Benedict Pond.

4.1 Rejoin the Benedict Pond Loop Trail and head right. Come near the pond dam and swim area, as well as a picnic area. A spur trail stays closer to the lake. Walk past the cascading outflow of the pond, then cross a part of the pond dam at a fishing area. Just ahead, near the swim beach with bathhouse.

4.4 Arrive back at the boat launch/picnic area, completing the hike.

24 ALFORD SPRINGS PRESERVE

This trek traverses a mountain range situated near the New York state line. On your figure-eight loop through Berkshire Natural Resources Council land, you will climb above the Alford Brook valley, crossing waterways feeding Alford Brook. Along the way, you will also pass several cleared views, where your eyes will feast upon Mount Greylock, nearby Mount Tom, and agricultural lands in the valleys below. Add in wildlife-attracting clearings and old farm evidence, and you have a parcel worth preserving—and exploring.

Start: Saddle trailhead
Distance: 7.3-mile figure-eight loop
Difficulty: Moderate to difficult
Elevation change: +/-1,440 feet over entire hike
Maximum grade: 4% downhill grade for 1.9 miles
Hiking time: About 4 hours
Seasons/schedule: Year-round
Fees and permits: None
Dog friendly: Yes
Trail surface: Natural surface doubletrack

Land status: Private preserve open to public
Nearest town: Great Barrington
Other trail users: Bicyclers, equestrians
Map to consult: Alford Springs
Amenities available: None
Cell service: Fair, better up high
Trail contact: Berkshire Natural Resources Council, (413) 449-0596, www.bnrc.org

FINDING THE TRAILHEAD

From Main Street in downtown Great Barrington, take St. James Street west for one block, then turn right onto Castle Street and follow it as Castle Street turns left. Stay with Castle Street for 0.5 mile, then keep straight, joining Alford Road. Drive Alford Road for 3.5 miles, then turn left onto Alford Center Road and follow it 0.2 mile to West Road. Turn right and stay with West Road for 2.8 miles, then turn left into the Saddle trailhead parking area. Be watchful, as the trailhead signage is small and the parking lot lies between residences. **Trailhead GPS:** 42.274919, -73.427083

THE HIKE

Part of the Taconic Range straddling the Massachusetts–New York line, the mountains lying within 899-acre Alford Springs Preserve provide a habitation of Berkshire beauty, where bears and other wildlife down the food chain can live out their lives in reforested lands of maple, birch, and oak, once cleared as crop and sheep farms. The preserve is best suited for what it is, a natural refuge where flora and fauna thrive and hikers like us can visit, appreciating both the natural world and a respite from that more hectic world from which we came.

The hike leaves the bucolic Alford Brook valley in field and forest, rising to a vista overlooking the lands below, framed by striking Tom Ball Mountain, forming the far side of the rich agricultural basin. You then enter a forest of red maple and ferns along with evergreens aplenty. Find a brook and the Father Loop, then curve up the watershed of this stream, coming within rock-throwing distance of New York state. Travel in young

This is but one of many views found at Alford Springs Reserve.

woods. The dynamics of meadows as well as forests young and old generate favorable conditions for wildlife. The more habitats, the more types of food that can thrive. More food, more animals.

And you reach such a fine meadow, with northward views of Mount Greylock. Back in 2016, the Berkshire Natural Resources Council cleared this 25-acre plot to create a successional habitat, where former woodlands would be cut down and then prairies allowed to develop with grasses and berries along with scattered tree cover—a food plot of sorts. Wildflowers color the clearing in summer. Still other vistas lie ahead after you top out on the hike's high point of 1,640 feet, a solid 700 feet above the trailhead. No matter whether the trail is sloped or not, the hike is made easier by the wide, foot-friendly doubletrack trails that course through the preserve.

Striped maples are common in Alford Springs Preserve. They are a smaller tree, easily recognized by the vertical-striped twigs on green bark and typical maple leaves, albeit larger than red maple leaves. Striped maple primarily grows throughout the Northeast, where it is nicknamed "moosewood," derived from moose feeding on its bark in winter. Deer, beavers, and rabbits also browse on striped maples during the cold season. Striped maples can be found throughout Massachusetts and Connecticut, save for the southeast Atlantic coast region of both states. Interestingly, striped maples stretch south along the spine of the Appalachians all the way down to Georgia.

You will come to the Mother Loop in a flat gap where old roads come together. Follow this trail south, passing the Old Village Road trailhead, then circling past former farm

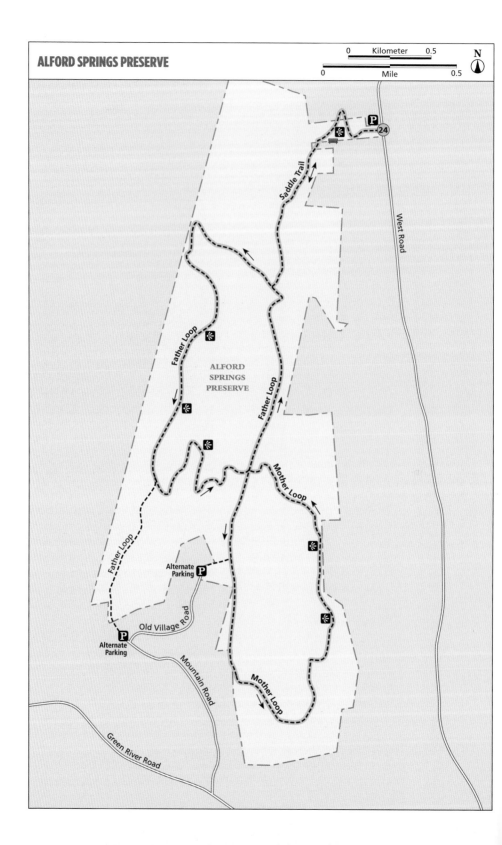

ALFORD SPRINGS PRESERVE

0 Kilometer 0.5
0 Mile 0.5

N

West Road

Saddle Trail

Father Loop

ALFORD
SPRINGS
PRESERVE

Father Loop

Mother Loop

Father Loop

Alternate
Parking

Old Village Road

Alternate
Parking

Mountain Road

Mother Loop

Green River Road

24

Wildflowers provide close up beauty at Alford Springs Reserve.

country with plenty of agricultural evidence to the discerning eye. Your northbound track negotiates a linear ridge offering occasional views to the east before the Mother Loop is completed. From here, keep on old farm roads, dropping past small streams before you complete the lower loop. From here, the Father Loop leads you north to complete the entire circuit. A final backtrack returns you to West Road and the trailhead.

MILES AND DIRECTIONS

0.0 Leave west on the Saddle Trail from the Saddle trailhead on West Road through a mix of field and wood, heading west on a right-of-way toward the eastern range of the Taconics. Sumac, paper birch, and brush line the path as it rises from the Alford Brook valley.

0.3 Reach a small clearing and a bench from which opens a view to the east across the Alford Brook valley onto steep-sided Tom Ball Mountain. Continue on the wide Saddle Trail into full-blown woods.

0.6 Pass through a gap—the saddle—of the Saddle Trail. Gently descend past stone fence lines, an old home site, and more evidence of this forest's agricultural past.

1.0 Intersect the Father Loop before reaching a noisy tributary of Alford Brook. Turn right, joining the Father Loop, climbing on a doubletrack in woods.

1.4 Cross the unnamed tributary via culvert. The trail turns south, skirting the New York state line. Climb a mountainside in young woods.

1.8 Open onto a meadow after ascending a mountainside. Views expand north clear up to Mount Greylock, Massachusetts's high point, 30 miles to the north.

2.1 Reach another vista after topping out on a high point. Looks open to the east. Ahead, pass through an almost-pure paper birch grove.

2.5 Come to an intersection. Here, the spur portion of the Father Loop leads south to the Father Loop trailhead on Mountain Road. Our hike heads left, surmounting a shoulder of the unnamed mountain just crossed. Angle down the east side of the mountain.

2.8 Come to another east-facing cleared view, with the Alford Brook valley below and Tom Ball Mountain in the distance.

3.2 Reach a gap, rock walls, and relaxing bench. From here, head right on the Mother Loop as it traces an old farm road south.

3.6 A spur leads right to the Old Village Road trailhead. Keep left on the Mother Loop. Descend along a creek valley with lots of rock walls.

4.1 The trail splits left as you near private property. Cross a small stream, then stay with the main blazed trail as faded unmarked connector paths spur off and on the well-marked main loop here.

4.3 Turn north in a pretty meadow sprinkled with old apple trees. Walk past a flat building foundation, then climb a southwest-facing slope rich with oaks and pines.

4.7 Level off and head briefly east then back north along the rim of a steep ridge.

4.8 Pass another cleared easterly view of the Alford Brook valley.

5.1 Reach another cleared view to the east. Soon turn westerly.

5.6 Complete the Mother Loop. Head right, northbound, rejoining the Father Loop. Execute an easy descent.

6.2 Bridge the main brook of the preserve by culvert. Climb.

6.3 Complete the loop portion of the hike. From here, backtrack toward the Saddle trailhead.

7.3 Arrive back at the Saddle trailhead, finishing the hike.

25 JUG END LOOP

This intriguing circuit hike delivers bottom-up views from a narrow and deep horseshoe-shaped valley bordered by six peaks, one of them being the actual Jug End. Leave open fields, heading up the Fenton Brook valley from its lower-end patchwork of meadows, old apple orchards, and rich forest. Enter deep woods, traipsing farther up the valley to find an old chimney. Circle around the headwaters of Fenton Brook before passing through and beside more fields, presenting stellar vistas of Mount Darby and Mount Sterling. The final part of the adventure leads you through a checkerboard of woodland, meadows, and orchards, with still more panoramas.

Start: Jug End parking area
Distance: 4.1-mile loop
Difficulty: Easy
Elevation change: +/-645 feet over entire hike
Maximum grade: 6% grade for 0.6 mile
Hiking time: About 2 hours
Seasons/schedule: Best from mid-May through Nov
Fees and permits: None
Dog friendly: Yes
Trail surface: Grass on lower loop, balance is foot-friendly natural surface

Land status: State reservation
Nearest town: Great Barrington
Other trail users: None
Map to consult: Mount Washington State Forest
Amenities available: None
Cell service: Good at trailhead, potentially sketchy deep in valley
Trail contact: Jug End State Reservation, (413) 528-0330, www.mass.gov/locations/jug-end-state-reservation-wildlife-management-area

FINDING THE TRAILHEAD

To reach the Jug End State Reservation trailhead from Great Barrington, take MA 41 south for 4.4 miles, then veer right onto Mount Washington Road. Follow Mount Washington Road for 1.7 miles, then turn left onto Jug End Road. Follow Jug End Road for 0.5 mile, then turn right into the large parking area, the site of the former Jug End Barn. The trail starts at the south end of the parking area.
Trailhead GPS: 42.148180, -73.450010

THE HIKE

Linked to Mount Washington State Forest and Mount Everett State Reservation, 1,158-acre Jug End State Reservation also features a segment of the Appalachian Trail (AT) traversing its eastern flank. (An AT access and parking area is located a short distance down Jug End Road from this hike.) The property was acquired by the state of Massachusetts in 1994. The name Jug End is derived from a Dutch German word, *jugend*, meaning "young" or "small," referring to the mountain forming the northeastern tip of the horseshoe valley dubbed Guilder Hollow. It was the Dutch family Guilder, who settled the area after purchasing the tract from the Housatonic Indians in 1736, that named the mount.

This hike visits a valley rimmed in mountains.

The six peaks that ring Fenton Brook and the Jug End Loop Trail are Mount Whitbeck, Mount Sterling, Mount Darby, Mount Undine, Mount Bushnell, and Jug End, all rising hundreds of feet above Guilder Hollow. These mounts form the north-facing horseshoe valley, once farmland of Guilder Hollow, that seemed a natural ski resort. A man named Hugh Smiley saw this possibility and acted on it.

The valley of Fenton Brook, glacially cut with steep-sided walls, is the centerpiece of this hike. A century back, ol' Mr. Smiley swooped into the area and purchased various properties, including Guilder Hollow, desiring to fashion an authentic New England village that was also complemented by recreational facilities from tennis to bowling to riflery—and a ski run. The ski run was to be the primary draw. Other attractions could hopefully make it a year-round resort.

Mr. Smiley undertook the project, but then sold out during the Great Depression of the 1930s. The destination passed through several hands, then was revitalized after World War II, including the addition of tow ropes to get powder enthusiasts up the mountain. Jug End continued snow ski operations, even adding a nine-hole golf course along the way. But the enhancements were to no avail. The gas crisis of the late 1970s, along with competition from other nearby ski areas, precipitated the downward spiral from which it couldn't recover, ending its run in the '80s.

Now we have meadows and mountains and a fine valley to explore. The large parking area was the site of the famed Jug End Barn, the original hub of Mr. Smiley's retreat. Once hiking, you will leave here then cross to the west side of Fenton Brook. The six peaks rise high above, including the radio towers of Mount Darby. A mix of hardwoods

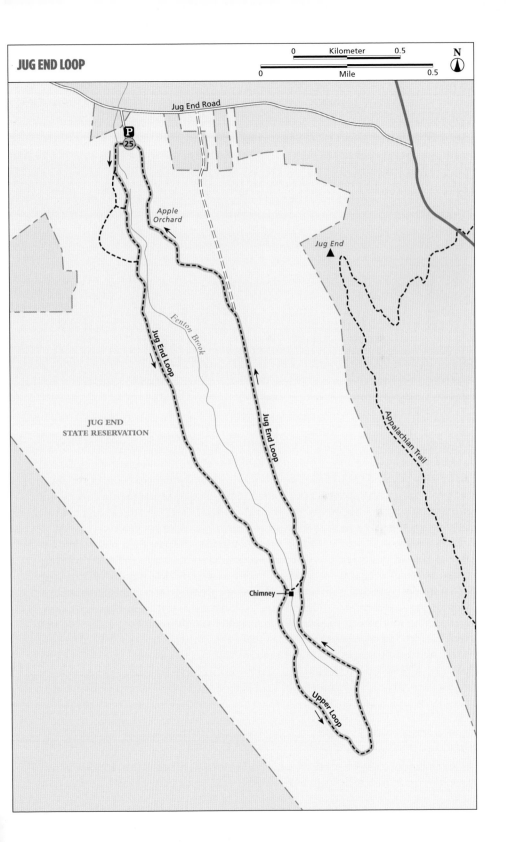

JUG END LOOP

Jug End Road

P
25

Apple
Orchard

Jug End ▲

Fenton Brook

Jug End Loop

Jug End Loop

Appalachian Trail

JUG END
STATE RESERVATION

Chimney ■

Upper Loop

0   Kilometer   0.5
0   Mile   0.5

N

Meadows provide near continual highland vistas.

and evergreens partially shades the trail. Daisies and other wildflowers brighten the track in summer.

Watch out as grassy spur paths, used primarily for winter cross-country skiing, extend east from the Jug End Loop Trail. The valley narrows and you join a former road under hardwoods of cherry, oak, maple, and witch hazel. The slope steepens but the ascent remains moderate. In some areas, lesser tributaries trickle over the path, creating troublesome wet areas.

After a while, meet the Upper Loop near a standing chimney from times past. The Upper Loop delves deeper into Guilder Hollow, and we take it to circle past trickling brooks draining the highlands above that collect to form Fenton Brook. After crossing Fenton Brook, begin a relaxed downward journey, once again joining the Jug End Loop. Here the trail alternates in and out of mown meadows that reveal superlative mountain vistas of Mount Whitbeck and Mount Sterling, displaying the height and depth of this gorgeous vale. The edges of these meadows are a fine place to spot deer or wild turkeys.

After wandering through alternating meadows and woods, you curve west and descend through a historic apple orchard. Local lore has it that these apple trees through which you pass were planted by Johnny Appleseed himself. A real person named John Chapman, the son of a missionary, Johnny Appleseed entered this world just before the Revolutionary War and lived until 1845, introducing apple trees from Massachusetts to the Midwest. Chapman was born in the Bay State, east of the Berkshires, and the family eventually moved west to Ohio. Throughout his years Johnny Appleseed not only spread the cultivation of apple trees, but also the Christian Gospel. Fort Wayne, Indiana, where Mr. Chapman ended his days, still holds an annual Johnny Appleseed festival.

MILES AND DIRECTIONS

0.0 With your back to the parking lot, facing south into Guilder Hollow, head right, west, on the Jug End Loop Trail. Quickly bridge Fenton Brook then head left, southbound, in a mix of meadow and woodland. Stay with the trail closest to Fenton Brook to avoid being swept into a mini-maze of mown paths that run through what was once the old resort golf course, now managed meadows.

0.2 Step over a tributary of Fenton Brook near a grassy spur intersection. Traverse fern meadows and willow thickets mixed with a screen of trees running alongside Fenton Brook.

0.4 Another grassy spur trail splits right. Stay left with the Jug End Loop. The valley quickly closes.

0.9 Step over another stream flowing down from Mount Darby.

1.0 The Jug End Loop Trail levels off and the hiking becomes a breeze.

1.3 Step over another stream.

1.5 Come to an intersection near a standing stone chimney. Here, the Jug End Loop Trail cuts left for a shorter circuit. However, our hike stays right, joining the Upper Loop to immediately climb a short, steep segment.

2.1 Reach the head of the cove. Above, steep wooded slopes upsurge more than 400 feet. Begin to curve back north, initiating a prolonged downgrade.

2.3 Cross a tributary. Below, sonorant Fenton Brook is picking up steam.

2.7 Intersect and rejoin the Jug End Loop Trail. Continue your downhill ride in hardwood forests.

2.9 Reach the first open meadows with fine panoramas of the peaks surrounding Fenton Brook.

3.2 Cut through a screen of trees, then enter another meadow with more vistas.

3.3 Return to woods.

3.5 Cut through another meadow. Note the blackberries growing along the edges of the meadows, a wildlife and hiker attractant.

3.8 Step over a tributary of Fenton Brook, then descend through an apple orchard. Purportedly the legendary Johnny Appleseed had a hand in its establishment. Enjoy the views—and the apples in season.

3.9 Enter scattered woods and meadows.

4.1 Arrive back at the parking area, ending the hike.

26 BASH BISH FALLS

Visit what is regarded by many as Massachusetts's most iconic waterfall. Hard against the New York state line, Bash Bish Brook (say that three times fast) drains the highlands of Mount Washington State Forest then tumbles through a steep canyon, fashioning Bash Bish Falls just before flowing into New York. This hike first climbs to an outcrop and a panorama of the Bash Bish Canyon and beyond, then you make the short but relatively steep walk to Bash Bish Falls, where you can look down on the twin-chute cataract. From there, follow the easy trail down along Bash Bish Brook to an alternative parking area in New York's Taconic State Park.

Start: Bash Bish Falls Massachusetts trailhead
Distance: 2.2 miles out and back
Difficulty: Easy; does have short rough patch to Sunset Rock
Elevation change: +/-600 feet over entire hike
Maximum grade: 20% grade for 0.3 mile
Hiking time: About 1.5 hours
Seasons/schedule: May through July for bolder falls
Fees and permits: None
Dog friendly: Yes, if coming from New York trail; otherwise no
Trail surface: Natural surface; rocky for first 0.3 mile, wide road-like trail rest of way

Land status: Massachusetts state park, New York state park
Nearest town: Great Barrington
Other trail users: None
Maps to consult: Mount Washington State Forest, Taconic State Park–Northern Section
Amenities available: Restroom at trailhead
Cell service: Good
Trail contacts: Mount Washington State Forest, (413) 528-0330, www .mass.gov/locations/bash-bish-falls -state-park; Taconic State Park, (518) 329-3993, https://parks.ny.gov/

FINDING THE TRAILHEAD

To reach the Bash Bish Falls Massachusetts trailhead from Great Barrington, take MA 41 south 4.5 miles then split right, joining Mount Washington Road. Follow it 4.4 miles, then turn right onto West Street and follow it for 0.3 mile. Turn left to stay on West Street and follow it for 1.2 more miles, then turn right onto Bash Bish Falls Road. Stay with Bash Bish Falls Road for 1.4 miles to reach the parking area on your left. If this lot is full, consider driving a little farther into New York and the Bash Bish Falls parking in Taconic State Park. **Trailhead GPS:** 42.114952, -73.491595

THE HIKE

Popular hikes are usually popular for a reason. And Bash Bish Falls is popular. The cataract spills 80 feet while splitting around an upstream rock jumble (other cascades tumble above this final drop). The view into the canyon of Bash Bish Falls adds to the rewards of the destination. I highly recommend the experience. Just make sure to avoid the busy times—weekends, holidays, and leaf-peeping season—to better enjoy the adventure.

Bash Bish Falls is a Berkshires classic cataract.

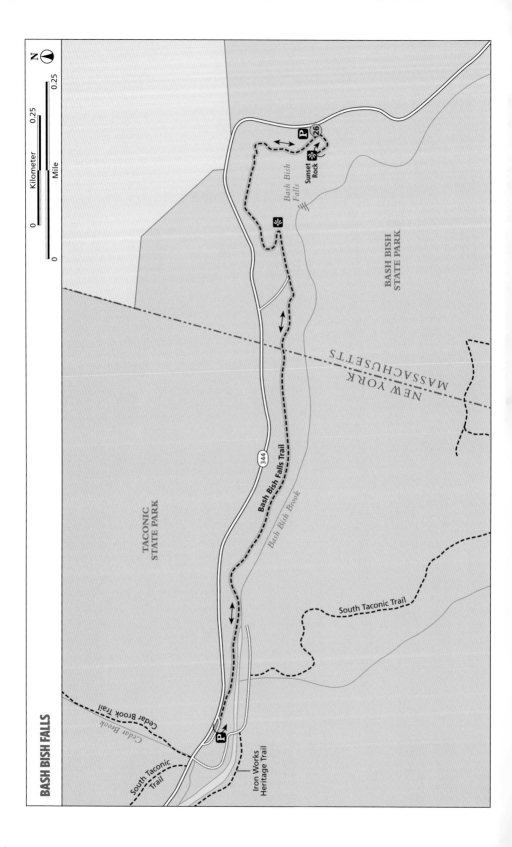

BASH BISH FALLS

TACONIC
STATE PARK

BASH BISH
STATE PARK

NEW YORK
MASSACHUSETTS

Bash Bish
Falls

Sunset
Rock

26

344

Bash Bish Falls Trail

Bash Bish Brook

South Taconic Trail

Cedar Brook

Cedar Brook Trail

South Taconic
Trail

Iron Works
Heritage Trail

N

Kilometer
0   0.25   0.25

Mile
0   0.25

Gazing down the Bash Bish Brook canyon

Morning is a good time to visit: The falls are less crowded and mountains to the east block the morning sun, enhancing photography opportunities.

Naturally, this popular pourover has two access points. Our hike starts in Massachusetts. The access here is steeper with more irregular rocky trail, dropping 300 feet in 0.3 mile. From this end you get there quicker. The New York access at Taconic State Park starts 0.8 mile from Bish Bash Falls, but the climb is only 230 feet and the trail is a wide regular track suitable for waterfall enthusiasts of all ages.

Though Bash Bish Falls is regularly bandied about as the highest falls in Massachusetts, Bear Rock Falls, also detailed in this guide, is clearly higher, dropping at least 200 feet. Even the most ambitious estimates of the entire length of Bash Bish Falls stretch only 200 feet, including the upper falls. Nevertheless, Bash Bish Falls has an aura of history, tradition, legend—and danger. Over the years at least twenty-five visitors have perished at the cataract, leading to increased visitation restrictions. The constraints started with no climbing around the falls, then no swimming in the falls pool, and in 2021 the lower stairs accessing the falls' pool was cut off, leaving a more distant view. Furthermore, on busy weekends, rangers plant themselves at the cataract to keep everyone safe.

Tourists have been coming to Bash Bish Falls for at least 200 years, and before that a now-muddled Mohican legend swirled around the cataract and led to its name. Seems a comely Indian maiden named Bash Bish was condemned to death by being strapped to a canoe and floated over the falls after being accused of adultery. Her body was never found, adding mystery to the account. However, she did leave a name for the falls, and tales persist of seeing the face of Bash Bish in the white froth of Bash Bish Brook.

In your eagerness to see the falls, don't neglect the view close to the trailhead. First take the short trail/scramble up to the overlook of Bash Bish Canyon. The outcrop is very rugged. The state of Massachusetts erected metal handrails, as careless visitors sometimes fell from the precipice. Once up here you can take in an extensive view of the canyon of Bash Bish Brook, widening and framing a westward panorama into the greater Hudson River valley.

After returning to the trailhead, you then join the Bash Bish Falls Trail, descending a heavily used, wide, wooded path delving into a dark forest of hemlock and white pine as well as yellow birch. The mountain slope is quite steep. Soon you find yourself at the Bash Bish Falls overlook. Enjoy a head-on view of the twin chutes of the 80-foot pourover.

Beyond the falls, go ahead and take the now-easy trail downstream, entering the state of New York at a sign. Bash Bish Brook tumbles loudly to your left through the woods. The trail comes directly alongside the stream before reaching the Taconic State Park parking area. If you want to explore more, walk to the nearby historic ironworks area, where a preserved mini-village from an iron foundry stands. You can also check out the Harlem Valley Rail Trail or the designated pond swim area, or continue on to climb to Sunset Rock, all at Taconic State Park. Otherwise, backtrack to the Massachusetts trailhead, having visited the Bay State's signature waterfall.

MILES AND DIRECTIONS

0.0 With your back to Bash Bish Falls Road, walk left, away from the Bash Bish Falls Trail, and climb the rock pathway, scrambling to a view through the Bash Bish Canyon into New York's Hudson Valley. Backtrack to the trailhead and begin the Bash Bish Falls Trail, descending toward Bash Bish Brook. Cross a tributary of Bash Bish Brook.

0.4 Reach the viewing area of Bash Bish Falls. Unfortunately, the falls' base access has been closed. Begin following the waterway downstream. Pass the ranger rescue road on your right.

0.6 Enter New York and Taconic State Park. The stream is crashing through the woods to your left. Ahead, pass the park rental cabins across the river.

1.1 Reach the Taconic State Park parking area. Backtrack to the Massachusetts trailhead.

2.2 Arrive back at the Massachusetts trailhead, completing the hike.

27 ALANDER MOUNTAIN

This bold hike reaps big rewards. First traverse field and wood, then come alongside Ashley Hill Brook and an old milldam. Rise through scenic woods, then return to a tributary of Ashley Hill Brook to find a backwoods trail cabin perched in a highland gap. From there, climb to the rock spine of Alander Mountain to discover an astonishing panorama of the mountains, valleys, and towns of three states near the site of an old watchtower. Part of your return route makes a loop along Ashley Hill Brook, delivering new terrain en route to the trailhead.

Start: Mount Washington State Forest headquarters trailhead
Distance: 6.7-mile loop with a tail on both ends
Difficulty: Moderate to difficult due to climb and somewhat rocky trail
Elevation change: +/-965 feet over entire hike
Maximum grade: 13% grade for 0.8 mile
Hiking time: About 3.5 hours
Seasons/schedule: Best from late May through Oct, open year-round
Fees and permits: None
Dog friendly: Yes, but trail has one short, steep, rocky segment

Trail surface: Forested natural surface, open rock at the top
Land status: State forest
Nearest town: Great Barrington
Other trail users: None
Map to consult: Mount Washington State Forest
Amenities available: Restrooms and picnic tables at trailhead
Cell service: Decent, better atop ridgelines
Trail contact: Mount Washington State Forest, (413) 528-0330, www.mass.gov/locations/mount -washington-state-forest

FINDING THE TRAILHEAD

To reach the Alander Mountain trailhead from Great Barrington, take MA 41 south 4.5 miles, then split right, joining Mount Washington Road. Follow Mount Washington Road (which becomes East Street along the way) for a total of 8.9 miles to the right turn into Mount Washington State Forest headquarters. The large parking lot is a little beyond the headquarter buildings. Address: 162 East St., Mount Washington, MA. **Trailhead GPS:** 42.086271, -73.462127

THE HIKE

Mount Washington State Forest, tucked into the southwest corner of Massachusetts where it meets New York and Connecticut, is one of the crown jewels of the Berkshires. The 4,169-acre preserve with clear-as-air streams links with other properties harboring other pathways stretching into the adjoining states, together creating a network of trails for hikers to behold. However, the trek to Alander Mountain is arguably one of the best in the area, where you top out on a long stretch of open mountain, where naked stone and low weather-stunted trees open vast vistas of the adjacent mountains and beyond, especially from the south slope of the mountain.

Furthermore, the scenery pleases the eye along the way. You will first walk past wooded old fencerows through small fields, vestiges of an agricultural past so often found in the

The rock outcrops atop Alander Mountain deliver expansive vistas.

Berkshires, before meeting lively Lee Pond Brook under a mantle of beech, yellow birch, maple, and hemlock. Ferns scatter through the forest.

After bridging Lee Pond Brook, the Charcoal Pit Trail leaves left. This path can become overgrown in summer, and thus not recommended as a loop option during the growing season. Better for a loop is the Ashley Hill Trail, which you meet, then find Ashley Hill Brook, a prototypical picturesque Mount Washington State Forest stream, dancing downward in white cascades. Look for the stone remains of an old milldam near the confluence of Ashley Hill Brook and Lee Pond Brook. This is a spot to linger before heading west for Alander Mountain.

After traversing a mountain slope, you turn up a tributary of Ashley Hill Brook. You will know this tributary well, hopping back and forth across it, as well as going directly up it at times, dancing on rocks standing above the diminutive creek. Here, the real ascent begins, gaining over 650 feet in the next mile, much of which is rocky. The brook peters out as you climb to a gap then reach Alander Mountain Cabin, a first-come, first-served shelter with a wood-burning stove, bunks, and a table inside. Water can be had from the brook just hiked along.

Then comes the short but steep assault up the east side of Alander Mountain. Here, the path scales a rock slope to level out and meet the South Taconic Trail, a slender track flanked by windswept brush. Pass the site of a former fire lookout tower—you can still see the footings. Here once stood the 60-foot metal lookout atop Alander Mountain. Though inside the Massachusetts state boundary, the post was erected and manned by the

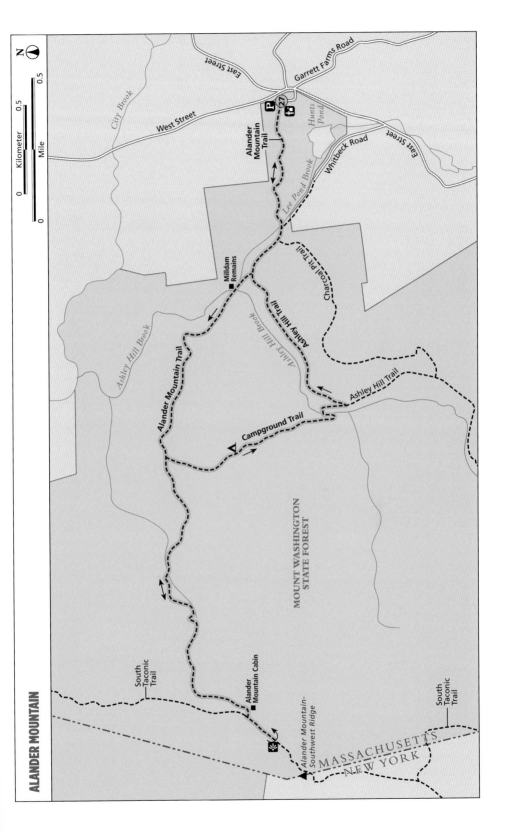

ALANDER MOUNTAIN

N

0   Kilometer   0.5

0   Mile   0.5

City Brook

West Street

East Street

Garrett Farms Road

P (27)

Hunts Pond

Lee Pond Brook

Whitbeck Road

East Street

Alander Mountain Trail

Milldam Remains

Ashley Hill Brook

Ashley Hill Trail

Ashley Hill Brook

Charcoal Pit Trail

Alander Mountain Trail

Ashley Hill Trail

Campground Trail

MOUNT WASHINGTON STATE FOREST

South Taconic Trail

Alander Mountain Cabin

Alander Mountain–Southwest Ridge

South Taconic Trail

MASSACHUSETTS

NEW YORK

The views from Alander Mountain go on for miles and miles.

state of New York, the state line a scant 0.2 mile distant from the tower site. Built in 1928, the tower was dismantled and moved after two years, eventually ending up on Beebe Hill in the Empire State. The Alander Mountain Cabin below was originally constructed as the tower watchman's cabin.

Ahead, you will see why the tower was constructed here. Incredible views open as you walk south, on the downslope of Alander Mountain. To the north stands Mount Washington, across Bash Bish Brook. To the east Mount Ashley rises across Ashley Hill Brook. To the south lies Connecticut's Washining Lake as well as hills and farmlands of the Housatonic River valley, and points south as far as the clarity of the sky allows. The wide-open terrain from where you stand is subject to excessive sun, wind, and precipitation. Be prepared.

Your return trip loops past a first-come, first-served backcountry campground, naturally located on the Campground Trail. Here, eight widely dispersed designated campsites are stretched along the path, each with bear-proof food storage box, picnic table, fire ring, and privy. If camping here, make sure to register at the sign-in board. The hike next joins lowermost Ashley Hill Trail, descending along the pretty brook before returning to the Alander Mountain Trail, where a simple backtrack returns you to the trailhead.

MILES AND DIRECTIONS

0.0 Leave the large parking area on the blue-blazed Alander Mountain Trail, westbound in oaks before bisecting a few small meadows. Hills rise to your left.

0.3 The Alander Mountain Trail curves left and descends.

0.5 Bridge Lee Pond Brook. Ahead, the Charcoal Pit Trail leaves left. Stay straight with the Alander Mountain Trail.

0.7 Intersect the Ashley Hill Trail. This will be your return route. For now, stay with the Alander Mountain Trail, potentially wet in places, descending to a bridge over cascading Ashley Hill Brook near some dam remains. This is the hike's low point. Begin ascending away from Ashley Hill Brook in mixed hardwoods and evergreens.

1.3 Turn west, wandering in dispersed tree cover rising among lush ferns on the north side of a hill.

1.7 Come near some old farm walls, then intersect the Campground Trail. For now, stay with the Alander Mountain Trail, passing small tributaries of Ashley Hill Brook.

2.0 Begin ascending along an unnamed tributary of Ashley Hill Brook. The path crisscrosses the small, clear watercourse, sometimes going up it directly. Mountain laurel, wild azalea, and oaks become more prevalent.

2.8 Come to the Mount Alander Cabin in a gap. The four-sided shelter with a wood-burning stove, bunks, and a table is open to camping, first-come, first-served. Stay with the Alander Mountain Trail to switchback up a sharp stone slope.

2.9 Meet the white-blazed South Taconic Trail atop the ridge of Alander Mountain. Head left, southbound, over exposed rock bordered by stunted aspen and brush. Pass the site of a former fire lookout tower and continue descending as vistas open wide before you.

3.0 The South Taconic Trail curves around a corner. This is a good place to turn around. Soak in the panoramas one more time, then backtrack.

3.1 Leave the South Taconic Trail, then descend past the Alander Mountain Cabin, rejoining the Alander Mountain Trail. Descend the stony track.

4.5 Return to the intersection with the Campground Trail. Head right here on new trail, rising gently in thick woods. Level out and pass the campsites strung along the trail.

5.3 Rock-hop Ashley Hill Brook. This may be a wet ford at higher stream flows. Climb away from the watercourse.

5.4 Head left on the Ashley Hill Trail. Follow an easy downgrade, trekking parallel to Ashley Hill Brook.

6.0 Rejoin the Alander Mountain Trail. Head right, backtracking.

6.7 Arrive back at the trailhead, completing the hiking adventure.

Looking south into Connecticut from Alander Mountain

28 RACE BROOK FALLS AND MOUNTAIN

You will be well rewarded while climbing over 2,000 feet on this combination waterfall and vista hike. Start in Mount Everett State Reservation, climbing along aptly named Race Brook to view two primary waterfalls, plus many other lesser cascades, then make your way past a backcountry campsite to meet the Appalachian Trail. From there, ascend over stone slabs—with a few steep sections—to top out on Race Mountain and indulge in some mountaintop vistas. In my opinion, the waterfalls are the stars of this hiking show. Try it out and see what you think.

Start: Race Brook Falls parking area
Distance: 7.0 miles out and back with 2 spurs
Difficulty: Difficult due to elevation gain
Elevation change: +/-2,081 feet over entire hike
Maximum grade: 19% grade for 0.6 mile
Hiking time: About 4 hours
Seasons/schedule: Apr through June for best waterfalls
Fees and permits: None
Dog friendly: Yes, along Race Brook, but not on rocky, irregular Appalachian Trail

Trail surface: Dirt, rocks, and roots on lower section; upper AT has naked rock slabs
Land status: State reservation
Nearest town: Great Barrington
Other trail users: None
Map to consult: Mount Washington State Forest
Amenities available: None
Cell service: Partial at trailhead, better on AT
Trail contact: Mount Everett State Reservation, (413) 528-0330, www.mass.gov/locations/mount-everett-state-reservation

FINDING THE TRAILHEAD

To reach the Race Brook Falls parking area from Great Barrington, take MA 41 south and stay with it for a total of 9 miles to the parking area on your right. If you reach Race Brook Lodge, you've gone just a little too far. Note: The parking area is a large paved pull-off. Be considerate about how you place your vehicle.
Trailhead GPS: 42.089814, -73.411193

THE HIKE

Race Brook certainly lives up to its name, dashing swift and fleet—and in stunning array—down the east slope of a precipitous mountain crest highlighted by Mount Race and Mount Everett, atop which the Appalachian Trail runs. The sharp slopes and erosion-resistant rock outcroppings result in Race Brook flinging itself headlong over the stone precipices, creating multiple waterfalls, cataracts, and cascades that attract Berkshires hikers like us to go and visit. By the way, if you are looking for a shorter, less strenuous hike, simply head to the waterfalls and back.

Though you may hear the term "Race Brook Falls" as if it were one cataract, you will find two named major spillers, along with three other noteworthy falls, with still other

This is an often overlooked cascade on Race Brook.

smaller cascades filling out the waterfall parade. You can view Lower Race Brook Falls from its base and from its crown using designated foot trails. The pourover is a tall spiller, around 100 feet, starting slender then fanning out as it plummets over a layered rock face, collects in a difficult-to-see pool, then makes a lesser, secondary drop. When you visit Lower Race Brook Falls from its crown, you can not only peer down at the lower falls, but also scramble upstream to another unnamed cataract dropping 40 feet into a deep glen.

Upper Race Brook Falls is my favorite. The cataract slices slender, faucet-like, 75 feet down a crevice, curving a bit as it makes a bold dash off the mountainside. Race Brook then mildly flows over the trail, then completely changes character, forming an angled veil-style waterfall of 25 feet. Then, as if to make up for moderating, it dives over a ledge, crashing white in a slender chute, down and out of sight. (Note: The Race Brook watershed is relatively small and steep. Water levels can be low and the falls disappointing from July through autumn. However, winter can be a delight, with higher stream flow and frozen cataracts.)

And then there are the overlooks. After making it through the steep slopes, the Race Brook Trail levels out on a rim overlooking the Housatonic Valley. Take in a distant view to the east. Then wander through the upper perched valley of Race Brook, passing near the top of one last waterfall, and enter the upper Race Brook valley, a literally cool place where hemlock and yellow birch reign. Next, you will find a backcountry campsite, used by intrepid backpackers tackling the wilds of Race Brook, along with Appalachian Trail thru-hikers doggedly trekking along the mountain spine of the East in their quest to walk from Georgia to Maine.

RACE BROOK FALLS AND MOUNTAIN

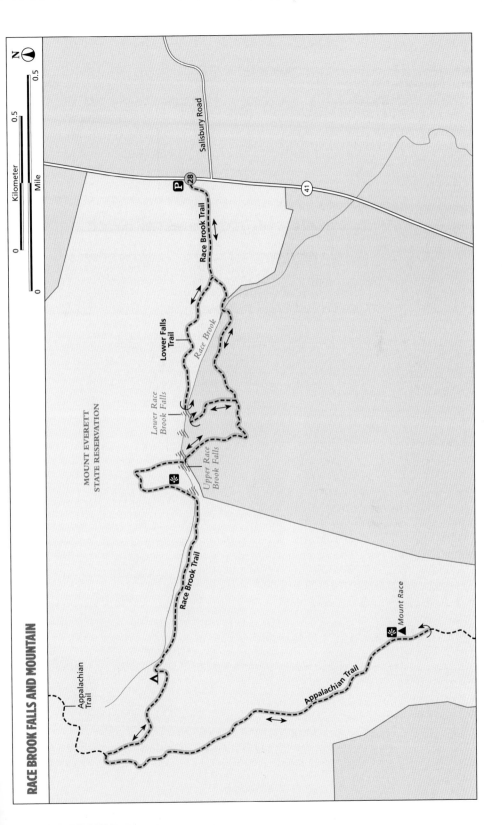

MOUNT EVERETT
STATE RESERVATION

Lower Race
Brook Falls

Upper Race
Brook Falls

Race Brook

Lower Falls
Trail

Race Brook Trail

Race Brook Trail

Appalachian
Trail

Appalachian Trail

Mount Race

Salisbury Road

Kilometer

Mile

N

Upper Race Brook Falls charges down a rock crevice.

And you too will join the Appalachian Trail, southbound, climbing to the summit of Mount Race. Be prepared for some steep sections over bare rock that may necessitate using your hands a couple of times. Once on the spine, squat storm-savaged pines flank the path. A widish rock slab crowns Mount Race, presenting distant views both east and west over the scraggly trees clinging to the stone here at 2,366 feet.

This hike is best done in dry conditions, enabling you to scramble around the falls and also navigate the angled rock slabs en route to Mount Race. The hike also demands an unhurried pace. Give yourself time to explore all the waterfalls, as well as the overlooks. Then you will be content as I have been while undertaking this endeavor.

MILES AND DIRECTIONS

0.0 From the parking area on MA 41, join the Race Brook Trail. Descend on a wide natural surface trail, crossing a spring branch near private property.

0.3 Take the spur right toward Lower Race Brook Falls.

0.6 Reach Lower Race Brook Falls in a steep canyon after working through stream braids. Enjoy the 100-foot spiller, then backtrack.

0.9 Resume the Race Brook Trail.

1.1 Rock-hop Race Brook. Continue up the valley with the stream in sight.

1.3 Come to an intersection. Take the lesser-used signed path leaving right toward upper Lower Falls.

1.5 Reach the rock outcrop at the crown of Lower Falls. If you scramble upstream a little bit, you can savor another cataract. Backtrack.

1.7 Rejoin the Race Brook Trail. The next section is the steepest.

1.9 Come to Upper Race Brook Falls, just upstream of the bridgeless trail crossing of Race Brook. Enjoy the view but also visit the waterfall below the stream crossing. After that, angle up the mountain slope away from Race Brook, at the base of a ledge.

2.1 Reach the rim of the ridge. Hike south.

2.2 A spur goes left to an overlook of the Housatonic Valley. Views open east and south. Continue on the Race Brook Trail, entering the perched valley of Race Brook. Here, the waterway tumbles over the mountain rim, forming the highest waterfall. From here, you can see it from the top down. Continue up the now-placid brook, bridging the stream then winding through groves of hemlock and yellow birch.

2.7 Come to the designated Race Brook Falls campsite, with several tent platforms and a privy.

3.0 Meet the Appalachian Trail. Turn left, southbound, rock-hopping through an upland bog, then climb, quickly reaching the first of many steep and/or irregular rock slabs that require dexterity to navigate.

3.5 Open onto a linear rock ledge bordered with stunted trees. Ledges become more common.

4.0 Reach the top of Mount Race after a short but quick jump on a stone slope. You can see Washining Lake below as well as valley farms and woods. Continue down the trail to gain additional views. Backtrack to the parking area, avoiding the spur trails.

7.0 Arrive back at the parking area, completing the trail adventure.

29 TRI-STATE VIEWS LOOP

This challenging yet rewarding circuit of superlatives takes you to stimulating views in three states—Connecticut, Massachusetts, and New York (including Connecticut's highest point). Start in Mount Washington State Forest, climbing steeply to stony Round Mountain and its vistas, then continue on to panoramas from Mount Frissell, using über-rocky and precipitous paths. Next, briefly enter New York and join the Taconic Trail, peering into the yon from atop Brace Mountain. Return via a more foot-friendly pathway, completing the circuit using quiet Mount Washington Road.

Start: Mount Frissell trailhead
Distance: 5.2-mile loop with spur
Difficulty: Difficult due to steep sections and rugged trail first 2.1 miles of hike
Elevation change: +/-1,157 feet over entire hike
Maximum grade: 29% grade for 0.2 mile
Hiking time: About 4 hours
Seasons/schedule: June through Nov, and when trails are dry
Fees and permits: None
Dog friendly: No; trail follows steep, naked rock slopes
Trail surface: Natural surface, lots of steep rock and irregular footing, then gravel roadbed

Land status: State forest, state park, private lands open to public use
Nearest town: Great Barrington
Other trail users: Bicyclists and drivers on Mount Washington Road
Maps to consult: Mount Washington State Forest, Taconic State Park–Southern Section
Amenities available: None
Cell service: Iffy at trailhead, better on peaks
Trail contact: Mount Washington State Forest, (413) 528-0330, www.mass.gov/locations/mount-washington-state-forest

FINDING THE TRAILHEAD

To reach the Mount Frissell trailhead from Great Barrington, take MA 41 south 4.5 miles then split right, joining Mount Washington Road. Follow Mount Washington Road (which becomes East Street along the way) for a total of 11.4 miles to the Mount Frissell trailhead on the right, just before crossing into Connecticut. The parking area is very small, but there is more parking on the left just into Connecticut. Note: The Connecticut parking area does not allow overnight parking.
Trailhead GPS: 42.050093, -73.466995

THE HIKE

On this hike you will pass a rock cairn marking the highest point in Connecticut, the shoulder of Mount Frissell at 2,380 feet, where it lies in the Constitution State. Connecticut is one of three states of which their high point is not actually a peak or hill, the others being Oklahoma's high point on the shoulder of Black Mesa and Nevada's Boundary Peak, on the shoulder of Montgomery Peak, just across the California state line.

There exists a whole class of people whose goal it is to visit all the highest elevations of every state. They are known as "high pointers." Some high points can be driven to, while others require challenging hikes like this. Still others require modest walks, like to West

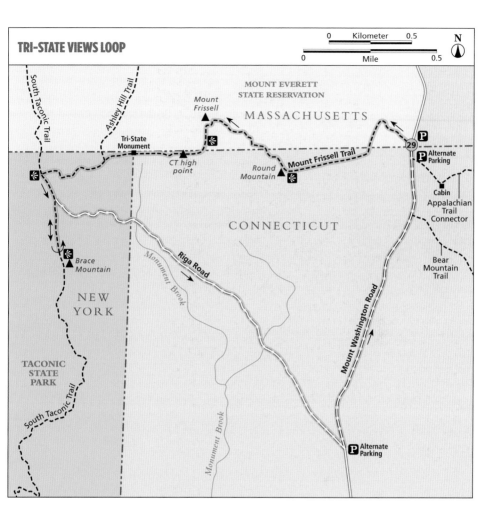

MOUNT EVERETT
STATE RESERVATION

Mount
Frissell

MASSACHUSETTS

Tri-State
Monument

CT high
point

Round
Mountain

Mount Frissell Trail

29

Alternate
Parking

South Taconic Trail

Ashley Hill Trail

Cabin
Appalachian
Trail
Connector

CONNECTICUT

Brace
Mountain

Monument Brook

Riga Road

Bear
Mountain
Trail

NEW
YORK

Mount Washington Road

TACONIC
STATE
PARK

South Taconic Trail

Monument Brook

Alternate
Parking

Virginia's Spruce Knob, Clingmans Dome in Tennessee, or Missouri's Taum Sauk Mountain, or a more substantial hike, like that to Virginia's Mount Rogers or Maine's Mount Katahdin. Some require mountaineering skills that your average hiker doesn't have—or need, unless you want to climb Washington's Mount Rainier or Alaska's Denali. That being said, many are high points that are significant only in context to being inside the boundaries of their given state—such as Britton Hill in Florida or Ohio's Campbell Hill.

The first high pointers began making such quests in the 1930s. To this day members of high point clubs or soloists on a personal mission will be found at places like Mount Frissell, completing another quest and checking off another state.

So maybe after reaching Connecticut's high point you will be inspired to become a high pointer. Massachusetts's high point of Mount Greylock also stands within the Berkshires—and you can drive to it or make it the centerpiece of a hike.

Superlatives aside, I guarantee you won't forget this loop. It starts out innocuous enough, just a stroll in the woods, then all heck breaks loose at the base of Round Mountain. You begin climbing—using your hands at times—making over 400 feet in a half mile, working up stone slopes and boulder jumbles in thin woods steep enough for a mountain goat to feel at home. The climb is relentless, and fun in a way, especially while you are fresh.

You will leave Massachusetts for Connecticut, but won't even notice. Open onto stone slabs atop Round Mountain, soak in your first panoramas, touch the summit's rock cairn, then make a slow stony descent to a gap lying betwixt Round Mountain and Mount Frissell. Catch your breath here because the stony ascent up Mount Frissell repeats the performance—you gain 289 feet in 0.2 mile! The top of Mount Frissell is wooded, and a short spur trail goes to a register for those who want to sign in. Resume the Mount Frissell Trail, circling around the south shoulder of the mountain. Big views open to the south along a stretch of trail, then you come to the Connecticut high point, marked with a cairn and survey marker. Sign in if you please, before beginning a steep rocky drop. Descents like this are best done in dry weather if at all possible. Slick rocks lead to slips.

The trail does level off for a bit, then you come to the next major highlight—the Tri-State monument, erected in 1898. Here, a rectangular concrete pillar marks where Massachusetts, Connecticut, and New York all come together. You can be in all three states at one time! Now, enjoy a stretch of "normal" hiking, rolling westerly to meet the South Taconic Trail—and flabbergasting vistas into the Empire State.

There's one more peak to bag. Here, we take the South Taconic Trail up to Brace Mountain and its open summit, where a rock pile atop a gently rounded peak usually is supporting a flagpole sporting Old Glory or another American symbol. The views up here are just grand: northwest to the Catskills, west into the Harlem Valley below, east into the Berkshires. A little backtrack leads to an old forest road that reenters Connecticut. From here you cross the Monument Brook valley then join quiet Mount Washington Road and make the final leg of the loop on easy gravel road, returning to the trailhead.

MILES AND DIRECTIONS

0.0 Leave west from the small signed parking lot on the Mount Frissell Trail. Traipse west through scads of mountain laurel on a stony singletrack path. Oaks, hickory, sassafras, and wild azalea complement the scene. Trillium and flowering dogwood brighten spring.

0.2 Reach the base of Round Mountain. The trail then radically ascends declivitous rock slope and rock jumbles.

0.6 Open onto a big stone slab bordered in pines, with views opening of Bear Mountain and points east. Stay with the blazes through the open stone slabs and low brushy aspens and oaks, along with blueberry bushes.

0.7 Top out on Round Mountain, marked by a rock cairn. Views spread of lakes and lowlands south into Connecticut, along with nearby mountains, including Mount Frissell. Descend northwest on a slow, stony path.

0.9 Reach a small gap below Mount Frissell. Note the old track running through the gap. Begin an arduous, abrupt climb up Mount Frissell.

1.1 Reach a short spur to the wooded top of Mount Frissell with trail register. From there, swing southwest around the side of the peak.

1.2 Panoramas extend south as far as the eye can see along a stretch of trail.

1.3 Reach a survey marker, big rock cairn, and trail register marking the high point in Connecticut. Though it is the state's high point, it is but on the shoulder of Mount Frissell.

1.5 Come to the concrete survey marker denoting where Massachusetts, Connecticut, and New York meet. Enjoy being in three states at once. Continue west, fully in New York.

1.6 Meet the Ashley Hill Trail in a gap. It leaves right into Massachusetts and Mount Washington State Forest. A trail used to go south from the gap but has been abandoned. We stay straight on the Mount Frissell Trail, gently climbing.

1.9 Meet the South Taconic Trail. Straight ahead are sweeping vistas west into New York. Traipse south on the South Taconic Trail in stunted vegetation toward Brace Mountain.

2.1 Old Riga Road angles southeast. This is your loop turn. For now, keep south on the South Taconic Trail in wind-stunted vegetation.

2.3 Reach the top of Brace Mountain with wide-open vistas on an open, mostly grassy summit. Backtrack.

2.5 Take the unsigned but well-used and well-maintained old Riga Road southeast, descending sharply on what becomes an ultra-stony track. Reenter Connecticut into Mount Riga, Inc. land, open to the public.

2.9 Step over a tributary of Monument Brook. The track becomes grassy and moderate.

3.5 Cross another tributary of Monument Brook. Gently rise. The trail is ridiculously easy compared to the first 2 miles of the hike.

4.0 Reach Mount Washington Road at an alternate parking area. Head left on the gravel road.

5.0 Pass the Bear Mountain Trail. Keep straight.

5.2 Arrive back at the trailhead after passing the large parking area just before returning to Massachusetts, a three-state trek under your belt.

30 SAGES RAVINE AND BEAR ROCK FALLS

This highly recommended hike uses the fabled Appalachian Trail to wander through cascade- and waterfall-rich Sages Ravine in Mount Washington State Forest, to then curve along the sharp rim of Mount Plantain to finally find Bear Rock Falls, tumbling hundreds of feet off the mountain edge, arguably the tallest cataract in Massachusetts. While here, savor distant panoramas east from a rugged outcrop adjacent to the falls' drop-off. Your return trip will reveal more unseen scenic treasures in Sages Ravine. Campers take note: On the way, you'll pass a cabin operated by the Appalachian Mountain Club as well as the designated Sages Ravine campsite and Laurel Ridge backcountry campsite, situated not far from Bear Rock Falls.

Start: Northwest Cabin parking area
Distance: 5.6 miles out and back
Difficulty: Moderate
Elevation change: +/-674 feet over entire hike
Maximum grade: 16% grade for 0.3 mile
Hiking time: About 3 hours
Seasons/schedule: Year-round
Fees and permits: None
Dog friendly: Yes
Trail surface: Natural surface
Land status: AMC club land open to public, state forest

Nearest town: Great Barrington
Other trail users: None
Map to consult: Mount Washington State Forest
Amenities available: None
Cell service: Iffy at trailhead and Sages Ravine, better on Bear Rock overlook
Trail contact: Mount Washington State Forest, (413) 528-0330, www.mass.gov/locations/mount -washington-state-forest

FINDING THE TRAILHEAD

To reach the Northwest Cabin parking area from Great Barrington, take MA 41 south 4.5 miles then split right, joining Mount Washington Road. Follow Mount Washington Road (which becomes East Street along the way) for a total of 11.5 miles, passing the Mount Frissell trailhead on the right. The parking area is on the left, just after crossing into Connecticut. Do not block the gate. Also, overnight parking is not allowed. **Trailhead GPS:** 42.049386, -73.466950

THE HIKE

Philosophers may argue the question "What is better: the journey or the destination?" The answer for this hike is a resounding "Both!" For on this trek you traverse gorgeous Sages Ravine en route to your ultimate goal—Bear Rock Falls and the view-rich outcrop beside the cataract. Consider turning this adventure into an overnight experience. There is a Connecticut Appalachian Mountain Club (AMC) cabin for rent early in the hike as well as two designated Appalachian Trail (AT) campsites, one in Sages Ravine and the other on Mount Plantain, a short piece away from Bear Rock Falls.

A tributary stream jumps into Sages Ravine.

Speaking of Bear Rock Falls, its absolute height is uncertain. The cataract drops off the cliffs of Mount Plantain, making it very difficult if not downright dangerous to reach its base. The water pirouettes in a series of spillers, making it problematic to determine exactly where it ends. Waterfall height estimates range from at least 200 feet to upwards of 400 feet!

The hike follows an Appalachian Trail connector from Mount Washington Road leading east to the Northwest AMC cabin, then onward to meet the AT at the northeast base of Bear Mountain. What became today's Northwest AMC cabin started in 1951 as a simple wood lean-to that evolved into a full-fledged cabin using local chestnut logs. It was named for being in the northwest quadrant of the AMC property here. The retreat, set in a hemlock grove beside a singing little brook, can be rented by visiting the Connecticut AMC website at https://ct-amc.org. (If renting the AMC cabin overnight, parking at the trailhead is allowed.)

Beyond the cabin, the connector meets the Appalachian Trail, and you turn into Sages Ravine, a wooded chasm through which flows a crystalline creek draining Mount Ashley and other peaks to the west. Look for small but picturesque waterfalls in the brook of Sages Ravine as well as on side streams. You will also find small but deep swimming holes, ideal for cooling off a sweaty hiker.

You will then cross the stream of Sages Ravine. When hiking along Berkshires streams and rivers, you will be faced with having to cross a body of water without the benefit of a bridge. Have a strategy for successfully crossing the waterway. For starters, every ford is different. The crossing may be deep, shallow, or some combination of the two. The stream may be flowing fast or slow, or somewhere in between. It may be rocky or have irregular boulders. Water temperature is another variable. In winter, your feet and legs can

SAGES RAVINE AND BEAR ROCK FALLS

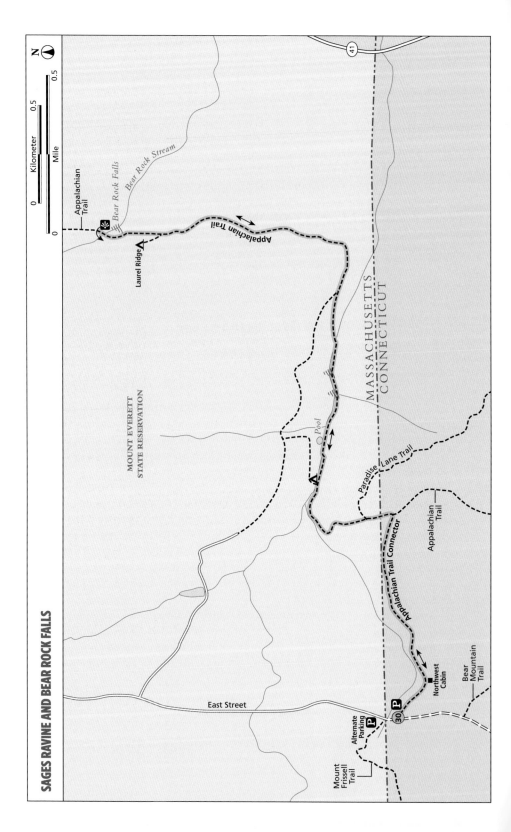

N

Kilometer
0   0.5

Mile
0   0.5

Appalachian
Trail

Bear Rock Falls

Bear Rock Stream

Laurel Ridge

Appalachian Trail

MOUNT EVERETT
STATE RESERVATION

Pool

MASSACHUSETTS
CONNECTICUT

Paradise Lane Trail

Appalachian
Trail

Appalachian Trail Connector

Northwest
Cabin

Bear Mountain
Trail

East Street

Alternate
Parking

30

Mount
Frissell
Trail

go numb before you're back on dry land. Finally, consider water volume. Is the stream flooding? If so, turn back. No hiking adventure is worth endangering your life.

So what are the best techniques for crossing creeks big and small? First, decide whether you can rock-hop the creek or it will necessitate a ford. Whether rock-hopping or fording, trekking poles help you maintain balance. Use a stout stick if you are pole-less. When rock-hopping, assume every rock may be slick. Factor in the weight of your pack when balancing atop a rock. Logs are especially prone to being slick. Be doubly careful when using a log to cross a stream. Logs with bark give better traction than those stripped of bark.

Whether rock/log-hopping or fording, plan out a route all the way across the stream. Remember, the widest parts of the stream are usually the shallowest, and still waters run deep. Therefore, go for the wider moving waters rather than narrower deep pools. While fording, face upstream to brace against the current, keeping at least two points on the stream bottom at all times—either one foot and one trekking pole or both feet. Try to pick the route with the least depth change. Go for gravelly or small-rock stream bottoms rather than open, slippery stone slabs or singular big boulders.

I often cross sans shoes. Sometimes I use a pair of sandals for stream crossings, but usually go barefooted if I want to keep my shoes dry, especially if I have but one or two total crossings for the entire trip, like this trip to Bear Rock Falls. Tie your shoe laces together and hang your shoes around your neck before crossing. On the other hand, if I have numerous crossings I wear hiking shoes I don't mind getting wet and staying wet the entire trip, crossing in shoes and socks every crossing. Having a strategy for successful creek crossings will help you have a successful hike.

Beyond the stream of Sages Ravine enter xeric deciduous woods dominated by chestnut oak, and work north through boulder-strewn woods, making your way along the eastern rim of Mount Plantain, where it drops precipitously to the greater Housatonic Valley. Views can be had through the trees. Ahead you will cross a small stream, then pass the spur trail to Laurel Ridge backcountry campsite. Ahead, you will hear then see Bear Rock Stream.

Head for the watercourse, cross it, then come to the grand easterly vista from the outcrop next to Bear Rock Falls. On a clear day it seems you can see to Boston! You can also peer down on Bear Rock Falls as the ribbon of white loudly crashes down, down, down, out of sight. Scaling down the drop-off to the base of Bear Rock Falls is not recommended. This area has been closed to camping. Enjoy the return trip back.

MILES AND DIRECTIONS

0.0 Leave the AMC parking lot, passing around an auto gate. Take the Appalachian Trail connector east in ferny woods.

0.2 Come to a stream with the AMC Northwest Cabin within sight on the other side of the brook. Continue east, skirting the steepening north slope of Bear Mountain, bridging another streamlet.

0.7 Open onto a flat, then meet the Appalachian Trail. Look back at this intersection, as the AT connector may not be signed on this end. Turn left, northbound on the AT.

0.8 Intersect the Paradise Lane Trail. It leaves right for the Undermountain Trail. We stay straight with the AT, descending hard into Sages Ravine, in birch, hemlock, and striped maple along a small stream. Enter Massachusetts.

Bear Rock Falls begins its descent hundreds of feet off Mount Plantain.

1.1 Saddle alongside the unnamed stream of Sages Ravine, a tributary of Schenob Brook, flowing through the ravine. Yellow birch and evergreens rise over the stream and trail. The path is very rocky and rooty. Take your time and enjoy the scenery.

1.2 Come to the spur trail crossing the stream to the designated Sages Ravine campsite and additional foot trails as well as group campsites. There may or may not be a bridge here to span the creek.

1.3 Pass a gorgeous pool and icy deep swimming hole.

1.5 Come to a side stream that drops off an 8-foot ledge, creating a waterfall as it makes a final drop into the brook of Sages Ravine. Just ahead, find a 10-foot slide fall on the main brook. The trail curves to present a fine upstream view of this chute.

1.7 Cross the main brook of Sages Ravine, sans bridge. This may be a wet ford. Begin the section of the AT managed by the AMC clubs of Massachusetts. Climb away from the brook, leaving Sages Ravine. The vegetation changes instantaneously to oak, mountain laurel, wild azalea, and sassafras.

1.8 An old road-turned-trail cuts acutely left and connects to other nearby trails, including the Sages Ravine campsite access trail. The AT briefly follows the old road then splits left, climbing near boulders and small bluffs on Mount Plantain.

2.5 Step over a small but perennial stream. A little bit ahead, come to the spur trail left to the Laurel Ridge campsite. It offers tent pads, a privy, and a bear-proof food storage box. Water can be had from the stream just crossed.

2.7 Join a spur trail leading right to Bear Rock Stream.

2.8 After crossing the watercourse, head out to the rock overlook delivering unobstructed panoramas to the east. To your right Bear Rock Falls is beginning its nosedive off the edge of Plantain Mountain, 200 feet or more and out of sight. Descending along the falls is not recommended. Backtrack to the trailhead.

5.6 Arrive back at the trailhead, completing the stimulating hike.

31 YORK LAKE LOOP

Enjoy a relaxing afternoon—and take a little hike—at this attractive pond set in sizable Sandisfield State Forest. Here you can picnic at a historic Civilian Conservation Corps (CCC) site, then make a fine circuit along York Lake and upper Sandy Brook, reveling in a woodland walk suitable for the entire family. Then when you return, take a dip at the designated swim beach.

Start: York Lake Picnic Area
Distance: 2.5-mile loop
Difficulty: Easy
Elevation change: +/-175 feet
Maximum grade: 7% grade for 0.2 mile
Hiking time: About 1.5 hours
Seasons/schedule: Year-round
Fees and permits: None
Dog friendly: Yes
Trail surface: Natural surface, has wet spots and boardwalks
Land status: State forest

Nearest town: New Boston
Other trail users: None
Map to consult: York Lake Loop Trail
Amenities available: Restrooms, picnic area, and swim beach at trailhead
Cell service: Okay
Trail contact: Sandisfield State Forest, summer (413) 229-8212, winter (413) 528-0904, www.mass.gov/locations/sandisfield-state-forest-york-lake

FINDING THE TRAILHEAD
To reach the York Loop trailhead from the intersection of MA 8 and MA 57 in New Boston, take MA 57 west for 4.6 miles to New Hartford Road. Turn left and follow New Hartford Road for 1.1 miles, then turn right onto Sandisfield Road and follow it for 2.3 miles to MA 183. Turn right and follow MA 183 for 2.3 miles, then turn right onto East Hill Road. Continue for 0.3 mile, crossing the York Pond Dam, then park on your left at the picnic/swim beach area. **Trailhead GPS:** 42.095614, -73.180677

THE HIKE
Situated inside the 9,500-acre Sandisfield State Forest, the York Lake Loop Trail and attendant facilities are the pride of the forest. Most of the facilities here were built in the 1930s by the 196 Company of the CCC, whose camp was located just south of what became York Lake. Part of decidedly rural Sandisfield town, York Lake, elevation 1,544 feet, provides a near-ideal Berkshire getaway where you can reconnect with nature by not only taking a family hike, but also partaking of the other facilities available at the trailhead, namely the picnic area, canoe and kayak launch, and swim beach. Bring your canoe or kayak and paddle the no-motors-allowed 35-acre lake, maybe even toss in a line for trout or largemouth bass. Trout are stocked in the lake during spring.

The hike itself is fine. Even Goldilocks of fairy tale lore would like the York Lake Loop Trail—it is not too short, nor too long, nor too steep, nor too flat, nor too hard, nor too easy and traverses a number of habitats from hummocky deep woods to marshy wetlands to open shorelines, fern glades, and piney woods. Though the trail does wind through marshy areas, numerous plank boardwalks have been laid out to keep your feet

A beaver lodge on York Lake

dry. Furthermore, the loop is a Massachusetts–designated Healthy Heart Trail, meaning it delivers enough exercise to keep your ticker pumping as designed.

You'll first pass directly by the swim beach, tempting on a hot summer's day. A grassy lawn overlooks the lakeside sand. The actual swim area is roped off by buoys, followed by lakeside picnic areas. (Another picnic spot is at the trailhead parking area.) After entering the woods, you will encounter occasional spring-fed streams feeding York Lake. When turning over their lands to Sandisfield State Forest, the Hoyt family expressly desired to have these springs preserved. Other properties were purchased from the Joyner and Willet clans, as well as the New England Box Company. Sandisfield State Forest came to be in 1926.

Continuing north up the east side of York Lake, you will cross more intermittent drainages in lumpy, hummocky woods of beech, birch, hemlock, and maple. The hiking at times is similar to snow skiing through moguls. The next part of the trail is striped with old rock walls. These walls were built using hard labor and a contraption known as a "stone boat." Here's how the process went: A horse pulled a low, flat sled on wood runners, guided by the farmer. When winter's frost upheaval pushed stones and rocks to the surface in a field, the farmer would pry out the bigger rocks with a lever (and good old-fashioned muscle) then load them onto the stone boat. The horse would then pull the stone boat to wherever the stone fence was being built, then the farmer (and perhaps other family members) would place the rocks together, building the wall. Though these

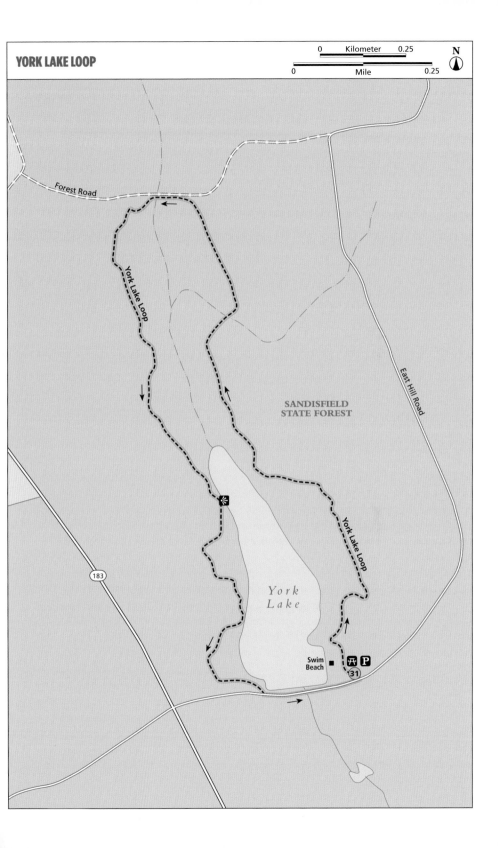

0   Kilometer   0.25

0   Mile   0.25

N

Forest Road

York Lake Loop

East Hill Road

SANDISFIELD
STATE FOREST

183

York Lake Loop

*York
Lake*

Swim
Beach

31

The swim beach at York Lake beckons.

walls were low, they were used not only to place rocks away from a field, but also to contain sheep and lesser farm critters.

Imagine this area as once cropland where potatoes, flax, corn, and rye were grown, and where apple orchards stood. It's all forest now. And like many other places in New England, these hard-won rock walls thread through much of former farmlands returned to forest.

Ahead, the lake is visible through the trees. The trail circles around the upper marsh before reaching a remote forest road, which it then uses to bridge the headwaters of Sandy Brook, at this point a sluggish, slow watercourse. You'll then turn south along the west shoreline of York Lake. Pass through old plantations of red pine, planted by the CCC. The young men even originated the trail upon which we walk. Piney hills run closer to the lake's edge, allowing the path to run closer to the lake, where you can enjoy more views. Look for beaver lodges along the shore. These industrious critters are numerous on York Lake. Other wildlife you may see include otters and waterfowl in season.

Reach a good overlook of open water. Gazing out over York Lake, realize this was formerly a vast swamp, much like the upper reaches of the impoundment are today. The dam built by the CCC raised the water level, fashioning the recreation area in its current incarnation. The trail then alternates between coming near York Lake and working around spring-fed wetlands over which plank boardwalks have been lain. These boardwalks allow you to hike through otherwise impenetrable and/or excessively mucky areas without disturbing the ecosystem.

The trail then pops out on East Hill Road. Begin crossing the dam on the road. This is not the original dam put in by the CCC boys back in 1935. Though it did withstand the downpours of the 1938 Great Hurricane, 1955's Hurricane Donna did it in. The dam you walk over was completed by the state forest, and in 1959 York Lake was reopened. Upon returning to the trailhead, have yourself a picnic, as I have, and even cook out on one of the CCC-built fireplaces, still in use after nearly a century.

MILES AND DIRECTIONS

0.0 From the East Lake Road parking area, walk through the picnic area toward the swim beach. Soon come along the restroom/changing facilities, then keep north entering woods on the signed York Lake Loop Trail. Make your way past picturesquely placed waterside picnic spots, then enter full-blown woods.

0.2 Bridge a pair of tributaries trickling into York Lake.

0.6 Come very near the upper end of the lake, trekking in pines. Ahead, pass old farmer-built rock walls.

1.1 After working around the lake's upper marsh, emerge on a primitive forest road. This is the hike's high point, though you will hardly notice it, since the trek is more level than not. Head left, bridging upper Sandy Brook by culvert.

1.7 Come very near York Lake. Soon find a rewarding lake view where open waters are visible to the south and vegetated marsh to the north. Scan for wildlife. The trail then turns away from the water, traversing wetlands on plank boardwalks.

2.1 Come very near the lake again, before once again turning away and working through wetlands on plank boardwalks. Ferns and viburnum can grow thick here in summer.

2.4 Emerge onto East Hill Road and head left, traveling east across the York Lake Dam. Expansive panoramas of the lake open, as well as of the nearer swim beach.

2.5 Arrive back at the trailhead, completing the hike. However, your recreation opportunities are far from done here. Consider swimming, fishing, paddling, or picnicking, making a day of it at York Lake.

32 **CLAM RIVER PRESERVE**

Take a walk on the watery side at this private preserve open to the public. Your hike first saddles along the Buck River, a tributary of the Clam River. Next, turn up the Clam, enjoying deep woods hiking in riverside flats where farms once held sway, and now anglers are found vying for trout. Make a surprise climb to a hilltop, circling around wetlands before dropping back to the river. Here, travel along pools and rapids encapsulated in a rugged mini-gorge. Loop back on quiet Hammertown Road before returning to a foot trail, finding an old home site with a strange cellar hole. The final part of the hike backtracks to the trailhead.

Start: Sandisfield Town Hall Annex
Distance: 6.1-mile double loop connected by an out-and-back
Difficulty: Moderate
Elevation change: +/-752 feet over entire hike
Maximum grade: 17% grade for 0.3 mile
Hiking time: About 3 hours
Seasons/schedule: Best from May through Nov, open year-round
Fees and permits: None
Dog friendly: Yes

Trail surface: Forested natural surface, often old roads
Land status: Private preserve open to public
Nearest town: New Boston
Other trail users: None
Map to consult: Clam River–Berkshire Natural Resources Council
Amenities available: None
Cell service: Good
Trail contact: Berkshire Natural Resources Council, (413) 449-0596, www.bnrc.org

FINDING THE TRAILHEAD

From the intersection of MA 8 and MA 57 in New Boston, take MA 57 west for 2.1 miles to turn right into the Sandisfield Town Hall Annex. The signed trailhead is on the east side of the annex building at woods' edge. Address: 66 Sandisfield Rd., Sandisfield, MA. **Trailhead GPS:** 42.108142, -73.108217

THE HIKE

When English colonists of early Massachusetts spread westward from the coast, they encountered increasingly rocky and less-arable ground, especially in the stone-pocked, hilly—and beautiful—Berkshires. Back then, settlers had an eye for arable lands, and the flats around the confluence of the Clam and Buck Rivers proved to be a find among these mountainous domains. And with dogged New England pluck, farmsteads were carved out of these possessions that once belonged to the Mohicans. The Clam and Buck Rivers also provided waterpower to run mills. Anglers fishing along the river will find remains of these milldams, only partially intact due to the floods of time.

Later, this land between the rivers was logged, yet after the cutting farmers returned, this time primarily engaging in sheep husbandry, along with growing garden crops. Eventually, the wool market collapsed and the farms were abandoned for good, left to reforest, leaving only relics behind, as the richer, unsettled lands of the Midwest beckoned

Traipsing through the pines and ferns at Clam River Reserve

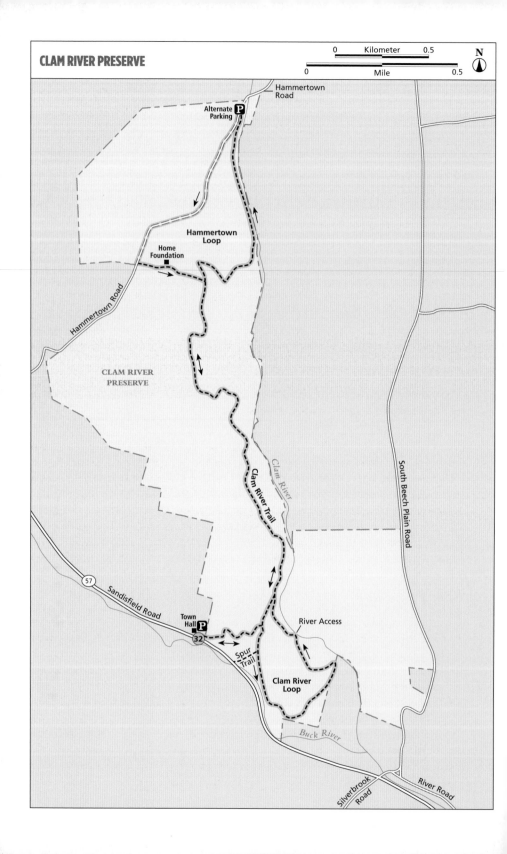

0   Kilometer   0.5

0   Mile   0.5

N

Hammertown Road

Alternate Parking

Hammertown Loop

Home Foundation

Hammertown Road

CLAM RIVER PRESERVE

Clam River Trail

Clam River

South Beech Plain Road

57

Sandisfield Road

Town Hall

32

River Access

Spur Trail

Clam River Loop

Buck River

Silverbrook Road

River Road

The Clam River shoots through a mossy evergreen forest.

the New England hardscrabble farmer. Wildlife returned to the Clam River valley, from trout in its waters to deer and bear roaming the terrain, calling the reforested tracts home.

The Berkshire Natural Resources Council (BNRC) recognized the value of protecting this 550-acre parcel that is Clam River Preserve. Today we can enjoy a hike displaying both the human and natural history of this Berkshire legacy property. From the Sandisfield Town Hall Annex trailhead, you join a singletrack trail, entering deep woods, instantly removed from today's frenetic electronic universe into a natural setting where life syncs with the seasons. Fragrant, regal pines rise high, spreading a golden carpet of needles on the forest floor, shared with oaks and hemlocks. A few upstanding erratic boulders recall the period of glaciation.

The trail forms a ribbon of discovery through the rumpled rocky woods, passing old stone fences and on forgotten farm roads, coming near the Buck River, a tributary of the Clam River, itself a feeder stream of the West Branch Farmington River, which flows south into Connecticut and the Farmington River, ultimately to give up its waters to the Connecticut River. The mighty Connecticut, the longest river in New England at 406 miles, then flows into Long Island Sound.

Next you will come alongside the Clam River, a fine trout stream. The waterway, about 25 feet wide at this point, takes its name from the freshwater mussels found along its bottom. The Clam River and Buck River are stocked with trout each spring by the state of Massachusetts (hunting and fishing are allowed on BNRC lands, in accordance with Massachusetts state game regulations). The shady banks make for a cool angling experience when summer's heat sweeps over the Berkshires.

Checking out the trouty Clam River

The Clam River Trail takes you north on an old road, occasionally detouring around wetlands. Suddenly the pathway climbs to a plateau 200 feet above the Clam River, and you are once again in former farm country, with stone walls lacing the woods. Ahead, join the Hammertown Loop, dropping 200 feet back to the Clam. But it's worth it. Here, the trail takes you along my favorite part of the hike—the part where the path runs along the edge of a stone-walled mini-gorge, with gray rock ramparts hemming in the gamboling waters of the river, strewn with moss-backed boulders. Hemlocks provide shady cover.

Unfortunately, the Berkshires' hemlocks are imperiled by the invasive bug known as the hemlock woolly adelgid. This critter from Asia has reached the United States and is beginning to work over Massachusetts and Connecticut. Hemlocks become infested with these bugs. Their signatures are tiny white "golf balls" on the undersides of hemlock needles. Trees die within five to seven years of infestation. The verdict is still out on the long-term viability of the hemlock, though they can be treated with a soapy insecticide or a ground injection absorbed through the hemlock's roots.

All too soon this segment is over and you turn left onto Hammertown Road, a quiet gravel track allowing you to make a loop. After a short ascent, the Hammertown Loop reenters the preserve, then finds a home site. The foundation, constructed of local stone, is unusual. It has the usual subterranean rock walls but also displays an elevated center, its purpose lost to time. Imagine the area around the home as cleared, with a vegetable garden, perhaps a corn patch, and sheep grazing in the yon. It's all forest now, rich with maples and pines.

Distinguishing between sugar maples and red maples is easy. Look at the leaf of a sugar maple. The curves between lobes of the sugar maple are U-shaped, whereas the curves between lobes of the red maple are at right angles. Massachusetts pioneers used whatever resources they could find in the great forests of the seventeenth and eighteenth centuries. They couldn't go to the grocery and get raw sugar or the myriad forms of artificial sweeteners we take for granted today. If they couldn't grow it or create it, they likely wouldn't have it. Today when looking at a sugar maple, we see a pretty tree producing golden leaves in autumn. The pioneers saw sugar and a trade product.

Even today maple syrup is made in Massachusetts. Over 60,000 gallons are produced each year by 300 maple syrup producers employing over 1,000 farm workers, the vast majority of producers being in the greater Berkshires region. Almost all of Massachusetts's syrup is sold within the Bay State. Massachusetts is the ninth-largest maple-syrup producing state in the Union.

First the sap must be tapped from the maple trees. This is known as the "sugar season." In Massachusetts, the season ranges from late February through March into early April. This is when the sap begins to move through the tree; it is collected in buckets (though hoses are used in the modern process) then boiled, removing the excess water, at the "sugar house," typically an on-site building where the sap is processed. The liquid is then lowered to a precise temperature before being put in containers. You then have not only good stuff for pancakes, but also a means to flavor sweet treats, make candy, and produce granulated maple sugar. The person who lived at the home site might've made a little maple sugar.

The final part of the hike stays in woods, finishing the Hammertown Loop then backtracking along the Clam River, before returning to the town hall annex, completing the trek.

MILES AND DIRECTIONS

0.0 Leave east from the Sandisfield Town Hall Annex, immediately joining the single-track Clam River Loop, rolling through pines.

0.3 Split right on the Clam River Loop. Pass the first of many rock walls from farms two centuries back. Ahead, a short spur trail splits right to MA 57, Sandisfield Road. Continue on an old woods road. Buck River comes into view, running clear in pools and shoals.

0.5 The Clam River Loop leaves left from the old roadbed, and within the property confines toward the Clam River.

0.9 The Clam River comes into view. Run parallel to the waterway, heading upstream.

1.1 Return to the Clam River. This is a good point to access the waterway.

1.3 Complete the Clam River Loop. Keep straight, north, joining the Clam River Trail, briefly climbing to a rise above the waterway. Rapids of the Clam drift into your ears.

2.0 Make a sharp climb uphill, leveling out on a plateau after a quarter mile. Keep north.

2.5 Head right on the Hammertown Loop. The path drops for the Clam River, descending 200 feet in 0.4 mile. Turn left and head up the fern-and-stone-flanked waterway.

3.3 Just after coming near an old home site, turn left onto quiet, gravel Hammertown Road. Make a gentle rise on the road, passing a small alternate parking area with room for two or three vehicles.

4.0 Leave left from Hammertown Road, passing around a pole gate and continuing the balance of the Hammertown Loop on a grassy doubletrack before entering full-blown woods, back on the plateau above the river.

4.1 Come to the signed home site, with its unusual foundation intact. Continue on the plateau.

4.5 Complete the Hammertown Loop. Head right, backtracking on the Clam River Trail.

5.7 Split right on the Clam River Loop.

5.8 Complete the Clam River Loop. Backtrack toward the trailhead.

6.1 Arrive back at the trailhead, completing the hiking adventure.

CONNECTICUT BERKSHIRES

Bulls Bridge Hike, page 226

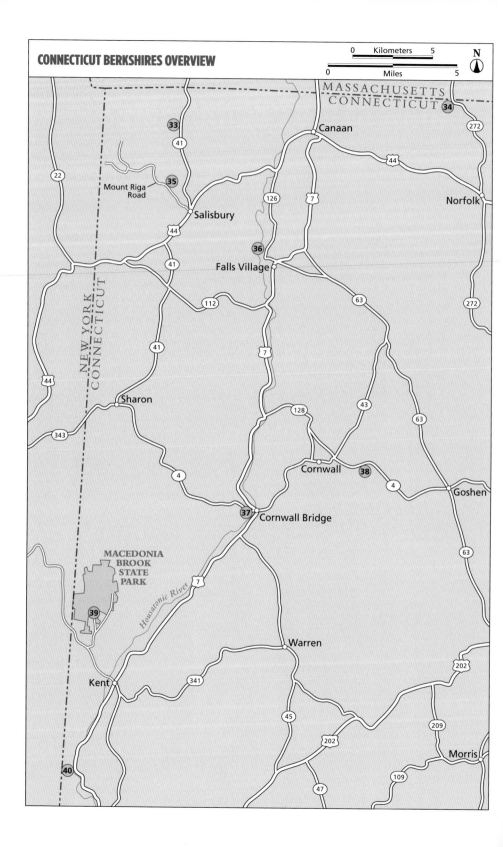

0   Kilometers   5

0   Miles   5

N

MASSACHUSETTS
CONNECTICUT

34

272

33

41

Canaan

44

22

35

Mount Riga
Road

126

7

Norfolk

Salisbury

44

36

41

Falls Village

112

63

272

NEW YORK
CONNECTICUT

41

7

44

Sharon

128

43

343

63

4

Cornwall

38

4

Goshen

37   Cornwall Bridge

63

MACEDONIA
BROOK
STATE
PARK

Housatonic River   7

39

Warren

Kent

341

202

45

209

202

Morris

40

109

47

33 BEAR MOUNTAIN LOOP

This first-rate hike takes you from the bottoms of Moore Brook on the Undermountain Trail into adjacent highlands to meet the Appalachian Trail. From there, climb onward and upward to Bear Mountain, elevation 2,316 feet, replete with incredible views and a rock-piled top, as well as bragging rights as the tallest mountain entirely within Connecticut. Drop precipitously from the Bear Mountain summit on open rock slabs. Enter Massachusetts then quickly return to Connecticut, joining the Paradise Lane Trail, much of which is paradise (for mountain hiking), gently rolling near highland bogs. After passing a camping area, rejoin the Undermountain Trail, returning to the trailhead.

Start: Undermountain Road trailhead
Distance: 6.1-mile lollipop
Difficulty: Difficult due to elevation gain
Elevation change: +/-1,788 feet over entire hike
Maximum grade: 29% downhill grade for 0.3 mile
Hiking time: About 4 hours
Seasons/schedule: Mid-May through Nov
Fees and permits: None
Dog friendly: Yes
Trail surface: Forested natural surface

Land status: State park, National Park Service Appalachian Trail corridor, state forest in Massachusetts
Nearest town: Salisbury
Other trail users: None
Map to consult: Connecticut Appalachian Mountain Club–Bear Mountain trail map
Amenities available: Restrooms and picnic table at trailhead
Cell service: Better on the ridgetop
Trail contact: Connecticut Appalachian Mountain Club, www.ct-amc.org

FINDING THE TRAILHEAD

From the intersection of US 44 and CT 41 in Salisbury, take CT 41/Undermountain Road north for 3.3 miles to the Undermountain Trail parking area on your left. Despite it being a large lot, the trailhead can be packed, therefore be courteous when parking. **Trailhead GPS:** 42.028697, -73.428918

THE HIKE

The northwest corner of the Constitution State, in my opinion, has the finest hiking in Connecticut. The Connecticut Berkshires are a land of superlatives—highest mountain entirely in the state, only area of peaks exceeding 2,000 feet, and home to the state's stretch of the Appalachian Trail (AT). You will experience all three superlatives on this hike that challenges right off the bat.

Bear Mountain was long thought to be the highest point in Connecticut until the United States Geological Survey came measuring in the 1940s. Though it is the highest mountain entirely within the state, the part of Connecticut along the slope of Mount Frissell (directly on the border with Massachusetts) is actually 64 feet higher. Five states may be seen from Bear Mountain on a clear day: Connecticut, Massachusetts, New York, New Hampshire, and Vermont.

Five states can be seen from Bear Mountain.

You will certainly notice the rock monument atop Bear Mountain. The mountain purportedly is so named because it was the last spot a black bear was killed in the state. The loss of wooded bruin habitat drove the bears from Connecticut, but with so many farms abandoned in New England and New York in the 1800s, mostly due to westward migration, the forests grew back and by the 1980s bears were being sighted once again in the Constitution State. In 2020 more than 8,500 bear sightings were reported to the Connecticut Department of Energy and Environmental Protection. Sightings were most numerous in the northwest, but reports came from all but a few towns along the coast and the far east of the state. Resident bears in Connecticut still number under 1,000, but are on the rise.

So maybe the monument atop Bear Mountain should be rededicated to the reappearance of bears in these parts. But to see the monument, you first have to hike there. The Undermountain Trail is your first leg. It leaves west from Undermountain Road, and you begin a 1,562-foot climb in 2.6 miles to the summit of Bear Mountain. Oaks, mountain laurel, and pines shade the track as you escalate into highlands.

You might even see some regenerating chestnut trees here. The American chestnut tree was once the dominant giant of the Appalachians. This tree formerly ranged from Maine to Mississippi, with Pennsylvania and West Virginia the heart of its range. The fruit of this tree was very important. Chestnut acorns were the staple food for everything from bears to birds. Of course, humans ate them, too. Remember the words from the Christmas carol, "Chestnuts roasting on an open fire"?

The tree also provided some of the best wood for everyday use by pioneers. It was also coveted by the timber companies, which harvested the giants. Just as the days of settlers

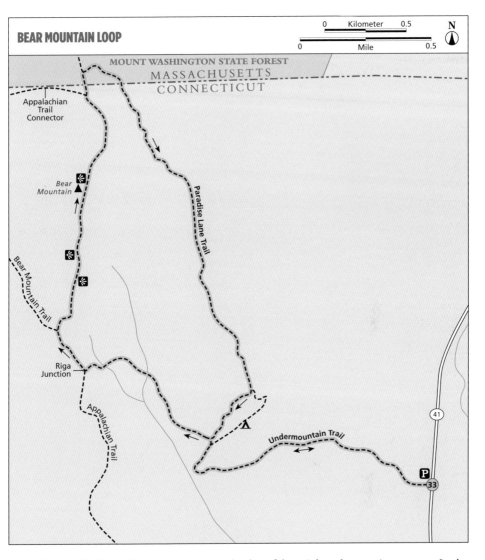

0   Kilometer   0.5   N

0   Mile   0.5

MOUNT WASHINGTON STATE FOREST

MASSACHUSETTS

CONNECTICUT

Appalachian
Trail
Connector

Bear
Mountain

Paradise Lane Trail

Bear Mountain Trail

Riga
Junction

Appalachian Trail

Undermountain Trail

41

P

33

clearing the Berkshire forests are gone, the day of the mighty chestnut is gone, too. In the early 1900s, Asian chestnut trees were imported to the United States, bringing a fungus with them. The Asian trees had developed immunity to the fungus, but the American chestnut was helpless. Before long, chestnuts were dying in the Northeast, and the blight worked its way south. Two decades later, the giant chestnuts were fallen.

But there is hope. To this day, chestnut trees sprout from the roots of the ancients, growing up but always succumbing to the blight. Hopefully, these chestnuts are building a resistance to the blight and will one day tower over the mountains again, long after we are gone. Scientists are expediting this process, and experiments are under way to graft American chestnut trees with the Asian chestnuts in an effort to develop a blight-resistant American chestnut.

The hike continues after passing the Paradise Lane Trail. Contour along the side of the stony mountain. Work past a few wet trail segments, passing a second smaller stream and

Looking east toward the Twin Lakes and the lowlands

a last chance for water for a while. Join the AT at Riga Junction. The climb steepens, and you run the ridgeline ever upward.

Views begin to open back to your south amidst squat trees and brush, and on open rock slabs. Then you top out, reaching the unmistakable remains of the rock monument at the summit. You will see an 1885 inscription stating that this is the highest ground in Connecticut. The stone structure, built by Owen Travis Mason, was the base of a small tower that subsequently collapsed. The tower was once visible from the lowlands. Repairs to the stone shrine have been attempted in the past, but you see what you see. Visitors climbing the rocks plus winter at 2,000 feet have taken their toll.

Nevertheless, the views are rewarding. Claim your five states seen from here. My favorite panoramas are to the north and northeast, though you can see Twin Lakes and agricultural fields to the east as well. The subsequent downhill is steep. Be careful navigating the angled stone slabs. After carefully working the descent, join the Paradise Lane Trail, amidst evergreens on a needle-covered track. Parts of the path skirt around bogs, and other areas have a rock base over which you trammel.

Much of the trail remains level, thus earning its name. Before you know it, the Paradise Trail ends. From here, it is a simple backtrack to the trailhead—all downhill.

MILES AND DIRECTIONS

0.0 Hike west from the parking area on the singletrack Undermountain Trail.

0.7 Skirt the base of a rocky slope rising sharply to your right.

1.1 Meet the Paradise Lane Trail just after passing the spur to a group campsite. The Paradise Lane Trail is your return route. For now, stay left with the Undermountain Trail, still climbing in xeric woods of pine, chestnut oak, mountain laurel, and maple.

1.6 Step over a small stream in rocky woods, then pass a second small brook.

1.8 Meet the Appalachian Trail at a spot known as Riga Junction. Head right, northbound on the AT in a corridor of sassafras, red maple, and witch hazel.

2.0 The Bear Mountain Trail heads left for Mount Washington Road. Stay right with the AT. Stone steps aid your climb into wind-stunted vegetation.

2.2 Enjoy views back to your south and west as you climb.

2.3 An open rock slab delivers westerly views.

2.7 Reach the piney peak of Bear Mountain. Savor the views, then begin a steep descent over angled stone slabs.

3.1 The trail eases up, sloping less amidst woods, then reaches a connector trail leaving left to Mount Washington Road. Keep straight on the AT, briefly entering Massachusetts.

3.2 Intersect the Paradise Lane Trail, curving east and south along the lower slopes of Bear Mountain.

3.6 Skirt around a bog, though the trail remains on rock. Scads of mountain laurel and ferns spread along the forest floor.

4.7 The spur to the group camp splits left. Stay right with the Paradise Lane Trail.

5.0 Complete the loop portion of the hike. Backtrack on the Undermountain Trail.

6.1 Arrive back at the trailhead on Undermountain Road, completing the challenging hike.

34 CAMPBELL FALLS

This short and easy trek leads you to not-to-be-missed 48-foot Campbell Falls. Here, the Whiting River finds a seam in an angled cliff, plunging over stone and bouncing off rocks then spilling over lesser ledges within the overall descent, making one final angled slide before the white froth ceases in a smallish plunge pool bordered with rocks where you can sit and observe the charming spiller.

Start: Spaulding Road trailhead
Distance: 1.0 mile out and back
Difficulty: Easy
Elevation change: +/-202 feet over entire hike
Maximum grade: 11% grade for 0.2 mile
Hiking time: About 0.5 hour
Seasons/schedule: Year-round
Fees and permits: None
Dog friendly: Yes
Trail surface: Forested natural surface

Land status: State park
Nearest town: Norfolk
Other trail users: None
Map to consult: Campbell Falls State Park Reserve
Amenities available: Picnic tables at trailhead
Cell service: Good
Trail contact: Campbell Falls State Park Reserve, (860) 482-1817, https://portal.ct.gov/DEEP/State-Parks/Reserves/Campbell-Falls-State-Park-Reserve

FINDING THE TRAILHEAD

From the intersection of US 44 and CT 272 on the north side of Norfolk, head north on CT 272 and follow it for 4.1 miles to Spaulding Road. Turn left and follow Spaulding Road for 0.2 mile to the Campbell Falls State Park Reserve parking area on your right. **Trailhead GPS:** 42.042302, -73.226384

THE HIKE

Consistently rated as one of the most scenic waterfalls in all of New England, much less the Berkshires, Campbell Falls is a sight to behold. And being a short trek, you have no excuse not to see it in person. If the mileage is too short for you, simply tack on another hike to your adventure agenda for that day.

Yet, the scenery of Campbell Falls will more than reward the minimal effort to reach it. Interestingly, though the trail to Campbell Falls starts in Connecticut, at Campbell Falls State Park Reserve, the actual waterfall is inside the Massachusetts border—just barely.

And the state line between Massachusetts and Connecticut has been in dispute since the days they were both English colonies. It all started when a pair of incompetent sailors named Solomon Saffery and Nathaniel Woodward delineated an error-filled boundary in 1642, making the boundary way too far south into Connecticut, which resurveyed the east–west boundary line in 1695. Of course, Massachusetts was unhappy with the 1695 line, since they lost territory, and protested the result. Therefore, surveyors from both colonies went out in 1702 and confirmed the 1695 boundary, yet Massachusetts clung to the favorable 1642 results.

Money talks, and finally Connecticut sold the disputed territory to Massachusetts. Problem was, the towns in that area wanted to stay with Connecticut, due to lower taxes.

Campbell Falls is one of the most picturesque cataracts in the Berkshires.

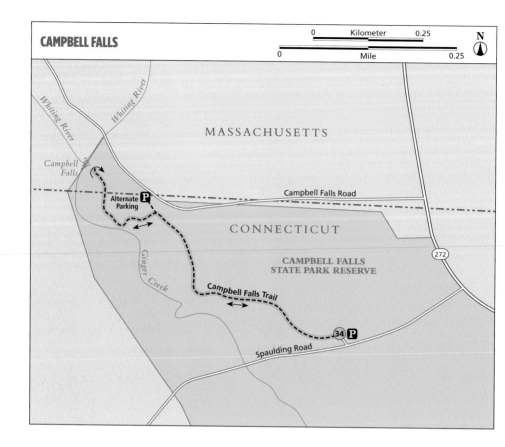

Kilometer 0 0.25

Mile 0 0.25

N

MASSACHUSETTS

Whiting River

Whiting River

Campbell Falls

Alternate Parking **P**

Campbell Falls Road

CONNECTICUT

272

Ginger Creek

CAMPBELL FALLS
STATE PARK RESERVE

Campbell Falls Trail

34 **P**

Spaulding Road

(Massachusetts was known for its high taxes even in the early 1700s!) In 1801, the two states finally settled their boundaries for good, with the southern edge of the town of Westfield remaining with Massachusetts, leaving what is known as the Southwick Jog, disturbing the east–west state line to this day. This jog is south of Southwick, Massachusetts, and north of Granby, Connecticut.

So, who knows in what state Campbell Falls may have ended up in if this interstate squabble had been settled another way? But there is no disputing the scenic splendor of Campbell Falls. It is worthy of being rated one of the best cataracts in the Berkshires or New England. The area near the base of the cataract is further enhanced by being adjacent to a 45-acre tract owned by the Berkshires Natural Resources Council, keeping this area just a little wilder, as the council tract forms a natural buffer, availing additional access to the Whiting River downstream of Campbell Falls, especially appreciated by anglers. By the way, the Whiting River is a tributary of the Housatonic River, Connecticut's master mountain waterway. The Whiting's headwaters flow off Woodruff Mountain east of New Marlborough in Massachusetts.

The hike starts at a parking area on Spaulding Road, complete with picnic tables in sun and shade. The path travels through a grassy area before entering tall woods, heavy with white pines, dropping their needles to fashion a golden carpet and perfuming the air with the pleasing aroma.

Eastern white pines, in my opinion, are the most regal of all the evergreens. They range throughout the Massachusetts and Connecticut Berkshires, and for that matter throughout New England, northeast into Canada and west to Minnesota. White pines stretch down the spine of the Appalachians all the way to Georgia. Arguably the most valuable timber tree of them all, they are so honored in Maine as to be the state tree. Old-growth white pines can rise up to 150 feet in height, with trunk diameters 4 feet across. Early American mariners prized the white pine as a straight, tall mast, leading to it being an early export to England, where it is known as the Weymouth pine. Commercially, white pine is used to make furniture, flooring, trim, and paneling, along with other millwork and construction uses.

And sometimes white pines simply shade a hiking trail. The pine needle path winds down along Ginger Creek, a tributary of the Whiting River, then meets a spur trail coming off Campbell Falls Road in Massachusetts. Next, the trail itself enters the Bay State, then levels out in a big flat with more white pines, into which Campbell Falls tumbles 48 picturesque feet. This flat presents ample room for lots of waterfall enthusiasts.

Waterfall photographers take note that this cataract faces south, thus can get a lot of sunlight in midday. Therefore, the best times to photograph Campbell Falls are early in the morning and in late afternoon. Luckily, a heavy tree cover keeps the waterfall decently shaded. The plunge pool is a little smallish, but deep enough to dip yourself when a summertime heat wave spreads over the Berkshires. And being a short hike makes a trip here in winter very doable—creating another time you could photograph this pourover splashing down while bordered in layers of water spray frozen onto adjacent rocks, and icicles finding their place in this amphitheater of primeval exquisiteness.

MILES AND DIRECTIONS

0.0 Leave the Campbell Falls State Park Reserve parking area, heading northwest through a brushy meadow to enter forest and cross a small brook. Maples, oaks, and ferns lie under tall pines. Step over intermittent streambeds draining the hill to your right.

0.4 A spur trail comes in on your right from Massachusetts and Campbell Falls Road. Stay left. The descent steepens. Ahead, pass a concrete post marking the Massachusetts-Connecticut state line.

0.5 Reach Campbell Falls in a deep valley, where Ginger Creek flows into the Whiting River. Here, the Whiting River makes its deep dive from an angled ledge. Various user-created trails fan out in several directions. Backtrack to the trailhead.

1.0 Arrive back at the trailhead, completing the short but highly rewarding waterfall hike.

35 LIONS HEAD VIEW

This short, easy, and rewarding hike starts off with a fine meadow view then leads along old farm roads turned paths to meet the Appalachian Trail. From there, make a final climb to a rocky knob with a first-rate panorama. The first part of the hike weaves around houses and private property, then you are suddenly in the back of beyond. Next thing you know, the stone perch of the Lions Head is within your grasp. And after scanning outward from the outcrop, you will agree the prize far outweighs the effort to reach this vista.

Start: Bunker Hill Road parking area
Distance: 2.4 miles out and back
Difficulty: Easy; does have steady climb second half of hike
Elevation change: +/-611 feet over entire hike
Maximum grade: 16% grade for 0.3 mile
Hiking time: About 1.5 hours
Seasons/schedule: Year-round
Fees and permits: None
Dog friendly: Yes

Trail surface: Forested natural surface, some rock
Land status: National Park Service Appalachian Trail corridor
Nearest town: Salisbury
Other trail users: None
Map to consult: CT Blue-Blazed Hiking Trails Interactive Map
Amenities available: None
Cell service: Good
Trail contact: Appalachian National Scenic Trail, (304) 535-6278, www .nps.gov/appa

FINDING THE TRAILHEAD

From the intersection of US 44 and CT 41 in Salisbury, head south on US 44 west for 0.1 mile, then turn right on Factory-Washinee Road and stay with it for 1.5 miles as it eventually first becomes Factory Street then Bunker Hill Road. Look for the narrow entrance to a gravel parking lot on your right. The parking area is limited. If you can't get in the lot, do not park on the side of the road. An alternate trailhead for this hike is on Undermountain Road/CT 41, 0.7 mile north of its intersection with US 44 in Salisbury. **Trailhead GPS:** 41.998836, -73.438000

THE HIKE

Have you ever wanted to take a lesser-able friend on a hike to a rewarding destination? Maybe you've considered a waterfall or an overlook, or a historic site? The Lions Head provides such a place. The panorama from the overlook is first-rate, presenting an open vista down to and beyond the Housatonic Valley, seemingly all the way to Rhode Island. Yet the hike to the Lions Head is not too difficult for older or younger or less-fit hikers. But they will be challenged—a few rocky spots and a short, steep section at the end create just enough work to increase the rewards.

However, exercise caution with children at the Lions Head. The first drop is a doozy. It is this vegetation-less falling away of rock that opens the landscape before you. However, there's enough room on the outcrop and adjacent rocky areas for you to relax and take in the aura of the Lions Head.

Avid hikers are often surprised to hear that Connecticut hosts 51.6 miles of the Appalachian Trail (AT), all in the Connecticut Berkshires. Within this segment, hikers will find

Even dogs love the view from Lions Head.

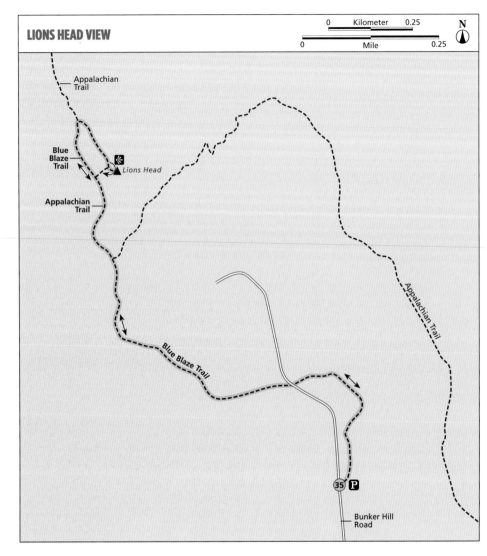

0   Kilometer   0.25   N

0   Mile   0.25

Appalachian Trail

Blue Blaze Trail

Lions Head

Appalachian Trail

Blue Blaze Trail

Appalachian Trail

35 P

Bunker Hill Road

seven trail shelters and nine designated campsites available for AT thru-hikers and other overnight enthusiasts. Fires are not allowed at these campsites and shelters. All camping along the Connecticut portion of the AT is at the designated sites and shelters only. The Lions Head is one of over a dozen major overlooks on the Connecticut AT.

Elevations of the AT in Connecticut range from 260 feet to 2,316 feet, the highest point being Bear Mountain and the lowest being along the Housatonic River. Most of the mountains through which the AT travels in the Constitution State were once ore-rich, and as a result iron was forged here. In fact, much of the weaponry used by the Patriots in the Revolutionary War was made in these parts, thus the Connecticut Berkshires are also known as the "Arsenal of the Revolution." Back then trees were cut down by the thousands to make charcoal to run the forges.

By 1930, when the Appalachian Trail was first routed through Connecticut, the trees were on the comeback from fuel cutting and overtaking abandoned farms. A man named

Arthur Perkins promoted the AT, while Ned Anderson actually constructed the original route. By 1979 the Connecticut Chapter of the Appalachian Mountain Club maintained the entire trail through the state, and continues to do so to this day. You may bump into a "ridge runner," a person who helps with trail maintenance and outdoor education, on your hike.

Back when the AT was being laid out in Connecticut, weather predictions were made by looking at the sky. Today we have much better options. Face it, Berkshires hikers live and die with the weather and the seasons. Reveling in the changes, we wait with anticipation as each season unfolds, along with its unique conditions, each potentially threatening in its own way—the storms of spring, the heat and lightning of summer, the first cold blasts of fall, the snows and frigid temperatures of winter.

Knowing the weather when hiking is paramount. Having an idea of what to expect, you can bring gear and clothing appropriate for the predicted situations—or call it off altogether. However, try to play the weather cards you are dealt. Avoid becoming a slave to the weather forecasts, reacting to their declarations as a servant to its master. I call it "weather paralysis," not knowing a course of action when the weather is iffy.

After all, what do you do when there's a 50 percent chance of rain?

Avoid weather paralysis, but be prepared and informed. Know the possibilities and have not only the clothing and gear contingencies covered, but also alternate plans if the weather gets dangerous, especially at an open overlook such as the Lions Head. If you are getting reception, your phone can be your best weather friend. You can get forecasts and even view precipitation radar. However, phones don't always get a signal. I recommend putting a portable weather radio in your pack. They come in small hiker sizes and weights, often with AM/FM radio bands included.

Weather radio broadcasts originate from the National Oceanic and Atmospheric Administration (NOAA), with over 1,000 transmitters stretching throughout the United States. They broadcast 24/7/365 over seven frequencies that require a special transmitter. NOAA not only predicts forthcoming weather, but also gives "short-term" forecasts, which, especially during thunderstorm season, can help you contend with strong, potentially life-threatening storms.

A weather radio also broadcasts sunrise and sunset times, as well as weather averages for the given day, temperatures, and conditions for regional cities. No matter what, check the weather before leaving home. Furthermore, learn weather averages well before embarking on your hike. That way you will be weather wise when setting out on your hike to the Lions Head or some other adventure.

The Lions Head hike first leaves the Bunker Hill parking area on a blue-blazed trail and immediately opens onto a field offering inspiring views to the south where Bunker Hill falls away, revealing Wetauwanchu Mountain just southeast of Salisbury. Enter woods of black birch, paper birch, aspen, and oak. The trail works around private property. Houses are in sight.

After a half mile the trail climbs away from the community on Bunker Hill. Maintain the uptick after joining the AT, northbound for Maine. Ahead, you run into another blue-blazed trail while the AT goes up a very short but rugged rock scramble directly to the Lions Head. Lesser-able hikers should take the blue-blazed trail straight, making an easy ascent to once again meet the AT, then head southbound, where the path opens onto the distinctive outcrop that is the Lions Head.

Enjoying the view from the outcrop that is the Lions Head

And what a view! From the Lions Head you can see the Twin Lakes to the northwest, the Berkshires of Massachusetts, and beyond. To the east drops the Housatonic Valley and the plateau upon which the Housatonic State Forest rises beyond it. To the southeast, it seems you can see—on a clear day—all the way to Long Island Sound.

MILES AND DIRECTIONS

0.0   Leave the Bunker Hill parking area on a blue-blazed trail, passing a view to the south, then enter youngish brushy woods. Soon pass an old home foundation to your left. Drift in and out of woods.

0.3   The blue-blazed trail crosses the private extension of Bunker Hill Road. Enjoy westerly views of the Taconics. Stay on the trail, then reenter woods.

0.4   Cross a small creek by culvert, still on mostly level trail.

0.5   Start climbing in woods, running parallel to a rock wall to your left.

0.7   The blue-blazed trail turns right, north, in very rocky forest.

0.8   Meet the Appalachian Trail as it makes a curve. Stay left with the AT, northbound. Keep climbing in woods.

1.0   The AT turns right and makes a scramble for the Lions Head. You can go this shorter way, but lesser-able hikers should stay straight, making a gentler, more foot-friendly ascent on a blue blazed spur side trail.

1.1   Rejoin the AT. Turn right, southbound.

1.2   Emerge at the Lions Head, reveling in distant panoramas of Connecticut and Massachusetts. Backtrack to the trailhead.

2.4   Arrive back at the trailhead, completing the hike.

36 **RANDS VIEW**

Start near the Great Falls of the Housatonic (a sight in its own right), then follow the Appalachian Trail northbound to Mount Prospect and find a view across the Housatonic Valley. From there, cruise the rim of the mountain to reach the unusual panorama at Rands View, where the Berkshires and beyond display their montane glory from a vast field. Finally, make your way to the unusual stone edifice that is the Giants Thumb, before returning to the trailhead.

Start: Great Falls Reservoir parking area
Distance: 6.2 miles out and back
Difficulty: Moderate
Elevation change: +/-1,099 feet over entire hike
Maximum grade: 14% grade for 0.4 mile
Hiking time: About 3.5 hours
Seasons/schedule: Year-round
Fees and permits: None
Dog friendly: Yes

Trail surface: Forested natural surface
Land status: National Park Service Appalachian Trail corridor
Nearest town: Falls Village
Other trail users: None
Map to consult: National Park Service–Appalachian Trail
Amenities available: None
Cell service: Good
Trail contact: Appalachian National Scenic Trail, (304) 535-6278, www .nps.gov/appa

FINDING THE TRAILHEAD

From the intersection of US 44 and US 7 in North Canaan, take US 44 west for 3 miles, crossing the Housatonic River, then turn left onto Housatonic River Road and follow it for 3 miles to the Great Falls Reservoir parking area on your left. If the lot is full, absolutely do not park on Housatonic River Road. You will be towed. The Appalachian Trail can be found crossing Housatonic River Road just a few feet south of the parking area. **Trailhead GPS:** 41.963702, -73.372231

THE HIKE

Most views had in the Berkshires are from mountain crags and other such overlooks. Rands View presents a different perspective. Although set on the upper slope of a mountain, this vista opens onto a mown meadow sloping downhill, revealing the near wall of Wetauwanchu Mountain to your left and an unnamed mountain to your right, while dead ahead, the void left by the vale of Garnett Brook opens north to a maze of mountains flanking the upper Housatonic River valley.

Though Rands View is the primary highlight of the hike, you will be rewarded from start to finish, with panoramas from Mount Prospect and the hike's turnaround point, the rock formation known as the Giants Thumb. The trailhead parking area is at Great Falls Reservoir Dam, where the Housatonic is slowed before rushing 60 feet over an angled slide. If the water is up and the Housatonic is flowing over the dam and down Great Falls, you are in for a loud and boisterous sight. Trails lead from the trailhead parking area to the base of the falls, should you want to take a look before your Rands View hike. (A portion of the AT just a little south along the river here is one of the few universally accessible segments of the world's most famous footpath.)

The meadow viewing stand that is Rands View

The Great Falls Dam is part of the greater Falls Village Generating Station. Water from the Housatonic River is diverted around the dam and sent down a canal paralleling the river, then is used to generate hydro power. The station and dam were built in 1914, before the Appalachian Trail existed. The operation is currently run by FirstLight Power.

To begin the adventure, we leave the reservoir parking area, then join the Appalachian Trail northbound, climbing past old structures now partly covered by vegetation, an American version of a Mayan ruin. This was part of the old Amesville Iron Works, opened in 1833, which manufactured cannons and cannonballs, train wheels and axles, and boat anchors, among other things. Over time the local iron-ore sources played out and newer methods of forging iron left places like the Amesville Iron Works to decay in wooded obscurity.

We now pass the once-bustling locale with a pondering glance, then emerge onto an open field that the Appalachian Trail crosses. Reenter woods in what was once farmland, passing a spring used by AT thru-hikers. Ahead, watch for an old home site and other evidence of a farming past. You then tramp up the nose of a rocky ridge clad in oaks. The ridge widens and the ascent eases. A final short climb takes you to the rocky crown of Mount Prospect, where an easterly vista awaits, as well as a shaded relaxing rock.

Beyond there, the hike is more downhill than not, as you work along the drop-off of Mount Prospect, then meet a spur trail that leads to the Limestone Spring trail shelter.

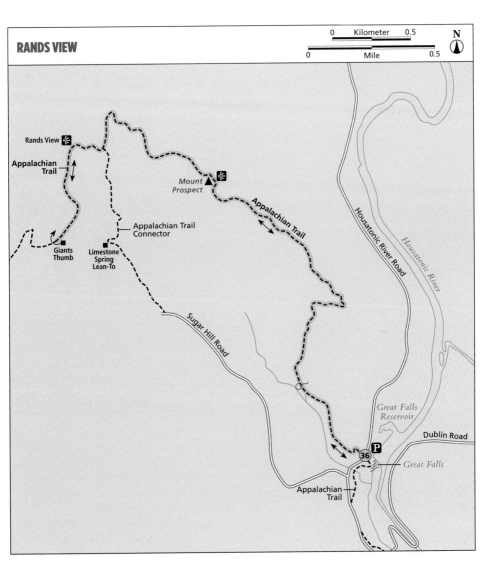

Rands View

Appalachian
Trail

Mount
Prospect

Appalachian Trail

Appalachian Trail
Connector

Giants
Thumb

Limestone
Spring
Lean-To

Sugar Hill Road

Housatonic River Road

Housatonic River

Great Falls
Reservoir

Dublin Road

Great Falls

36

Appalachian
Trail

By the way, the 0.5-mile trail to the lean-to and spring makes a descent (and subsequent climb back out) dreaded by AT thru-hikers tuckered out at the end of a long day. However, the aquatic upwelling is cool and reliable.

After this intersection, descend through woods to run along the edge of a field. Here you find Rands View, opening north across the field, a sublime melding of mountain and meadow and worth every step of the hike. Yet one more highlight lies ahead—the Giants Thumb. It isn't far. Cut through a stony gap of sorts then gently top out on Raccoon Hill, where this strange 8-foot gray stone protrusion bursts from the forest floor like a trail sign. You can't miss it. On your return trip, try to look for other highlights on this fair and fulfilling trek in the Connecticut Berkshires.

Looking into the Housatonic Valley from Mount Prospect

MILES AND DIRECTIONS

0.0 Leave the Great Falls Reservoir parking area and walk south a few feet, then cross the road to join the Appalachian Trail northbound. Climb into cedars, vines, and brush, shortly coming up to the ruins of the old Amesville Iron Works.

0.1 Open onto a field bordered by sumac and white pine. Return to woods.

0.4 Come to a piped spring to the right of the trail shortly after crossing the outflow of the spring. Keep weaving upward in pines and hardwoods.

0.6 Curve past an old home site to your left.

1.0 Turn up the nose of the ridge leading directly to the top of Mount Prospect.

1.8 Reach the crest of Mount Prospect. Here, a cleared view opens east across the Housatonic Valley to Bradford Mountain and the Housatonic State Forest. A nearby shaded rock outcrop makes for a well-used relaxing place.

2.5 Meet the spur trail to Limestone Spring shelter. It heads south to a refuge and water. We stay with the AT, descending rapidly.

2.7 Open onto Rands View. Here, a mountain meadow slopes away to reveal the Berkshires in all their glory. Shortly reenter woods and climb a bit.

3.1 Reach the unmistakable Giants Thumb to the left of the trail. It's a trailside photo opportunity few pass up. Backtrack to the trailhead.

6.2 Arrive back at the trailhead, completing the hike.

37 PINE KNOB LOOP

The Pine Knob Loop is a Connecticut Berkshires hiking tradition. And deservedly so, for on this circuit you travel a picturesque trail leading to multiple overlooks delivering montane postcard panoramas across the Housatonic River valley. And you also get to enjoy a waterfall. This particular hike adds to the Pine Knob Loop by starting on the Mohawk Trail to savor a fine view from Bread Loaf Mountain. Next join the Appalachian Trail, then connect to the Pine Knob Loop, making a good thing even better.

Start: US 7 parking area near Cornwall Bridge
Distance: 6.5-mile lollipop
Difficulty: Moderate to difficult due to elevation changes
Elevation change: +/-2,063 feet over entire hike
Maximum grade: 22% downhill grade for 0.5 mile
Hiking time: About 4 hours
Seasons/schedule: May through early Dec
Fees and permits: None
Dog friendly: Yes
Trail surface: Forested natural surface

Land status: State park
Nearest town: Cornwall Bridge
Other trail users: None
Map to consult: Housatonic Meadows State Park
Amenities available: None at trailhead; picnic area and restrooms north on US 7 at state park
Cell service: Good
Trail contact: Housatonic Meadows State Park, (860) 927-3238, https://portal.ct.gov/DEEP/State-Parks/Parks/Housatonic-Meadows-State-Park

FINDING THE TRAILHEAD

From the intersection of CT 4 and US 7 in Cornwall Bridge, take CT 4/US 7 west across the bridge over the Housatonic River, then after 0.2 mile split right with US 7 and immediately look for the Mohawk Trail parking area on your left.
Trailhead GPS: 41.821525, -73.375943

THE HIKE

Entrenched deep in a steep gorge from which rise craggy mountains, Housatonic Meadows has been a Connecticut state park tradition for nearly a century. And it seems that every outdoor enthusiast in the Berkshires has a camping, fishing, paddling, or hiking story that took place in the state park. I even know a guy who buried a time capsule in the park four decades ago and can't remember where he buried it. (Don't do this!)

The beautiful setting is augmented by a desirable campground and picnicking and paddling facilities, along with fine trails enhanced by a segment of the Appalachian Trail (AT) and the Mohawk Trail. Hiking is our thing, and this trek takes you all over the park. After making this loop, perhaps you can set up at the campground, then enjoy some of the finest fly fishing in New England or float your kayak down the waterway. Adventure is the name of the game here at Housatonic Meadows. You can then join the legions who have a Housatonic Meadows State Park story.

This outcrop opens panoramas down to the Houatonic River.

Start at the trailhead on US 7. Take the Mohawk Trail west, uphill, toward its intersection with the Appalachian Trail on a carpet of golden evergreen needles. Make your way up the southeast slope of Bread Loaf Mountain. The terrain becomes rockier and steeper the higher you climb. It is a solid ascent—you are gaining 558 feet in the first 0.7 mile. After summiting Bread Loaf Mountain, you can split left for a southerly view across Guinea Brook to Silver Hill and forested lands to the south and southwest. A fainter trail leads right, downhill and northeast, to a smaller outcrop with a look down into the Housatonic Valley and across the river.

Next you join the Appalachian Trail, northbound on its 1988 reroute, well entrenched by thousands of footfalls as the master path of the East. It works along the slope of the gorge in oaks and other hardwoods. Look in the woods for charcoaling locations—level spots on the mountain slope where colliers cut and burned wood very slowly, usually covering the smoldering fires with dirt, to create charcoal for use in ironworks. Cornwall Bridge Iron Company operated along the Housatonic River just south of this hike's trailhead from 1833 to 1897. You can still see the stone remnants of the furnace stacks to this day. Therefore, it is no surprise that these slopes were once timbered, but have since recovered to such a degree that most hikers would never think the area was logged.

Continuing north in the gorge the AT leads past Hatch Brook, then takes you to your next vista at an outcrop above a declivitous drop-off. Here, a panorama opens down the

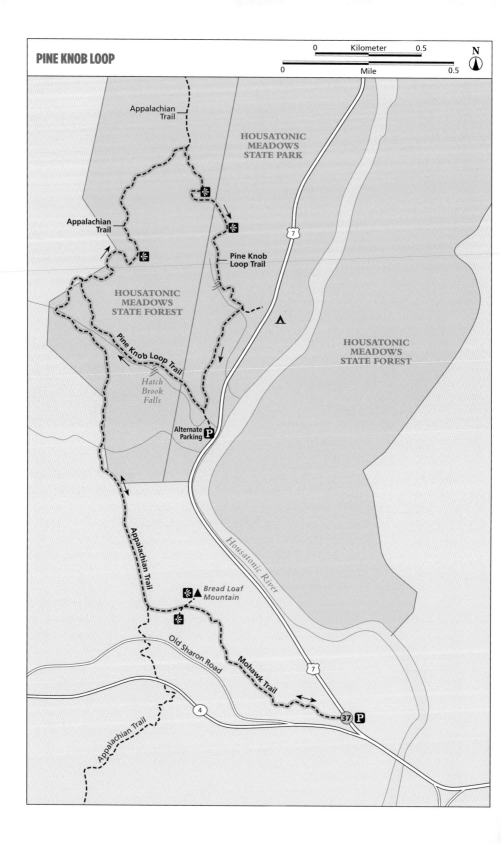

PINE KNOB LOOP

0 Kilometer 0.5

0 Mile 0.5

N

Appalachian Trail

HOUSATONIC MEADOWS STATE PARK

7

Appalachian Trail

Pine Knob Loop Trail

HOUSATONIC MEADOWS STATE FOREST

Pine Knob Loop Trail

HOUSATONIC MEADOWS STATE FOREST

Hatch Brook Falls

Alternate Parking P

Housatonic River

Appalachian Trail

Bread Loaf Mountain

Old Sharon Road

Mohawk Trail

7

4

37 P

Appalachian Trail

You can see why the Pine Knob Loop is a classic Berkshires adventure.

Housatonic Valley and beyond to hills rising southeast of the watercourse. The AT turns away from the slope, then rolls to its next intersection and you join the Pine Knob Loop, going over a stone knob that qualifies as a low-grade rock scramble. But the rewards are great at the next outcrop, where a naked stone slope reveals mountain and river topography that makes overlooks like this worth hiking to.

After you reach the river bottoms, the hiking levels out for a while in rich woods. Next, climb along singing Hatch Brook to visit Hatch Brook Falls. It is not easy to reach the base of the spiller, but if you do, you can get a bottom-up look at the angled 30-foot classic slide cascade. The lesser-flowing stream is more lively from April through June, or after rainstorms. Finally, you climb back to the Appalachian Trail, then backtrack to the Mohawk Trail and conclude the Housatonic Meadows State Park classic hike.

MILES AND DIRECTIONS

- **0.0** From the parking area on US 7, take the Mohawk Trail west and uphill in woods on an old roadbed, roughly paralleling CT 4 just to the south. Quickly pass an old home foundation and spring outflow. Ascend in piney woods.
- **0.7** Reach an outcrop and view to the left of the trail, after topping out on Bread Loaf Mountain.

0.9 Meet the Appalachian Trail. Here, head right and northbound along the inside slope of the Housatonic gorge.

1.4 Cross a small unnamed brook after passing three consecutive charcoal-making flats.

1.8 Turn into the vale of Hatch Brook. Come alongside the stream, gently climbing.

1.9 Rock-hop Hatch Brook. Cross lesser tributaries ahead.

2.0 Meet the Pine Knob Loop. Here, stay straight on the Appalachian Trail, which forms a leg of the circuit. Make a steady climb along a steep slope of the mountain.

2.4 Come to another overlook to the east and south down the Housatonic Valley. Continue with the AT.

2.8 Reach an intersection. The AT keeps straight, Maine-bound, while we split right on the Pine Knob Loop. Just ahead, make a short rock scramble over a knob, possibly involving using all fours.

3.0 Come to another overlook. This is the finest overlook on the hike, standing atop a sloping open rock slab. The Housatonic Valley forms the low centerpiece of a wooded mountain wonderland stretching to distant horizons. Begin a long, steep downgrade in woods and rocks.

3.2 Pass a lesser view. Continue descending. Look for the state park campground in the flats below.

3.4 Come along a small stream with a single drop cascade directly by the trail.

3.5 Turn right, down the flat of the Housatonic River in thick tall pines, as a spur goes left to the park campground. Enjoy the easy, almost level walking.

3.9 A spur leads left to alternate parking and a good starting point if you want to hike only the Pine Knob Loop Trail. Our hike stays right, climbing along cascading Hatch Brook.

4.1 Pass 30-foot Hatch Brook Falls on your left. Look for a lesser slide cascade just a little upstream. Ahead, curve along a tributary of Hatch Brook.

4.5 Meet the Appalachian Trail, completing the Pine Knob Loop. From here it is a 2-mile backtrack to the trailhead, via the AT and Mohawk Trail.

6.5 Arrive back at the US 7 trailhead, completing the view-rich hike.

38 MOHAWK MOUNTAIN VIA THE MOHAWK TRAIL

This highlight-filled hike uses some of Connecticut's longer pathways to scale Mohawk Mountain, where views extend in nearly all directions. Along the way you will pass trail shelters for overnight use, beside a mountaintop ski resort, and to an old stone lookout tower on the way to the denouement—the vistas that can be had atop Mohawk Mountain.

Start: CT 4 parking area
Distance: 6.0 miles out and back
Difficulty: Moderate
Elevation change: +/-694 feet over entire hike
Maximum grade: 12% downhill grade for 0.2 mile
Hiking time: About 3 hours
Seasons/schedule: May through early Dec
Fees and permits: None
Dog friendly: Yes
Trail surface: Forested natural surface

Land status: State forest
Nearest town: Goshen
Other trail users: None
Map to consult: Mohawk Mountain State Forest–Northern Section Summer Use
Amenities available: Picnic area and restroom near trailhead
Cell service: Fair
Trail contact: Mohawk Mountain State Forest, (860) 424-3200, https://portal.ct.gov/DEEP/State-Parks/Forests/Mohawk-Mountain-State-Forest-State-Park

FINDING THE TRAILHEAD

From the intersection of CT 4 and CT 63 in Goshen, take CT 4 west for 4.1 miles to the trailhead parking area on your left, near the intersection with Toomey Road. Note: Just off Toomey Road lies a small loop road with picnic tables and restroom. **Trailhead GPS:** 41.844079, -73.289923

THE HIKE

The top of Mohawk Mountain features a first-rate panorama that was originally used by local Paugussett and Tunxis Indians to send smoke signals to warn their people when the fierce Mohawks were on the warpath. As with other areas in the Connecticut Berkshires, the slopes of Mohawk Mountain were cut over by colliers making charcoal to fuel the iron furnaces. Later, these treeless views were enjoyed by locals, especially after the mountaintop became part of a state preserve in the 1920s. The forest slowly replenished itself over time. Adjacent lands were added to the state preserve until today the Mohawk State Forest covers in excess of 3,300 acres, through which the Mohawk and Mattatuck Trails travel.

And it is the Mohawk and Mattatuck Trails that we use to make our way to these fine panoramas. But in full disclosure, you can drive to the top of Mohawk Mountain during the warm season. However, don't let that be a deterrent, for you can enjoy plenty of sights along the way that those who access the top of 1,683-foot Mohawk Mountain by vehicle can't see.

Local Indians used to watch out for warring Mohawks from this very perch.

The Mohawk Trail was born when a segment of the Appalachian Trail (AT) in Connecticut was rerouted to the west of the Housatonic River valley in the late 1980s. The old AT then became the Mohawk Trail, and now is part of the greater Connecticut Blue Blaze Trail system, managed in grand fashion by the Connecticut Forest & Park Association. The old AT/Mohawk Trail starts atop Bread Loaf Mountain near Cornwall Bridge and makes an arc before rejoining the AT near Falls Village, a distance of 24.3 miles. If you are interested in a 37-mile-long backpacking loop in Connecticut, combine the Mohawk Trail and the Appalachian Trail.

Our hike begins at the parking area on CT 4 and travels near the adjacent picnic area past the site of Camp Toumey, where the Civilian Conservation Corps was situated starting in 1933. They built many of the roads and trails here, as well as planted trees. The Mohawk Trail is bordered with sassafras, mountain laurel, and oaks.

Sassafras trees are easy to identify. Sassafras leaves have three basic shapes: oval, three-lobed, and mitten-shaped. Mature sassafras trees have a reddish-brown, deeply furrowed bark. Sassafras is known for its aromatic scent. Scratch the bark away from a twig, and the sweet smell is unmistakable. Native Americans used sassafras for medicinal purposes. Pioneers, and even people today, make tea from boiling sassafras roots. Birds eat the berries. The leaves can be added to soups and sauces as a thickening agent. Dried and ground leaves are used in Cajun cooking, down Louisiana way. The wood of sassafras shrinks when dried and is used for fence posts and hand tools. Massachusetts is near the northeast

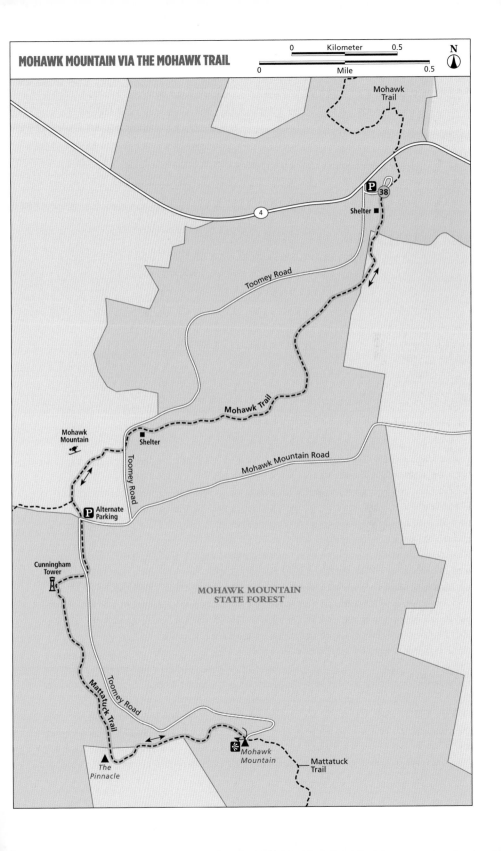

0   Kilometer   0.5

0   Mile   0.5

N

Mohawk
Trail

P

38

Shelter

4

Toomey Road

Mohawk Trail

Mohawk
Mountain

Shelter

Toomey Road

Mohawk Mountain Road

Alternate
Parking

P

Cunningham
Tower

**MOHAWK MOUNTAIN
STATE FOREST**

Mattatuck Trail

Toomey Road

Mohawk
Mountain

Mattatuck
Trail

The
Pinnacle

This old stone lookout tower was in use a century back.

edge of the sassafras's range, which extends west to Missouri and southeastern Texas and on south to northern Florida.

The hike quickly takes you to a trail shelter, then rolls over a knob before coming to a second shelter. The lean-tos are open to first-come, first-served backcountry camping, though in reality both of them are very near roads. Higher up the mountain, the hike runs along a ski resort. This is a privately run ski area on state-owned property, also named Mohawk Mountain. In operation since 1947, the ski area's founder, Walt Schoenknecht, worked with area engineers to create the very first viable snow-making machines, whose use spread around the globe. And it all started right here on Mohawk Mountain.

Beyond the ski area you join the Mattatuck Trail, a 42-mile-long path also maintained by the Connecticut Forest & Park Association. Return to Toomey Road and an alternate parking area before rejoining the trail through the woods to reach the Cunningham stone lookout tower. Today, this tower is roofless and minus its former windows. Imagine this spot back in the 1920s. The forest would have been cut down all around the tower, and part of a sheep farm. Therefore, the treeless peak was a fine place for a view, rather than the view today, where all you can see from the tower area is trees.

This rock edifice was built by the fledgling Mohawk Tower Association in 1913, spearheaded by Seymour Cunningham. Earlier the group had built a wooden tower and adjacent hut atop Mohawk Mountain, but that tower collapsed. Today, Mohawk Mountain sports communication towers and such, but no official observation towers. In truth none are needed, as the rock outcrops and a mown peak reveal a host of rumpled wooded highlands.

Keep south beyond the Cunningham Tower, cruising through woods to surmount The Pinnacle. The forested crown offers no views. After roller-coastering through a gap you make the final ascent to Mohawk Mountain. And what views! The Berkshires to the north and west open in the distance, while other looks spread south. Towers and small buildings cover part of the historic peak, first used by aboriginals as a point of communication and still in use today for the same purpose, plus a fine reward for a fun and interesting hike.

MILES AND DIRECTIONS

0.0 From the parking area on CT 4, follow the spur road toward a small picnic area, then pick up the signed Mohawk Trail heading south. Quickly come to a three-sided, wood, Adirondack-style lean-to. Climb into attractive woods of sassafras, mountain laurel, and pine.

0.2 The Mohawk Trail climbs onto a knob. Shortly descend from the knob, dropping 135 feet in 0.2 mile.

0.8 The trail heads westerly at the base of a mountain slope rising to the south.

1.3 Come to another trail shelter. This one is backed against a hill, facing west. Ahead, join Toomey Road, heading south. Big views open to the west, toward New York.

1.4 Split right, westerly, from Toomey Road, back on singletrack footpath.

1.5 Emerge at the top of the Mohawk Mountain ski area, coming near the wheels of the lift. Stay with the blue blazes here as roads and ski trails spur off.

1.7 Intersect the blue-blazed and signed Mattatuck Trail. Stay left with the Mattatuck Trail as the Mohawk Trail descends right.

1.8 Return to Toomey Road, reaching alternate parking and a picnic area. Keep south with the road and shortly split right from the road, back on singletrack trail in fragrant pines.

2.0 Reach the historic Cunningham Tower. Explore the stone edifice, then continue in birch woods with a ferny understory. Pass an old hand-pump well ahead in level, boggy woods with spruce.

2.5 Top out on "The Pinnacle." The peak is wooded with no views. Turn east and drop to a gap.

3.0 Make the top of Mohawk Mountain. The primary views extend north and south. Benches provide a good respite for the weary hiker. Maybe you can play up being sweaty and thirsty, beseeching a drink off visitors who arrived here by vehicle. Backtrack to the trailhead.

6.0 Arrive back at the trailhead, completing the mountain hike.

39 **MACEDONIA BROOK CIRCUIT**

You will be surprised at the challenging terrain on the first half of this view-laden loop at Macedonia Brook State Park. The Macedonia Ridge Trail leads from Macedonia Brook onto a stony and incredibly steep track with sections of sloped sheer rock that make for tough but rewarding hiking, for the rewards are reaped among the views aplenty of the nearby Berkshire Hills as well as distant peaks and valleys. Parts of the hike include scrambling that necessitates using your hands in places. Your return route takes you on a mercifully level road built by the Civilian Conservation Corps then turned into a pleasant trail.

Start: South Macedonia Ridge trailhead
Distance: 4.5-mile loop
Difficulty: Difficult due to terrain
Elevation change: +/-1,154 feet over entire hike
Maximum grade: 33% downhill grade for 0.2 mile
Hiking time: About 3 hours
Seasons/schedule: Best when trails are dry
Fees and permits: None
Dog friendly: No; too many steep sections and open rock slabs

Trail surface: Forested and rock natural surface
Land status: State park
Nearest town: Kent
Other trail users: None
Map to consult: Macedonia Brook State Park
Amenities available: Restrooms and picnic tables at trailhead
Cell service: Best on the ridges
Trail contact: Macedonia Brook State Park, (860) 927-3238, https://portal.ct.gov/DEEP/State-Parks/Parks/Macedonia-Brook-State-Park

FINDING THE TRAILHEAD

From the intersection of US 7 and CT 341 in Kent, take CT 341 west for 1.8 miles to Macedonia Brook Road. Turn right and follow it for 1.5 miles to the Macedonia Ridge southern trailhead, on the left side of the road just after Macedonia Brook Road bridges Macedonia Brook. **Trailhead GPS:** 41.760806, -73.493715

THE HIKE

Plan to have a very slow first half of your hike. The going is rough but well worth the trouble. The setting is Macedonia Brook State Park, under protection as a preserve for over a century. Home to the Scatacook Indians, then later the site of an iron foundry along Macedonia Brook, the bulk of the park was deeded over to the state of Connecticut in 1918. Today, the 2,300-acre preserve presents not only a fine network of hiking trails, but also streamside camping, trout fishing, and picnicking.

Part of our hike climbs Cobble Mountain, the must-see highlight of any hike here at Macedonia Brook State Park. On the slope, look for shagbark hickory trees. You will be able to pick them out without problem. Shagbark hickories look like what their name implies, with their loose-plated bark sloughing off the main trunk, looking like they could use a trim, much as shaggy-haired humans. The loose bark plates run vertically up the trunk of the tree.

Open outcrops reveal views of surrounding rugged mountains

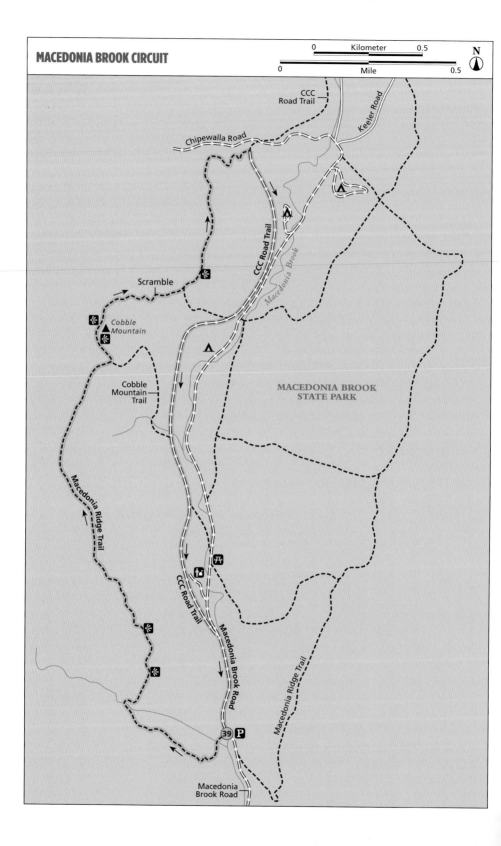

MACEDONIA BROOK CIRCUIT

0   Kilometer   0.5

0   Mile   0.5

N

CCC
Road Trail

Keeler Road

Chipewalla Road

CCC Road Trail

Macedonia Brook

Scramble

Cobble
Mountain

Cobble
Mountain
Trail

MACEDONIA BROOK
STATE PARK

Macedonia Ridge Trail

CCC Road Trail

Macedonia Brook Road

Macedonia Ridge Trail

39 P

Macedonia
Brook Road

Found in lower-elevation, south-facing mountain forests of the Connecticut Berkshires, shagbark hickories were an important food source for aboriginals, who sought out their surprisingly sweet nuts. The nuts were used by colonial pioneers much as you would use a pecan. However, attempts at commercial propagation of the shagbark hickory have been unsuccessful. In the wild, nut production varies considerably year to year.

The thinner shell and greater nutmeat make shagbark hickory nuts an attractive choice. Indians even made hickory nut soup. They also broke the nuts, collected the meat, and pounded it down, releasing oils in the nut. They would then form the meat into balls, with the oil of the nut keeping the pulverized acorns intact. These "nutballs" were an ideal way to store the food for later use, since they could be quickly and easily eaten, as opposed to breaking the shells and removing the meat.

The best time to collect the nuts was soon after the acorns fell and before the first frost of autumn. Bird and mammals competed with the Indians in getting to the sought-after nuts, especially in times with the shagbark's nut production was down. Shagbark hickories also aided the Indians in obtaining food another way. The strong wood was fashioned into bows, with which they could hunt game. Early colonists used the tough yet resilient wood for everything from axe handles to wagon axles.

After identifying the shagbark hickories, you then can identify ranges on the horizon from Cobble Mountain. Here, views stretch in all directions, including New York's Taconics and Catskills, with nearer points as well. But to get to Cobble Mountain we first join the Macedonia Ridge Trail, rising away from gurgling, clear Macedonia Brook. The ascent is nothing out of the ordinary, not giving away any hints of what is to come. Ahead, you join an earlier route of the Appalachian Trail. The path steepens and traverses angled rock slabs that are frankly challenging to hike. Yet, the tree-free stone outcroppings also render views down the Macedonia Brook valley in the near and wooded ridges beyond.

The track rolls in and out of woods, then climbs Cobble Mountain. The stony open summit delivers first-rate panoramas that make it worth every step. Landscapes open primarily to the west into waves of ridges. After soaking in a series of vistas from Cobble Mountain, your descent from this peak is incredibly steep as it runs over angled rock slopes that can be downright treacherous in wet conditions, including a very short scramble. That is why it is best to make this hike on a dry day. Avoid snowy conditions as well.

You continue the slow but eye-pleasing hike, passing other views while surmounting an unnamed mountain. Switchbacks ease the descent from this mountain, and you end up at a picturesque old road bordered with hand-laid rock walls. This old road is now a trail. It was built from 1935 to 1937 using local materials by members of Civilian Conservation Corps Camp 1191, who developed much of the park we see today. Now called the CCC Road Trail, the path runs along the base of Cobble Mountain on a mild and steady grade. While on the trail, you can't see the artistic stone retention walls facing toward Macedonia Brook. Make sure to drop off the track to view these handsome rock walls.

This trail is as easy as the Macedonia Ridge Trail is difficult. Enjoy the wide, foot-friendly, and historic track. Along the way you will pass tempting park facilities. At the end of the CCC Road Trail, you walk a short distance on Macedonia Brook Road to complete the loop.

Finally, while in the area, make sure to visit Kent Falls State Park. There you can take the 0.4-mile trail to view Kent Falls as it cascades a total of 250 feet in a series of waterfalls to the Housatonic River.

Parts of this hike require a little rock scrambling.

MILES AND DIRECTIONS

0.0 Leave from the south Macedonia Ridge Trail parking area at the south end of the state park and head west, passing the trailhead outhouse, then bridge a tributary of Macedonia Brook. Hike underneath witch hazel, red oak, and black birch, with ferns aplenty. As you leave the stream, mountain laurel becomes more prevalent. Once up high, chestnut oaks and other xeric trees take over.

0.2 Pass a mountainside flat, once a locale used to make charcoal to fuel the iron furnace located just beyond the southern park entrance.

0.4 Cross the upper end of the tributary of Macedonia Brook. Rise to more-rocky terrain with partial views. Keep climbing.

0.6 Open onto the first full-fledged view. A vista opens southeast, down the Macedonia Brook watershed and wooded ridges to the east. Blueberries grow near the trail. Keep climbing.

0.8 A view opens to the north as you level out. Here, keep hiking north in scrubby hardwoods. The trail rolls up and down.

1.2 Cross an unofficial abandoned trail.

1.3 Level off in a gap, then begin ascending the south side of Cobble Mountain. Note the shagbark hickory trees.

1.6 Meet the Cobble Mountain Trail. It dives a steep half mile down to Macedonia Brook. Our hike ascends the southeast slope of Cobble Mountain on a naked outcrop with views.

1.7 Reach the crest of Cobble Mountain. Here, the trail takes you to westerly open rock vistas into New York as far as the eye can see, framed in scrubby oaks, hickories, and pines. Ahead, views open of the Catskills. Make a breakneck descent over sloped stone slabs. Use extreme caution.

2.0 Reach a short rock scramble off an angled ledge. Follow the blazes closely here. Just ahead, reach and cross a normally dry drainage, then climb again.

2.1 Meet a green-blazed trail descending toward Macedonia Brook. Stay straight with the Macedonia Brook Trail, making an uphill scramble in rocks.

2.3 Another stellar view opens on a rocky clearing. This vista is to the east across the vale of Macedonia Brook.

2.7 Reach the CCC Road Trail. It initially resembles a road, and it was. Head right on the wide track southbound, lined with hand-laid rock and stone retention walls. Ahead, come near one of the park's camping areas.

3.2 Come to an intersection. Here, a green-blazed trail leads right to Macedonia Ridge, while another trail leads left to Macedonia Brook Road. Stay straight with the CCC Road Trail.

3.7 The Cobble Mountain Trail leaves right.

3.9 A short spur trail goes left to a park picnic shelter. Ahead, come near the park maintenance shed, then pass behind the park office.

4.3 The CCC Road Trail ends. Keep south, joining Macedonia Brook Road.

4.5 Arrive back at the trailhead, completing the view-filled hike.

40 BULLS BRIDGE HIKE

This hike treks along the wild Housatonic River, first spanning it via a historic covered bridge. Next, join the Appalachian Trail (AT), wandering by whitewater rapids amid former farmland. Stop by an AT shelter before leaving the Housatonic River for Tenmile Hill and a view. Your return route loops by an old home site.

Start: Bulls Bridge parking area
Distance: 4.7 miles out and back with a loop in the middle
Difficulty: Moderate; does have 720-foot climb
Elevation change: +/-970 feet over entire hike
Maximum grade: 11% grade for 1.5 miles
Hiking time: About 2.5 hours
Seasons/schedule: May through Nov
Fees and permits: None
Dog friendly: Yes

Trail surface: Natural surface but follows paved road at first
Land status: National park
Nearest town: Bulls Bridge
Other trail users: None
Map to consult: National Park Service–Appalachian Trail
Amenities available: Restroom at parking area
Cell service: Good
Trail contact: Appalachian National Scenic Trail, (304) 535-6278, www .nps.gov/appa

FINDING THE TRAILHEAD

From the intersection of US 7 and US 202 in New Milford, take US 7 north 9 miles to the hamlet of Bulls Bridge and Bulls Bridge Road, at a traffic light. Turn left on Bulls Bridge Road and follow it a few feet to turn left into a parking area just before Bulls Covered Bridge. **Trailhead GPS:** 41.675606, -73.508228

THE HIKE

The community of Bulls Bridge, where this hike starts, is named after the covered bridge located here. The one-lane bridge, part of this hike, spans a channel of the Housatonic River. As we all know, George Washington got around in his day, and it is said that the general lost a favored horse crossing the Housatonic at the bridge site, and had to pay a hefty bill of $212 to get it retrieved from the rapids. The 109-foot covered bridge was built in 1842, long after Washington's day.

Revel in both human history and natural beauty on this trek. After crossing the power-generation canal dug by First Light Power Generating Company, you will stroll through Bulls Covered Bridge, which is open to cars but regularly walked through by tourists and hikers alike. In fact, to get from the trailhead parking to the trail itself, you must hike through the dim wooden structure rising above frothing torrents of the Housatonic River. Ahead, a trail splits left to a view, where separate channels of the crashing Housatonic come together. Observe the whitewater extravaganza and daring whitewater boaters plying their craft, while others head for adjacent riverside rocks to watch the boaters and/or fish. Swimming is not allowed hereabouts, even for sweaty hikers.

You then pick up a connector to meet the Appalachian Trail (AT). Your southbound hike leads along the Housatonic River gorge, an impressive mix of motionless stone and frenetic aqua. Enjoy more watery wonders in the form of the Tenmile River, which you

Looking out on the confluence of the Housatonic and Ten Mile Rivers

cross on an impressive iron span. The sandy confluence of the Tenmile and Housatonic Rivers beckons you to linger. A designated AT hiker camp is located here, and the Tenmile trail shelter is nearby. The three-sided wooden structure faces a field. The open meadow delivers a perspective of what this area looked like before reforestation shaded the amazing number of stone-fence-lined fields. Scan for old farm implements near the shelter, further evidence of a previously peopled past.

The campsites and trail shelters are used by thru-hikers, typically attempting to trace the Appalachian Trail from Georgia to Maine, trekking through the Berkshires in summer. We often see them along the trail, looking a little gaunt and sometimes smelling a little grungy. Thru-hiking the AT isn't easy. And that's how "trail angels"—people who help thru-hikers—came to be.

One way to be a trail angel is to position yourself somewhere on the Appalachian Trail, usually near a trail junction, road crossing, campground, or parking area, with a smorgasbord of edible goodies for the hikers. The good eats can be extravagant, such as grilled hot dogs, hamburgers with all the fixings, ice cream, or some perishable dessert, or a simple setup of fresh fruit (too heavy for the hikers to carry as part of their daily meals) and soft drinks. Cookies and candy bars are always on the menu. Hikers seem to crave sweets and can't get enough. And when they do have them, the treats don't last long enough.

Other angelic deeds you can do are charging their cell phones, giving them a ride to the grocery store, or mailing no-longer-needed items back home for them. I highly

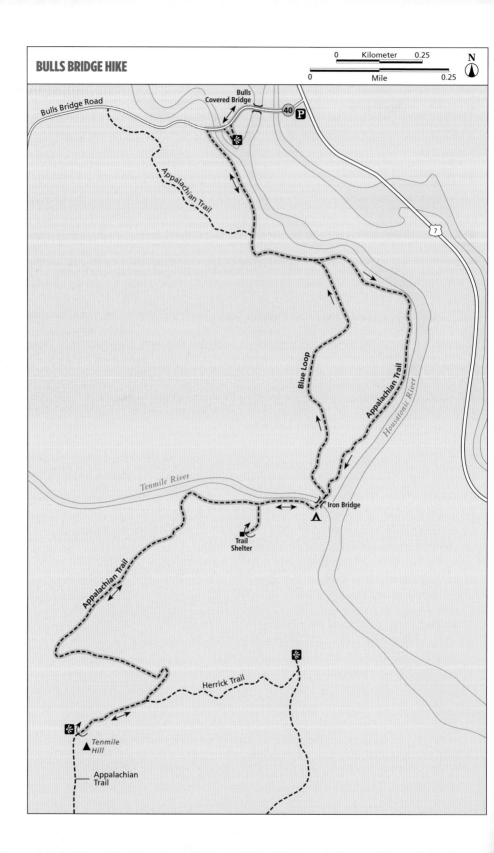

0   Kilometer   0.25

0   Mile   0.25

N

Bulls Bridge Road

Bulls
Covered Bridge

40 P

7

Appalachian Trail

Blue Loop

Appalachian Trail

Housatonic River

Tenmile River

Iron Bridge

Trail
Shelter

Appalachian Trail

Herrick Trail

Tenmile
Hill

Appalachian
Trail

Cross this bridge over the Ten Mile River on your hike.

recommend becoming a trail angel. It is an opportunity to show Berkshires hospitality. I promise any small act of kindness will be so graciously received that it will have a far greater impact on the giver.

After exploring the shelter/camping area, continue on the Appalachian Trail to the crest of Tenmile Hill through deep towering hardwoods shading a mossy, ferny, and stony forest floor. Switchbacks ease the climb. A short spur at the top of the 1,000-foot peak leads to a stone outcrop amid sturdy oaks and hickories. Here, peer northwest into the Tenmile River valley and the state of New York. From this vantage, make the descent back to the Housatonic/Tenmile River confluence, crossing the iron span again. This time, an alternate loop leads up a low hill on a timeworn former farm road. Here, more stone fences appear and a keen eye will spot a pair of standing chimneys, one brick and one stone, all that remain of a Housatonic Valley farm.

Before reaching the trailhead, you get one more chance to walk through Bulls Covered Bridge, with its undersized windows letting in just enough light to make your way.

MILES AND DIRECTIONS

0.0 Leave the Bulls Bridge parking area and walk west toward Bulls Covered Bridge. Cross an outflow canal of the power plant visible just upstream. Dip to enter the historic covered bridge. Watch for cars. Beyond the bridge, trails lead right, but you stay with Bulls Bridge Road. Ahead, look left for a little loop leading to an observation deck overlooking the Housatonic. Continue along Bulls Bridge Road.

0.2 Reach a trailhead kiosk on the left. Leave Bulls Bridge Road and head left on a blue-blazed wide connector trail, entering forest. Cruise downstream with the waterfall-laden Housatonic River to your left and hilly terrain rising to your right. User-created spur trails lead to the Housatonic.

0.4 Meet the white-blazed Appalachian Trail. Head left, southbound and uphill, still on a wide old roadbed. Rise to a bluff overlooking the wild waterway. Good views can be had from this perch.

0.5 Come to another trail intersection. Here, the Blue Loop splits right. This will be your return route. For now, stay left with the AT, negotiating rugged terrain along the river gorge.

1.1 Reach the Tenmile River, an iron span, and the other end of the Blue Loop. Keep straight, bridging the river. Immediately enter an AT hiker camping area (no fires allowed) in a flat at the confluence of the Tenmile and Housatonic Rivers. Turn right with the AT, heading upstream along the Tenmile River, flowing to your right.

1.3 Follow the blue-blazed trail leading left and uphill toward the Tenmile trail shelter, overlooking a field. Backtrack to the AT and continue southbound, upstream along the Tenmile River.

1.6 Leave the Tenmile River and begin ascending Tenmile Hill.

2.3 Reach a trail intersection. Here, the lesser-used Herrick Trail leaves left. Stay straight on the AT, making a final push up Tenmile Hill, entering oak woods.

2.4 Come to the signed spur to Tenmile Hill. Revel in the view from emergent rocks into the Tenmile River valley and beyond. Backtrack on the AT.

3.7 Return to the Tenmile River. Cross back over the iron bridge, then leave the AT, heading left on the Blue Loop. Briefly hike along the right bank of the Tenmile River, then turn from the waterway, tracing an old farm road through former fields, where cedar and tulip trees now dominate the woodscape.

4.0 Pass stone and brick chimneys on trail left, remains of a farmhouse.

4.2 Rejoin the Appalachian Trail, heading left, northbound.

4.3 Leave right from the AT on the connector path, backtracking along the Housatonic.

4.7 Arrive back at the Bulls Bridge trailhead, completing the scenic and historic hike.

HIKE INDEX

THE TEN ESSENTIALS OF HIKING

American Hiking Society

American Hiking Society recommends you pack the "Ten Essentials" every time you head out for a hike. Whether you plan to be gone for a couple of hours or several months, make sure to pack these items. Become familiar with these items and know how to use them. Learn more at **AmericanHiking.org/hiking-resources**

 1. Appropriate Footwear

 6. Safety Items (light, fire, and a whistle)

 2. Navigation

 7. First Aid Kit

 3. Water (and a way to purify it)

 8. Knife or Multi-Tool

 4. Food

 9. Sun Protection

 5. Rain Gear & Dry-Fast Layers

10. Shelter

PROTECT THE PLACES YOU LOVE TO HIKE

Become a member today and take $5 off an annual membership using the code **Falcon5**.

AmericanHiking.org/join

American Hiking Society is the only national nonprofit organization dedicated to empowering all to enjoy, share, and preserve the hiking experience.